Truth Out In The Open

BY

Dr. J. E. Murdock

Table Of Contents

Unless otherwise indicated, all Scripture quotations are taken from the King James Version of the Bible.
Truth Out In The Open
ISBN 1-56394-263-1/B-JEM-12
Copyright © by Dr. J. E. Murdock
All publishing 2003 rights belong exclusively to Wisdom International
Editor/Publisher: Deborah Murdock Johnson
Published by The Wisdom Center · P. O. Box 99 · Denton, Texas 76202

CORNER POSTS

by

DR. J. E. MURDOCK

CORNER POSTS...
The Fear Of God...A Firm Foundation.

COMPILED BY DEBORAH MURDOCK JOHNSON

FOREWORD

I walked along-side my daddy with an ax, hammer and some other tools to be used by my dad in building a fence around the seventy-eight acre farm. We had to mark off pasture land or areas for planting grain. I noticed that he put down special posts marking the corners of the areas he wanted to enclose.

Although my dad didn't talk very much he did call to my attention the reason behind putting the special posts down on the corners. He said the whole wire fence was supported by the *Corner Posts*. The *Corner Post* was to be special because there was a lot of strain on the corner. I listened to all the information he took the time to explain. This information was helpful to me because I grew up and lived on a dairy farm and I had a lot of fencing to do.

Putting down *Corner Posts* and bracing them properly was important to me. My uncle was impressed with my fencing, which made me feel good about my *Corner Posts*. Learning the difference between the *Corner Posts* and the line posts helped make my future building successful.

Always understand the importance of
the *Corner Post*.

Age 15...

It was evening. My aunt brought my mother and three of my sisters home from a prayer meeting. My ten year old sister was speaking in the Spirit. (I had never heard of such a thing!) My aunt said to me, "She's filled with the Spirit and we're going to have prayer here (my house) tomorrow evening." I said to myself, "I'm going to be in the prayer meeting"...*and I was there.*

Three months later...

It was eleven o'clock when I left the front room where my sister Reba, and my first cousin Loye, had been in prayer in our home. After I laid down I felt like if I stayed up all night and sought the Lord I would be filled with the Spirit. I got up and went into the living room and said to my sister, "I believe I will be filled with the Spirit. Will you and Loye pray with me?" They did. Fifteen minutes later I began speaking in a heavenly language.

At that time Loye said, "Isn't it wonderful?" For about two-and one-half hours it was heaven on earth.

The next day...my first time to witness...

I went to town and told my Grandpa Skidmore about my experience with tongues. He seemed to be shocked and said no one had an experience like that except for the twelve disciples and that was because they had a special work to do.

I said, "I don't know about that Grandpa. All I know is I spoke in the Spirit about two and a half hours last night."

He said, "You did?"
I said, "Yes."
Then he said, "That won't last."
It has been seventy-one years since that experience, and as Jesus said, "The Holy Ghost would be within us as rivers of living water."

A surge of convictions...

My thought life began to be dealt with. There wasn't a preacher telling me the do's and don'ts of this new experience I had. I was aware of another power that had come into my life. I soon realized that if I was to continue on in this new found joy and hope that I would have to deal with these new feelings of right and wrong that were racing over me. I felt that if I gave myself to prayer and worship, the Holy Spirit could more than match the opposition that would come against my new life in the Holy Ghost.

I repented on the spot...

Still just a boy on the farm, I was plowing in my dad's field when the mule that pulled the plow decided not to walk where he was supposed to. Anger kept rising in me...yet I knew that I should not feel such anger...but it got the best of me anyway. So I stopped the mule and went around and hit him in the head with my fist. My fist hurt. Most of all I knew God had not wanted me to fly off the handle, losing my temper like that. I walked behind the plow and down on my knees I fell, crying out to the Lord to forgive me and to help me not to grieve Him. He forgave me...but I never forgot how bad I felt that I had grieved the Lord.

Married a few short weeks...age 17

The task of married life for a little wife of fourteen years of age and myself, just seventeen years old, caused me to fret. I knew I shouldn't be fretting against my little bride because I was a Christian, filled with the wonderful baptism of the Holy Ghost. The Lord moved in one night as I let go of some words of complaint. He said, "Stop this way of doing *now*." Suddenly a fear of God moved through me. It was another time of repenting on the spot.

I had to talk back...

Working on my brother-in-law's house with a carpenter that, for sure, was hard to please...I knew where my place was...being a Christian, but that ole temper just kept raging. He seemed so hard to please, I said to him (an elderly man), "I wish I could please you."

He looked at me and said, "I'll knock you in the head with this hammer."

I had to talk back but when I did my conscience struck me and by the next day while in prayer at home, the Lord told me to ask forgiveness. I reasoned with the Lord, but to keep the wonderful flow of His Spirit in me I had to be sorry and repent. I did go to him that day and ask forgiveness for talking back. This too, I never forgot.

I felt bad...

Standing on the sleeping porch talking to my mother, I was saying a few things about my brother who was preaching in Florida. The Holy Spirit convicted me. I stopped at once and said, "Mama, I feel bad talking about my brother, he has had enough battles fighting the devil. Let's pray for him." We joined together in prayer right there on the spot and prayed for him instead of talking against him.

Yes, I was only a young boy, but when the *Holy Spirit* is free to work in us, He'll do things that you will not forget.

I was 18...

Saturday evening I caught a ride over to my first cousin's house, who lived eight miles away. I spent the night and was enjoying my visit and our prayer time. The next day, about the middle of the evening, I felt the need to return home. There was no traffic going from that community towards my home that day because it was Sunday.

While I was thinking about the long walk, my uncle gave me directions; a trail that led through the woods which would cut my walk to half the time. He made it plain to me where, up the road a mile, there would be an old dipping vat. There I would turn to my left and follow the trail until I came to the place where there had been an old sawmill. To my left would be a lot of old tin buildings. My uncle said, *"Don't* turn to the left, but *here,* turn to the *right."*

When I came to the old tin buildings I decided to go and take a look around them. The sky became covered with clouds...I was soon aware I needed to be on my way. I started toward the trail I had *left,* but for some reason I couldn't find it.

"And this I speak for your own profit;and that ye may attend upon the Lord *without distraction"* (1 Corinthians 7:35).

I've lost my way...

Soon I knew...I was lost. Well, being a Spirit-filled boy, I began to pray while I walked... becoming more and more fearful as the moments went by. I prayed...I stopped and listened...I hollered...trying to get someone, somewhere, to hear me and respond. By this time I had my shoes in my hands walking, then running and praying, only to find that I was running in circles. I could see my tracks here and there where I had already been.

Finally I decided to kneel down by an ole tree stump...one knee up and the other on the ground ready to spring back on my feet. I said a quick prayer and went back in the circle again. At last I began to talk to myself. "You are lost—only the Lord knows where you are and He's the only one who can lead you out." So down on *both* knees I went—giving up—fully *persuaded* I must *let God lead* me out.

Becoming unbelievably still I spoke quietly to the Lord. "I'm lost Lord. I can't find the way out. You know the way and you know where I am." I barely got those words out when a peace came over my mind. I almost forgot I was lost. I got up on my feet with a deep feeling of peace and spoke aloud, "I feel at peace to turn to my right." I quickly stepped into a clear trail. I stopped, looked both ways and said aloud again, "I feel peaceful to turn to the right."

I was now traveling *under the banner of peace.*

Moving at a steady pace I came to a tree that had fallen across the trail. The big limbs of the tree held its trunk off the ground about three feet. I stopped and looked at it, thinking, I'll walk around this tree and come back to the trail on the other side. Immediately I was met with the thought—*Remember??? You lost your way when you turned aside at the old tin buildings.* This settled my mind, quick.

I said aloud, "I'll not leave the trail." I got down on my knees and crawled under the fallen tree. *I'll stay on the trail. I did.*

When I stood up, the thought came to me, you're still in the woods, so I bowed my head and said aloud, "I feel peaceful to go on ahead." Soon I came out of the woods...just across the highway from my house on top of the hill.

"Be still, and know that I am God:"
(Psalm 46:10).
"Fear ye not, stand still, and see
the salvation of the Lord," (Exodus 14:13).

I was 23...

The sun had gone down and a beautiful moon had risen. My wife and I decided to go out on the hill for a while to pray, leaving our one and a half year old daughter, Barbara, in the house.

I had been busy fixing up things around our new home, the home my uncle had built for us. He had also given me a job on the dairy farm. Things seemed to be coming in order for us.

I had brought in cedar from the woods to use as posts for our yard fence, tying the two front posts with cedar at the top and putting the hanging gate inside the split cedar post. I knew that cedar would last a long time.

I routed a spring of water to run through our backyard and through the garden. I loved to be around water and anywhere things were growing. The shadow of the trees were reflected across the yard, the little houses silhouetted in the moonlit night.

I had a desire to work for the Lord...some way...somewhere...some day. But how??? When??? This was my heart's desire as my prayer was going up to the Lord. I turned my head and looked toward the house, admiring the place there in the country. I could see a future here—when these words came to me, "These things shall pass away...but he that turns many to righteousness shall shine as the stars forever and ever."

In just one week all stakes were uprooted, our plans for a future in the country, dissolved. It had to be God's timing...His doings. A door opened and into a ministry that has lasted for over a half a century; we went.

Beautiful things have happened along the way. Many times so much discouragement has been entwined with the good that, at times, pulling aside seemed to be the only thing to do. When I would begin thinking along these lines the Lord would help me to *remember those Corner Posts*. The Lord knew where to place them in my life.

As Peter said to Jesus,
"To whom shall we go? Thou hast
the words of eternal life" (John 6:68).
"Labour not for the meat which perisheth,
but for that meat which endureth
unto everlasting life, which the Son of
man shall give unto you:" (John 6:27).

God's Corner Posts give direction to us and help us to make the best choice...God's will.

*Age 36...The quiet hour that turned
into a battle...*

The telephone at home or in the office at church seemed to always have a way of hindering my much needed prayer time and reading of the Word, so to capture that special time I needed, I fixed up a small room upstairs in the church. It was only seven feet square with a small window facing outside. I would be away from the phone and no one would even look for me in this little room. I placed a piece of carpet on the floor and had a small desk with a chair. With the light on, it appeared to be the perfect place for a quiet prayer meeting...nothing more.

On my third trip to my little prayer room something happened. Satan came along too. That is the only way I can describe it. Such wrestling and testing went on inside of the room I became afraid and got up to go away. My thoughts were...people on the streets don't know God nor do they want to know God...but do not feel like this! Then as I started to run out the voice of the Lord seemed to say, "You'll have to face it sometime or another."

With that I knelt back down in the little prayer room. As I knelt down such a feeling of desperation came over me...I would spring up on my knees and fall against the wall, then a suggestion would come to my mind..."Why don't you jump out the window?...See if what you've got is real," just as satan said, "Jump off the pinnacle...and the angels will bare you up" (Matthew 4:5). Oh what a test! I left the room once again but heard the same voice, "You'll have to face it sometime or another." On hearing this I turned again and knelt down. A peace came over me and I felt organized and calm as though nothing had even happened.

I got up to go visiting for the rest of the afternoon and forgot what had happened earlier. I went into the office later that evening and bowed my head at my desk. With a prayer and my hand on the Bible I said, "Lord, give me a word for the people tonight." I opened the Bible and my eyes fell upon this scripture:

"He that dasheth in pieces is come up
before thy face: keep the munition,
watch the way, make thy loins strong,
fortify thy power mightily" (Nahum 2:1).

As quickly as I read these words my mind went back to

the battle I had fought in the prayer room. Then I understood what had happened in that prayer time.

In the service that night I ministered to the people... "The enemy comes against the people who call on the Lord. *Expect it* and *be prepared."*

If we allow the enemy to steal our time with God we will be the loser...but the promise is...

"...When the enemy shall come in like
a flood, the Spirit of the Lord shall
lift up a standard against him"
(Isaiah 59:19).

So don't let anything steal your prayer time with the Lord and your battles will be won *ahead* of you.

"...and thy Father which seeth in secret
shall reward thee openly" (Matthew 6:6).

God's Corner Posts

God places things all along the way in this walk of life; most of them we tend to forget. The things that He speaks to us...those unforgettable things...are God's *Corner Posts.*

God brought Moses and Israel to Mt. Horeb; for there He would speak to them in such a manner that when they heard Him they would *fear Him all the days of their life.*

When Israel crossed Jordan the Lord told them to "...take twelve stones out of the place where the priest's feet stood firm; Bring them and place them on the bank of the river." These would be *corner posts* for the future generations as a reminder that God brought them across Jordan. Those twelve stones will speak when other messages will have long been forgotten.

Jesus—The Corner Stone And The Master Builder Of The Christian Life

What is a *corner stone*??? Much like the Corner Post, it is the basic or main part...the foundation of a building.

It has been said that Jesus was the carpenter's son. Jesus spoke of building your house on the rock so when the storms came and the winds blew against it, they would not prevail...and your house would stand firm.

The Good News of the Gospel of Jesus Christ, our Lord, is to build our human life back into a lasting relationship with God. After the fall of Adam our hearts were rent from God and we were without hope in this world—but God, through His Son, made a move...one that would save us and redeem us again to a lively hope.

Jesus is our *corner stone*; no other corner post has stood so long.

The Simplicity...A B C's

The A B C's were learned in the first years of school...oh, so simple...yet all walks of life depend on them. As simple as my experiences may seem they have become the guidelines for Christian living and a continual growing relationship with our soon coming King, Jesus Christ.

It's IMPORTANT to Remember...

▶ When the Holy Spirit is reproving you...*hear Him*

and *respond* to *Him* on the spot.

▶ Don't let the sun go down on your wrath.

▶ Make straight paths for your feet.

Can you recall Corner Posts in your life?

What did He speak in His Goodness...His Severity...?

Hear what the Holy Spirit is saying to your heart.

Obey...if you expect your relationship with Him to continue to grow.

Life Without *Corner Posts*...

Corner Posts...The Fear of God... A Firm Foundation.

Learn To *Hear*
The Voice
Of The Lord...
Learn The *Value*
Of His Voice...
Learn To
Understand His
Voice.

-J. E. Murdock

FATHER'S TALK

VOLUME 1

by

DR. J. E. MURDOCK

TABLE OF CONTENTS

– 1 –

IS MY FAMILY ON THE SAFE SIDE?

There's nothing, I suppose, that's ever touched me more concerning my family than the experience I had one night about 10 or 11 o'clock in a little town called Grapeland, Texas. We owned an old pickup truck and had been to a service and had my oldest little daughter, Barbara Ann, the only daughter that we had at that time, in the seat of the pickup with us. We pulled into Grapeland and parked in front of my aunt's house for just a few moments.

We got back in the truck and had to cross the highway to turn around so we could get to where we lived. When we got out in the very center of the highway the pickup went dead. Then I struggled quickly to try to start the truck to get off the highway because a large truck was coming around the corner, just about 50 or 60 yards away. It was dark and the truck had a long trailer that was loaded and it was coming toward us. I just knew that I had to get us out of the road because we could very easily get run over.

It looked to me like the driver of the truck had time to see us and to stop, but I could tell that he was coming on and was not slowing down. I thought, how am I going to get out of the truck, go around and help my wife *and* our baby girl to get out before they get run over? I had such a terrible feeling and was so concerned.

I jumped out! As I did, I had just enough time to move off to the side when the truck came right on and bumped into the back end of our pickup. When he did, I just knew that he had crushed my wife and little girl...I'd never had such a feeling. In fact, I went through death for them for the next five seconds.

Then, I ran around to the other side and saw that the truck wasn't damaged, but it was knocked around and facing the other way. I didn't know what had happened to my family. When I walked around on the other side, I saw the thing that thrilled my life...I can still feel the thrill of it...my wife, without my knowing, had opened the door to her side and had taken Barbara Ann and was standing on the other side of the highway. *She had gotten out before I did!*

It was all over with...that terrible feeling. They looked so good over there beside the road and she was holding Barbara Ann in her arms. The man got out and made sure we were okay.

I just had to share the feeling that I believe God wants us to have towards our family...the care. *Are you safe...are you on the safe side?*

Moving on to a more serious area than that...a family could be lost...eternally separated from God according to the scripture. We've felt concerned that that could really happen to your family...and mine.

That's why we have spent so much time in prayer for our household. It was no more the truck that was giving us the problem...no more just someone on the highway or careless driver that was approaching, but it was actually a revelation of disobeying or rejecting the Lord that would cause us to spend eternity away from God.

Listen Friends, those things touch the heart of God. He saw that picture to the extent that He went all out to save humanity...to get the good news of His salvation, His strong arm, to save us even when we were disobedient children, even away from God. His concern moved Him to make a great sacrifice to see us saved.

That same concern comes into the heart of a true father about his family. We will not just feel the need of buying them clothing...buying them food. We'll not just look for the pleasure of seeing them do well on the job, but our whole desire and the deep purpose of our life today should be to see them come to the place where they can say, "Even so, come, Lord Jesus," looking for the return of the Lord...having faith in God to help them fear Him...giving them hope for the world to come. There is no way to paint the picture of the reality, the concern and the intercessory prayer that can come to a father or mother concerning their household and their children.

The Bible shows that we, a lot of times, live far apart from the real vision of care for the soul. The scripture is quoted like this, "No man cared for my soul." Think of that...yet that's the important part of our being...our soul. Our soul returns back to God. God has said, "All souls are Mine."

My effort today is not just to tell a story about one experience in the pickup when the truck ran into us, but I am gravely concerned, yet filled with hope, that the Lord is able to save our household...our children and our family. As David said in the Psalm, "I'd have fainted unless I had believed enough to see the goodness of the Lord in the land of the living." And we do know that through our prayers, our interceding, we have the promise that He has made...that He is going to change our lives so that we can rejoice in the return of Jesus.

The Bible says the whole creation is groaning for the manifestations of the sons of God, the children of God. Most people are already far enough along in life to know where we belong. *We're not going to stay here...are we ready to go...what will things be like after life here?* We find in the Scripture that the soul never dies. We are going to spend eternity somewhere.

With a touch of God's love and the compassion that He has for us, we will find ourselves travailing in prayer for those towards whom the storm is headed.

One more thought I'd like to share. This happened literally in the land of Egypt whenever the Lord was visiting the people with the death angel. He told His people, "The death angel is going to pass over every home. What you must do to prepare for the death angel is that you shall kill a lamb and sprinkle the blood over the doorpost of your home. You shall eat this lamb and stay inside the house until the death angel passes over because if the blood isn't on the doorpost when the death angel comes, the firstborn in that home will be destroyed."

Knowing that the death angel is coming towards us can move us quickly like it did when the truck was coming towards my family and me. You'll find yourself seeking for God's way to make it different for your family.

Disaster is on its way and sin is moving in, in such a measure to destroy our loved ones. Don't allow the sun to go down without seeking to have full confidence that all is right with you and God if, tomorrow doesn't find you here in this life.

May the Lord help you to take the experiences that you've had...the cautions, the warnings that you've had concerning your household and *give your heart to the One who can make you profitable to your family* by being faithful to talk to them, share with them, the graces of God and the will of God for their lives. Don't hide from it any longer. Tell them God is able and we must have help, for the wages of sin is death. Is your family on the safe side?

–2–

Should I Talk About My Brother?

We are very loose with our talking. Especially before the Holy Spirit begins to move in our hearts and lives. **It's just amazing what the Holy Spirit will do with *our speech* and attitude toward others.**

I never shall forget an experience...I meant no harm by what I did, but it was certainly wrong. I was standing in our homeplace in Grapeland, Texas, talking to my mother and I began to relate to her a little bit of faults. The reason I call it a little bit of faults is because I did like a lot of times people do when they're talking about somebody...they try to say it free of any kind of prejudice or jealousy or criticism...try to say it in a Christ-like way. I don't mean we're trying to be hypocritical about it, but when the Holy Spirit truly has its way with the believer, it will make him very *sensitive to a more perfect way* to talk, *a more perfect attitude towards others.* This experience stayed with me, for my heart was so touched by it.

I was relating the little things that led to my being different than my brother in the church that he was ministering and pastoring. It's so easy to do that, but when we do, we don't realize the harm until a little suffering begins to strike us in those areas.

My brother was already experiencing a real warfare against the enemy and was trying to keep the courage to stay in the ministry. He was a young convert and hadn't been saved all that long and as I spoke those words of criticism the Holy Spirit moved so deeply into my heart...I felt so sad about it...felt sorry for my brother. A compassion came over me and I said, "Oh, mama, I feel so bad that I'm talking about my brother. I feel the Lord is grieved with it. He has enough battles to fight without me talking about him. Mother, let's pray for him." And we prayed earnestly for him.

That experience has lived on ever since.

Be careful of what you say about anybody.

If you can't say it in the right spirit, if you can't say something that's profitable, pray that the Lord will bless them and meet their every need.

We've certainly lived long enough to know that people are all about the same everywhere unless the Lord is in charge of their life. In other words, if the Lord turned loose of you and left you alone, you would certainly say and do things that would grieve the heart of God. So, it didn't just stop me from talking about my own fleshly brother, but it stopped me from talking about everybody and anybody. God wants you and I to be useful, helpful, thoughtful, mindful...a blessing to one another and He has a way of making it happen.

Don't talk about your brother.

— 3 —

Be Ye Angry, But Sin Not

I want to relate another experience while working on a job with an elderly man putting wood shingles on a barn. The shingles were running a little crooked on the roof. This elderly man (I was just a young person then) got after me several times blaming me for the crooked line of shingles. I really didn't feel I was the cause of those shingles laying there wavering on the barn crooked because there was another person that was on the roof between us and he was really the one who was causing them to waver.

I hated anyone to find fault with me. I began to feel that little old Irish nature rise and I didn't like it because I knew I would feel the Lord was grieved.

The Lord helped me and we finished the barn work. I was so glad because I felt like it was about time to go home and then I wouldn't have to put up with this man who was coming against me, finding fault with me. But about an hour before quitting time he suddenly spoke up and said, "We got about an hour before quitting time. We're going to work around on the front of the house and put up a form for a concrete walk."

Oh, I dreaded it because it seemed like he was so hard to work with and found fault in everything we did and didn't mind expressing it. Then I prayed, "Lord, help me keep right." So I got some little stobs ready to stob down the form for a cement slab and he began to gripe about the way I was aiming those little stobs that were to hold the form together for the cement to be poured.

Finally, it seemed like it was just more than I could bear, so I said to him, "I wish that I could please you." And I said it in a *wrong tone* of voice...I felt bad about it.

He looked up at me as he was on his knees driving the

stobs down in the ground and said, "I'll knock you in the head with this hammer."

Well, I was just young enough, you might say, just in the stage that I didn't like that at all.

Anyway, I calmly said, "You'll not be Mr. Willis either when you do."

And when I did, I knew that I had answered him wrong, for this man had stood out on the street several times while I was out there singing and witnessing for the Lord. And the thought came to me: the next time he sees me on the street he'll remember me talking back to him.

I went around the side of the house crying and my sister asked me what was wrong. I told her and she said, "No one gets along with him. Don't worry about it."

Nevertheless, what could I do about it? But, when I knelt down in prayer the next morning, the Lord spoke to me and said, *"I want you to go to that man and ask his forgiveness."*

Well, I'll tell you, really, I knew enough about that man that he could care less about my apology, and what would he say?

But the Lord just seemed to put it upon my heart.

And I said, "Lord, if you'll let me see him whenever I get to town, I'll sure ask him to forgive me."

The very next morning I went to town and he was one of the first people I saw...in that little country town where they tie off their teams in the back alley and stand around and talk to one another. He was back there talking to somebody and I thought to myself, "Well, I'll wait until he quits talking and ask him to forgive me later."

But the Lord must have known that was the best time and something just seemed to almost get a hold of my collar and pull me over there.

So I said, "Listen, Mr. Willis, I'm trying to live a Christian life and I'm sorry that I talked back to you yesterday evening."

He said to me, "Well, you had no business doing it."

I said, "I know it and I want you to forgive me for it." He just turned away and walked over and started talking to the man again.

But, did I feel better? *Yes, I felt better.*

I've used these experiences as guidelines as time has gone

by. **The more room we make for the Lord, the more He puts in our heart: the same feelings that He has towards others.**

So, don't fall out with one another. Find a place in the Lord that you can share with others the Christ-likeness that you want the Lord to share towards you.

Give it a try...it's worth it.

The Testings In Today's Experiences, Are Actually An Arm... Reaching Out To Things Eternal, Things Of Tomorrow.

-J. E. Murdock

– 4 –

THE GREAT BONFIRE

You never know just what may come alive in your spirit and mind if you give God a chance to talk to you.

A great bonfire took place a few years ago at a church in Lake Charles, Louisiana. This was more than just an experience…it truly became a way of life for the believer. It is mentioned in the 19th chapter of Acts, verse 19, "Many of them also which used curious arts brought their books together, and burned them before all *men:* and they counted the price of them, and found *it* fifty thousand *pieces* of silver. So mightily grew the Word of God and prevailed."

You'd be surprised to know how many things are written that we never see. But if we're in search of a deeper walk with the Lord…to be more what He'd have us to be and make our calling and our election sure, we'll do like the early church did and begin to search the Scriptures to see if those things that the minister is talking about are really true.

That scripture goes on to relate to us the conditions that Paul found in the church and among the people that he ministered to…to find that conviction of the Lord had come upon those who were reading materials, books and things that were actually harmful to the believer. The Holy Spirit had begun to point out the things that were not good for them. The Word tells us how *they decided to do something about it.*

Many of them who had books and wrong literature brought them together and they were worth around fifty thousand pieces of silver. That was a pile of stuff, no doubt a bonfire! So they had this fire burning and to prove that God was certainly in it, *the church grew mightily.*

And while in search of a closer walk and spiritual growth to establish us in Him, it came to my mind to go into our homes, into the bookshelves and into the places where we had materials that were not Christ-like or helpful to spiritual growth.

I said, "Let's dedicate our life to the Lord and let's prove it so by bringing in those books and we'll have a book burning right here beside the church." And listen, Friends, it was not what you'd call a big fun game, but it was a time of serious commitment to God.

Quite a few of those people had expensive books and a lot of them actually thought more of those things that fed the natural, the carnal man, than they thought of their own Bible. And so the Spirit of God awakened their hearts.

That evening we built the fire and watched the different ones bring some of their materials that they felt the Lord had deemed were not good for their souls, and we burned them. Though that's been a few years ago, I can actually still see something on their faces, how they looked as they put their books into the fire and destroyed them. They were saying, "Lord, I don't believe You approve of this kind of literature; I don't believe that You are pleased with it and we're going to do like they did in the book of Acts." They brought them and they burned them, destroyed them. And their work grew. And now we're doing this in order that the church can grow spiritually and the Holy Spirit can move in His own way and can condition our hearts and help us to discern right reading and wrong reading.

They brought these things in and, remember, this wasn't just to show off, just a make-believe that we were spiritual, that "We're right and this will make us ready for heaven," but this was actually to show us the difference between the carnal nature of man and the spiritual side of man, which is Christ. These books were feeding the carnal nature of man and, while doing that, it blocked spiritual growth and revelation that God wanted to give to the believer. God was moving and the hearts of the people were reaching out, He was able to draw their attention to destroy these things...putting them away so they would not be an hindrance or be a place where the enemy could deceive.

I would like to say again, seriously, conscientiously, and even respectfully to people who are not seeing the need of destroying those things that do not feed your soul and inspire your life spiritually, that I have a feeling that there are many, many homes in which there are reading materials like that, and they scarcely read their Bibles. For if we would read our Bible enough, we would run across a scripture like the one I just related in Acts 19:19, and find what the early church did in the face of conviction about things that they were reading that did not edify their souls and bless their lives.

In the love of God and in the fear of God, look again and say, *"Many of them also which used curious arts brought their books together, and burned them before all men: and they counted the price of them, and found it fifty thousand pieces of silver."*

Begin to separate yourselves from those materials, even to the extent of burning them, destroying them.

You'll never be sorry.

When We
Recognize
Our Imperfection
We Will
Automatically
Reach For A Cure.

-J. E. Murdock

– 5 –

PRAYER WORKS FOR OUR LOVED ONES

Different experiences that we have in this life are an extension of things *eternal.*

Oh, if we could grasp that! The testings in today's experiences, if we'll let them, are actually arms reaching out to things eternal, things of tomorrow.

Let me tell you about my brother. It was during the time that I had been saved and filled with the Spirit and I did love to talk about the Lord and felt like I should witness for Him. My brother, seven years older than me, belonged to a church, but he really had no testimony of God's presence...God's grace. He didn't talk about those things, but he was a hard worker and he had made a statement to one of my sisters that he wouldn't give me a job even if I went hungry. When I heard that, I knew that I couldn't be mad at him, but I wanted to find out if he had really said that.

So, I walked into his shop one day shortly after I heard about it and I said, "Earl, I don't want to start a fuss or anything, but I heard you had said something and I just didn't believe that you had said it, but I want to ask you if you did. I heard that you wouldn't give me a job even if I was going hungry. Did you say that?"

He said, "Yes, I said it. I don't want anyone around here who's always talking about the Lord. You're always talking about the Lord."

I said, "All right, Earl. I just wanted to find out if you said it."

He turned to go to his work in the shop and I turned to walk away and, of course, I was real tender towards the Lord and towards my brother, too. So, I had to weep a little bit as I walked out. That was a breaking experience, but at the same time I was spending a lot of time praying for him...that he would be saved and the Lord would deal with his life. That was the inside story about my brother at that point.

But as time went on, it wasn't long until the Lord called my wife and I into the work of the Lord.

We had our little girl, our first child, who was about a year and a half old at that time. We went into the work of the Lord, for a door had miraculously opened up for us, and the pastor had sent word that they would come and move us there. The church had discussed us coming and working with the young people and helping the pastor in the services. Both of us played instruments. I played the guitar and my wife played the accordion and we sang. We loved to worship the Lord in that way. The Lord opened that door immediately.

I wasn't out in the Lord's work but just a very few short weeks when I got a letter from my twin sister which said, "John, pray for our brother. The Lord's dealing with him. He went to church last night."

"Well," I said then, "If he went to church, God is really working."

It wasn't three or four days after that that I got a letter from my brother who had *never* written me a letter, never really held a real conversation with me, being seven years older than me. This letter said, "John, I am now serving the same Lord you are and I'll pay your expenses if you'll come home and stay a few days. Our little church is in a revival and I'd like for you to come." *Well, that was the thrill of my life!*

My wife and I got into our little '31 Model Ford and took off. About 145 miles later we walked into the little church that had been built in our hometown just to find my brother down at the altar. The day after that service my brother turned his shop over to the helpers that he had in the shop. Then, he and I drove out about three or four miles outside of Grapeland, Texas, where I had worked on a dairy before I went into the Lord's work, and we sat down on the side of a creek that wound through the dairy farm and spent most all day talking about the Lord.

While we were sitting there I asked, "Earl, what happened that you decided to turn to the Lord?"

He said, "Well, you know John as long as you were at home around here, I resented hearing you talk about the Lord. But whenever I heard that you had gone on out into the Lord's work, I knew it must be real. So, I turned to the Lord." That's actually the beginning of a glorious experience of *how God answers prayers on behalf of our families.*

There Is More In
The Secret Place.
If We'll Talk
To God,
He Can Change
The Picture.

-J. E. Murdock

– 6 –

WHEN I MISSED GOD

When we went in the Lord's work, we spent the first year and a half working with the young people, playing and singing, going to prayer meetings at the church every morning at nine o'clock, visiting the sick and working for the Lord full time. But there came a real desire over me...I wanted to preach as well as sing the gospel. And it got to where I didn't care all that much about singing because I just wanted to get up and preach what the Lord was giving to my heart.

Back in those days, they said a person who wanted to get up and preach had the *"preacher's itch."* Well, when the Lord calls you to do something, you're going to find that real satisfaction comes as you obey and do what the Lord has called you to do.

So, that desire to preach was down inside, but the pastor where we worked wanted us to play and sing for him and to help him in his services while he preached. After I experienced this desire to minister, I prayed the Lord would open a door. Of course, the pastor discouraged us from making such a move, but, nevertheless, the desire was so great and I prayed earnestly.

A young man named Jack McCullough from Hartburg, Texas, (I had no idea where Hartburg was) wrote the pastor and said, "Brother, I wonder if you would let your singers come and hold a meeting for me?" He gave me the letter so I went to this community and started a revival.

After we had preached there a week, this pastor wanted to go away somewhere and hold a revival and wanted us to stay there and fill in at his church until he got back. Well, three weeks went by and we hadn't heard from him...a month went by and we got a message, he said, "Brother Murdock, I believe the Lord is through with me in Hartburg. Why don't you just take the pastorate there?" So, that was a door that opened for us to pastor. Just think...a door had opened that *I could preach!* I didn't just pray and sing...*I could preach.* I got more satisfaction out of the ministry then than ever before!

After being there about six months, the pastor that we had been working with in Cameron, Texas, sent me word that he had bought a tent and was going to do some out-station work in other small towns around Cameron, Texas, and said, "If you'll come and help me, we will build you a good church up here around somewhere close to us." That sounded really good then because I'd pastored enough now, I'd preached all my sermons, and I was about ready to make a little change! At the same time, I really felt I shouldn't go...that I should stay with that little church because God had opened the door and everything was working beautifully. But I went against that feeling and conviction and drove on up to Cameron, Texas, and on up to Buckholts where the pastor had already put up the tent and was waiting for us to get there.

I drove up on the lot where he had the tent up and he walked out and said he was so glad to see us. My wife knew that I was already in *the dumps,* what we call "in the valley." I had told her I thought I was missing God and should not leave that little church. She told the pastor that I felt that way and that I felt like I should go back there. The pastor said boldly, "You're right where God wants you...nobody's gonna run off with your little church. And whenever the summer is up, we will have you a little church built here near us and we can have fellowship together up here." That really sounded good, but it didn't erase the terrible, deep conviction that I should not have left that little church.

We began the revivals around in the different places, but the summer was up, still no church was built. Another pastor had taken the little church that we had left in Hartburg and now I was out there...*stranded.* No excuses were made why we hadn't built the little church like we had been promised, but there I was.

So, I parked the trailer just at the edge of Cameron under a peach tree and connected my lights up to a friend's that worked in the church there. I kept praying, of course, seeking the Lord. *Now I was without a church to pastor...out of a place to work for the Lord...stranded from everything.*

So, while sitting there, the pastor had decided that he would build a new church in a new, better location for them right there in Cameron.

He told me, "John, if you'll just come and help me we'll give you two dollars a day to work on the church and that will give time for the Lord to open up something for you. You'll have to have something to live on."

Well, really I didn't want to work for money...I knew I had to have money, but I didn't want to work for money...I just wanted to preach and work for the Lord and let just whatever happened take place.

I went to work digging in the foundation of black dirt there. On the second day I noticed I had rubbed a blister in my hand with a shovel digging into that black dirt.

By the fourth day I could not use my hand. It swelled up and it looked like poison was going to set up in my hand. I lost three or four nights sleep...just couldn't rest...trying to pick this open so that it would heal up, but I couldn't. The bruise was too deep.

So, we went to a doctor at night after office hours.

We went to his home and he said he'd have to operate on me. He called the druggist to prepare some kind of medicine that I should take before he put me to sleep to operate the next morning. Well, I went to the drug store and told the man I really didn't want to take the medicine...I wanted to *"trust the Lord"*...(and I didn't have any money either!) The friend that took me there, Brother Joe Danna, said he would take care of the three and a half dollars for the medicine...that's what it cost back then. But the man said, "No, if you're not going to take it, I can sell it to someone else." That was just what I wanted to hear.

I walked into the doctor's office the next morning and

stood beside the little bed that I was to lie down on to be put to sleep. The doctor said, "Did you take the medicine?"

I said, "No," and I wanted to give an excuse.

When he said, "Well, get up on this bed here. You should have taken it. I wanted you to take it to prepare you for the operation." And that's all he said.

I laid down and was soon put to sleep and when I woke up, my hand was all wrapped up. He had operated on me and everything was taken care of and I went home to the little trailer that we were living in.

In one week's time, I went back to have my hand checked. He had run this little gauze through the hole in the two openings on my hand...on the backside and on the inside...so it could drain. When he unwrapped my hand and reached to pull out that little piece of gauze, it just turned me sick.

He said, "Well, it's not time. I'll have to wait a few days."

He waited one week and I went back and he pulled the gauze out...it didn't hurt me. Then he wrapped it up.

I asked him, "Now, what do I owe you?" He said, "Well, an operation like that is usually $30.00 or $35.00, but since you are a minister, I'm only going to charge you $8.00."

I never really got over that.

Whenever I think of how I felt about having to go to work...I'd left the little church...I couldn't go back to it.

Now I was on the side of the road and the winter months were on there and I was, we might say, just crippled to where I couldn't do anything with my hand and I had only worked four days.

Why didn't the doctor say, "You owe me ten dollars?" Why didn't he say five dollars? Well, if he wanted to be nice, why didn't he say fifteen or twenty? Why did he say *eight dollars?*

Since I had worked four days and made eight dollars and the bruise cost me that, that has "talked" to me and said a lot of things and has actually been instrumental in helping me to *seek hard* to hear the voice of God in whatever I did from that day forward.

The Lord has been gracious, though, using those places

where you miss God and such chastening comes. In fact, the pastor told me, "Well, nobody's going to run away with that little old church anyway." But they did, and I'll tell you the door that God opened was never opened again for me to go back to that little church.

The suffering was so that one day even years later I was thinking about how miserable, how wretched, I was whenever I left that little church in Hartburg against the conviction that God had put on my heart knowing that I should stay there.

The Lord spoke to me again, "I didn't chasten you like that just because you left the little church, *but I wanted to teach you the importance of staying in My will and not being moved by anything else.*"

I guarantee you I got a lesson then that kept me in places where, really, in the natural, you'd think it was time to run. But if God didn't tell me to run, I didn't run. I remembered the chastening that God gave me because I left that little church *contrary to the conviction* that I should stay there.

Friends, God loves us enough to *chasten* us, but I'll tell you that your *chastenings are hard to forget.*

God knows just how to do it and no one can keep you from it when God gets ready to chasten you for something that you have overlooked or something that you have failed to obey.

Thank God for the chastening rod.

He didn't kill me, but I thought a few times I had come to the end of the road, but how good the Lord has rewarded me by just staying in The Secret Place seeking the face of God...*there's always a better way for us.*

Between this experience of "missing God" from the other little church and the experience we had working four days and paying the eight dollars to the doctor for lancing the blister I got while I was digging in the dirt, we kept praying, of course, seeking the Lord.

I felt that if I ever went back home to the dairy farm that I had left going into the Lord's work that something may happen and I'd never get back out again. I was afraid that I would never be able to launch out again as God had opened the door so wonderfully prior to this experience. The Lord kept working in our hearts and during that summer we were supposed to build a little church after holding revivals.

We had a good revival in a little town about 20 miles away from Cameron called Rogers, Texas. So, we decided that we would rent a little house up there that we could get for eight dollars a month. And I could put two church benches (we had some old benches that we used under the tent) in one room and two in another and we would have church in that and we would live in the back end of this old house just off of the main street.

We got the house, but we had sold our furniture and had bought a new Gibson guitar. Now we didn't have any furniture to move into this house, but a friend of ours in Cameron, Texas, had some old furniture that she had put in her garage.

We were stepping very slowly at that time when we got ahold of this old furniture there. One of the young men that had worked with us in the youth service there in Cameron prior to the time when we first went into the Lord's work had taken his pickup and gotten the old furniture. I gave him a dollar to bring it up to Rogers, about 18 miles away, and put it in the back two rooms of this building to see if we couldn't get our church started in there.

We had had a wonderful revival there in the early part of the summer and then we left there and since we never did do anything else, we thought we would give it another try. So, I unloaded the furniture and we straightened it up and found that the mirrors of the old dresser were all broken, the rocker was broken, the old bed looked like it had been worn out for many years and the old chair looked as though it wouldn't hold anybody.

I looked at my little wife and told her, "I don't believe that I can take it. We had nice furniture and now look what we've ended up with here."

She just looked at me as if to say, "Well, whatever you feel like doing."

So, I told the boy, right then and there, to load it right back up and take it back to Cameron!

I had a little something else in my mind then. I decided that I would catch a ride...which I did...and go about 145 miles to where I was raised and where I had lived before we went into the Lord's work. I decided that I would go over there and *spend a little time in prayer and see what I could get from the Lord.*

When I got there, I went into a little service and knelt down and prayed at the altar and sought the Lord...we had quite a bit of freedom to pray at that time. The little group of people who were there made it very easy just to pray, however, I didn't tell them what I was experiencing concerning moving this old furniture. But I did get up and tell them what I really felt while I was praying there at the altar...that the Lord laid it on my heart to go back and gather that old furniture up again and take it to Rogers. I felt a peace from the Lord to do that. Then they praised the Lord with me, and prayed that the Lord would direct me.

I caught a ride back to Cameron, Texas, where my wife was staying with the pastor and his wife while I was making my trip to Grapeland, Texas. We gathered the old furniture right back up and took it to the house there that we'd rented and put it up in the two little rooms in the back of the house and, honestly, you could not believe it, but it looked really good. That old furniture that had looked so bad that I couldn't take it the first time...I was surprised how good it looked. Actually, I felt *peaceful.*

So, we might say there is more in The Secret Place if we'll turn back and talk to God. *He can change the picture* and that's exactly what had happened.

Then we began to try to gather people into the service (it was the winter months), but no one came out except one elderly man. We were certainly on the mercies of the Lord.

We didn't feel like telling anybody about the hardships of it...just felt like God had the answer if we would just seek His face and have faith in Him that we'd know what to do.

The old enemy had already spoken to my heart. I knew it was the enemy because he said, "You'd better fast and pray or your little girl is going to go hungry." We won't go into details about how close poverty had come to our door, but I just thought to myself, *No, the enemy doesn't want me to fast. He just wants me to be afraid...to doubt God.* So, I told my little wife that we still had a few jars of canned stuff and weren't out of everything yet. The thought came to me...I said we're just going to look to the Lord and see how far we are from going hungry. We'll just seek the Lord and not be afraid because I could tell the suggestion of fasting because our baby girl was going to go hungry was to make me afraid...make me *doubt*.

Just about that time, the pastor had sent word to us that they were coming by our house the next day, a Saturday. "We're going to Davilla, Texas, to a little church up there; they're having a fellowship meeting." I can remember this as if it were yesterday.

I told my wife, "Isn't that wonderful? We will go up there and we'll have a good time in the Lord. We'll have something to eat and we can bring back something for our little Barbara Ann." So, I felt very good about it...the Lord was very real that day.

We brought some food back home with us and when we got out of the pastor's car before going into the little house he said, "Brother Murdock, how are you doing?" I said, "All right, Brother, I'm doing just fine." He got back in his car and pulled out fifty cents. I thought to myself, *Isn't that wonderful!* We hadn't told him how bad a shape we were in. We went inside and figured out right quick what we could buy to eat with that fifty cents and did we thank the Lord for it!

We had planned when we first went to Rogers that we would have services on the streets...hopefully someone would give an offering. But the weather was so bad that there was no one for us to minister to. But I left the house and went to the post office...walked on up there with my summer suit on.

No one knew just where we were at, so we didn't get any mail and walking back home from the post office I met an elderly lady. She looked at me and said, "Aren't you Brother Murdock?"

I said, "Yes, ma'am."

She said, "You don't know me but I was in your tent revival in the spring here and I belong to another church, but I feel like the Lord wants me to give you this."

She reached in her purse and gave me a dollar bill. You've heard of dollar bills that look like wagon wheels...well, that's exactly what that dollar bill looked like. I rejoiced as never before! I went to the house and told my little wife and she took that dollar bill and got busy figuring out what all we could do with that one dollar bill!

If you haven't been there, you just don't get the feel of that, but at the same time there was still somebody in The Secret Place praying..myself along with my dear wife while watching over our little girl. Somehow or another, the Lord helped us to seek the mind of Christ...whether to sit still or exactly what we should do. The pressure, of course, hadn't turned loose...it was still on.

We had been there about three months and no one was coming out to church. I kind of felt impressed to leave there and decided to catch a ride to Orange, Texas. There was a dear man working there in Cameron, but he had a job now at the shipyard in Orange and he came home on the weekends. So, I caught a ride with him down to Houston. I had heard about a young pastor there and stopped off and, of course, did a little fasting...praying...seeking the Lord. He wanted me to stay two or three days. I did and then I caught a ride on down to Orange.

I'll tell you the true stories are all in there. It would take a while to share them with you, but I do want to say this, Friends, that by spending time in The Secret Place or getting before the Lord and giving your heart to Him, the problem will be solved. The Word speaks, "I had fainted, unless I had believed to see the goodness of the Lord in the land of the living" (Psalm 27:13). So, always add faith to your prayer in The Secret Place...*that's the only thing that makes us different*

from anyone else...faith in the Lord. And certainly it was time
to believe or faint...but the Lord was working in our hearts in
a most precious way.

When I got over to Orange, I went to a little church there.
It was my first time to be down in that area.

I got up and testified and at the end of the service a dear
sister in the Lord whom I'd never met before came to me and
said, "Aren't you a minister?"

I said, "Yes, ma'am."

She said, "Are you looking for a revival?"

I said, "Well, if the Lord opens up one, I'm ready for a
revival."

She said, "I know of a friend, a pastor in Orangefield.
He's a night watchman there in Beaumont, but he has a little
church and I really do feel like he'll give you a revival. I believe
he'll let you preach. I'll take you out there to see him in the
morning."

So, we rode out there about six or seven miles to
Orangefield and met this Brother Ellesor and told him who I
was and what we were there for.

He said, "Well, I don't have a large church. I don't think
you could hurt anything and I believe we'll let you come here
and hold a revival."

Immediately, I accepted. Got back on the road to Cameron
to get my wife and bring her down there and we went into this
revival.

The Lord began to bless us. In just two weeks of revival
we had been given a total of about $65.00. We owed a little bit
at a dear friend's grocery store in Cameron, so we shared about
half of that in paying our bill and rejoiced with what we had
left.

Then...the revival was over...now what were we going to
do? We went in the trailer over to Vinton, Louisana. We had
never been in that little town, except in passing through, and
I thought maybe I could find a place for revival. We found an
old building and the man let us rent it for three dollars a week
and we had to pay our own light bill. Of course, we could see

the Lord in that.

Then I traveled all over that town for three evenings and covered about every place and invited them out to our revival meeting there in the old store building. Most everyone said they would come, but would you believe only about a half a dozen came? Then the rain came and water began to gather around our trailer and it looked like there would be no chance for revival at all. While sitting there *"in the dumps,"* I was kind of getting low again and had to just stay before the Lord.

There was a dear preacher friend of ours who heard we were there who drove up in the rain and said, "Brother Murdock, I'm glad to find that you are here. I didn't know you were down here in Louisiana. I've got a little place over in Hackberry where I've held a revival in a theater building. We have bought an old bar there and would like to get a church started. We would like for you to go over there and try it out and see what you think about it." Of course, we were just waiting for God...whatever the Lord said.

We ended up going over there immediately. We stayed with some friends there in Hackberry until we could get the little old building cleaned up, get the pews made and could fix up a little barge that had been pulled out of the river and was sitting right beside this bar. It wasn't really livable, but there was a lumberyard close by so I got busy and fixed it up so we could move out of our friend's house...trying to pastor and get a little church started there.

Honestly, talk about blessed!...I have sat there on an old couch in that little 12x22 house that we had fixed up...a living room and bedroom together along with a little kitchen and dining room and just cried and *rejoiced* for *the peace* that began to fill our souls. After the road we had been over since we had left that little church in Hartburg, I'll tell you, it seemed like a real refreshing had come to us. I wished that some of my loved ones could enjoy the peace that began to come over our souls right there.

We saw the Lord work there. These experiences came about because *God wanted to do things in our lives and the only way He could do them was for us to stay in the prayer place, The Secret Place, before the Lord.* We had already experienced God moving in a miraculous way so we were not afraid that God couldn't lead us on although our little church was just a very small handful. As far as finances were concerned, three or four dollars a week was doing well, but at the same time, we didn't go out for the money...we went out to do what God wanted us to do and felt like the Lord would take care of the rest. And did He...He certainly did! He does it in His own way and that's the only way for you and I to come to know Him anyway...*let Him do it the way He wants to, then you will see the hand of the Lord.*

Now we were looking forward to a new baby and were hoping that the Lord would bless us with a boy, since we had a little girl. And so, while waiting for this to come about, groceries were very low...very poor. But one day a man, who worked in the oil field, and his wife drove up right out in the rain and brought a great big sack of groceries and set it there on the porch and from that time on, every week, they would give us groceries or give us a very small paycheck, but it sustained us.

The time came for the baby to be born, but we certainly didn't have what it took to go to the hospital, so we stayed right there in this little two-room house and called for the doctor. While the doctor was there, he decided it would be a day or two before the baby would be born. But I happened to have an aunt that had come over from Orange and was staying with us and she had a lot of experience with mothers who were confined with a new baby. She said immediately, "No, no, that baby's ready to be born." Before the doctor could go back to his house, why things shaped up so *that he decided it was true.* It wasn't but a few minutes, then, until I hollered out at the foot of the bed, "It's a boy!"...and we still have that fine boy who has a fine little family today. We saw the mighty hand of the Lord in those days.

Listen, Friends, we have told you, more or less, one side of the picture, but there may be some who will read and find out there are two sides to the picture. There's one thing about it, though, that through all of these things that seemed to be very pressing, *we were praying and seeking the Lord and came to know Him more in a real way.* And that's why we're not afraid to tell you, if God says to jump, *jump.* If the Lord says to be still, *be still. Whatever He saith unto you, do it, and things will go better.* Don't forget where you get it...seek the Lord with all of your heart, all of your soul.

Whenever You Relate
The Hand Of God,
Whether It Was
Yesterday Or
Years Ago,
There Is Something
About The
Relationship With
God That Will Still
Bless You...
Refresh You...
Encourage You.

-J. E. Murdock

FATHER'S TALK

VOLUME 2

by

DR. J. E. MURDOCK

Table Of Contents

~ 1 ~

HE IS HEALED!

It seems like when you begin to get directions or God begins to direct your life, the path behind you has been so testing, so trying, that you begin to walk more carefully. In the scriptures, Elijah, the prophet of God, had grown weary and it looked like he just wasn't going to make it when the Lord appeared to him and said, "Arise, Elijah, and eat. Your journey is too great for you." So he arose and the angel of the Lord fed Elijah and he sat down again.

That seemed to be the experience that we were having *until* we got over to Hackberry. For about five or six months, we actually rested there, delighting ourselves in the Lord along with that new baby boy...what a rejoicing we had! Though the congregation was not big enough to support us, we looked to the Lord and saw how He began to work there.

The pastor who had started the work in Hackberry was in Lake Charles and also had an out-station in Big Lake, Louisiana, about four miles across the lake from Hackberry. But to get to Big Lake, you'd have to go about 30 miles around to get there. He wanted us to go over to Big Lake and hold a revival meeting, so we went and the Lord blessed us in such a way...he asked us if we'd pastor that church.

It didn't have a parsonage to live in and we didn't have anything but a little bit of furniture, so we moved our furniture over to a building we rented in Big Lake and started pastoring the church there. Immediately, we had such favor with that nice little congregation...began to experience such fellowship and harmony with the people and truly enjoyed the services, worshipping the Lord with prayer meetings daily. Then we borrowed money at the bank and built a nice little parsonage.

Things just grew sweeter in many different ways. I can't

help but believe that the roads we had traveled a few months before certainly helped to make the experience in Big Lake taste a bit sweeter. That happens...the Lord gives you and I experiences, some of them we bring on ourselves, but if we'll follow on and stay before the Lord they will prove to be profitable to us. *Learning to **hear** the voice of the Lord...learning the **value** of His voice...learning to **understand** His voice is so important.*

The church began to grow and we had another little boy born into our family while living there in Big Lake, and this time we were able to go the hospital in Lake Charles. We brought him home and were so blessed for about a year and a half and then this newest little boy, Michael Dean, (in fact, the nurse suggested that his name be Michael; kind of a Bible name we understood then, so that's what we named him) had taken a spell of sickness. We won't go into details about it, but we truly almost lost him. We'd come to the place where we just said, *Lord, if you're going to take him, Your will be done. If You will him to live, we'll praise You for that.* We tried to surrender to God's precious will.

During that time, a dear sister, who walked across the street everyday to prayer meeting, who couldn't read or write but certainly had a relationship with God in The Secret Place, told us more than once, "The old enemy wants to destroy that baby, Michael Dean, but God is going to use him and that's why the enemy wants to destroy him." She said that with such confidence. When she spoke that it seemed to help us believe that certainly God did have a plan. And so, prayers began to go up and many wonderful things began to happen during the next few months.

I'd like to go just a bit farther. We had announced that we would hold a brush arbor meeting in Orange, Texas, a few miles out of Orange. They built it during the time that Mike was so sick and the only nourishment he would actually take in was cocoa. And, of course, we still hear a little bit about cocoa, in fact, he still signs his letter when he writes to me, "Your cocoa kid." He doesn't remember the cocoa as much as he remembers us *giving* him cocoa. He couldn't eat anything else and didn't want anything else, but he had to have something and we found that he liked cocoa.

We experienced such a low place with Mike and it looked like we were about to lose him, but I told my dear wife, "I'm going to go ahead and hold this brush arbor meeting." I had promised to do it so they got it ready for us.

During the first three nights of the meeting, a lady brought her little baby there who had a terrible disease and wasn't expected to live. She brought the baby before us and we prayed *earnestly* for it and the Lord healed the baby. In just a few days the healing was evident, even years later we found out the child stayed healed and has become a fine young man.

But what was going to happen to our baby, Mike? We prayed, the church prayed, and we sought the Lord earnestly, but I can't say that we really ever prayed to the point that we could say the Lord wanted to take him home to be with Him...or heal him.

So, I told my little wife on a Friday night after a service, "They have an all night prayer meeting every Friday night at the Full Gospel Temple and I'm going there, after our services are over, to the prayer meeting where others will be praying and I'm going to pray through." Back then that meant we prayed till we touched God and got His answer for our prayer request.

So, I went up there about 10:30 p.m. after the services...others were praying and worshipping and seeking the Lord for different needs...I knelt down quietly before the Lord and, all at once, there was a sweet annointing that came up over me. I had come there to wait the rest of the night and to pray through and find out what God really wanted and planned to do concerning our baby.

The annointing struck me and I began to say these words, *"Thou art a mighty God."* And by the time I said that about three or four times, there was a *heavy* annointing upon that, and I said it again, "Thou art a mighty God." I found myself standing up on my feet and saying it again and as I said those words it seemed like it was not a vision that you could actually see with your natural eye, but the Spirit of the Lord that let me see Mike was in the hands of satan and there was no fear that gripped me.

I said again, "Thou art a mighty God."

And as I repeated those words, I actually, in the Spirit, saw the Lord walk over very gently and *calmly take Mike out of the hands of satan just like you would take a baby out of the hands of a mother or somebody.*

He didn't jerk the baby out of his hands, He didn't say anything, He had just taken him out in such a way that something registered right then, *he is healed.* And from that moment on, I could not even say, "Lord, heal Mike."

I knew he was healed, and *immediately* he began to be restored back to health.

So, it was a precious experience in Big Lake along with a good group of people who prayed with us...stood by us in the midst of that trial. And we have seen God work and bring him right on through and use him for years now in the work of the Lord...sharing the Gospel in the most unique way...contacting and encouraging people and having favor with people in an unusual way.

It's hard not to see a mighty miracle taking place in the life of that young boy called Michael Dean at the age of nearly three years old when we almost lost him.

But *how beautiful it is to follow on and see God work and find out how to get things from God...it is most wonderful.*

– 2 –

CAMERON NOW IN VIEW

Stepping out of the prayer room one day there in Big Lake where we were pastoring, I suddenly began to have a real desire for a revival there and thought maybe that we'd be able to get an evangelist in and it would help the church.

And the people began to spend a little time in fasting and prayer that the Lord would direct us concerning a revival. Would you believe that at the close of about two weeks of prayer and fasting, the Lord laid on our hearts to pray for the revival to be held down in Cameron, Louisiana?

Cameron was a nice little shrimping town filled with fishing boats and shrimp sheds. They had no full gospel work at all in that town. I'd already heard a lot about that little town. It was said to be the most wicked little town on the Gulf and it was said so much and by so many different people that I decided it must be very wicked. So, as the Lord had impressed us, we went to check out this little town to see if we could find a building and get a place to hold a revival.

Immediately we found a dear elderly man that we became acquainted with, a Mr. Roger, who had lived there for many years. He had a big building that was used for a theater building and it held quite a few people. He said we could use that building for a revival and that was the hand of the Lord because, from what we'd heard about the people down in that area, they wouldn't want to know that a preacher even came through town...but we found favor *immediately*.

We started the revival meeting and were going back and forth about 40 miles to Big Lake, but we soon got an old house and moved in so we could stay down there while we were holding the revival.

The first two weeks in this revival we only preached how

to be saved...how to trust the Lord for forgiveness of their sins...why the blood of Jesus was shed. We actually felt like that was the part of the gospel that they needed first of all.

The little building just filled up and people were standing around on the outside and then we began to preach to them more about the closer walk with the Lord and the baptism of the Holy Spirit. The results were so wonderful that we immediately began to look for a lot on which we could get a church started...right there on the Gulf of Mexico in Cameron, Louisiana.

We couldn't find land anywhere. It looked like every door was closed when suddenly an addition opened right up on the highway on the edge of town that none of us knew about. We bought two little lots and started building. We found an old building down on the bank of the river that we could buy for $175.00.

So, we began to tear it down and get something started up there on our lots. And the Lord blessed in such a way that, as soon as we got it fixed up and could begin services, it was a *beautiful* sight to see a nice group of children along with a few teenagers standing there an *hour before* church, waiting for us to open the door...they were so hungry!

Relating another beautiful experience we had, shrimp season came around and people in our church made a living that way...heading and packing shrimp during the shrimp season and the men who were operating the two shrimp sheds said, "Why don't you come on down and bring your guitar and your accordion and just sing to us while we're heading shrimp."

That sounded good to us, so we dismissed our service and went down there and played the accordion and the guitar to the folks along with those who were coming into our church. It felt like we were having a little revival...we enjoyed that very much.

So, along with working on our church, we just decided we'd give the people a chance to give so that we could put screens on the church, do some painting and make it more complete.

We went to a dear man who had a bar there in Cameron and would you believe that immediately the Lord gave us such favor with that man? We didn't beg him but just told him we were receiving gifts in order to complete the little church that he was already aware was being built and in which services were being held. He said, "I'll tell you what, I'll pay for all the screens that it takes to screen your church." From that time on, it was no problem at all to complete that little church.

Time went on by and we saw that there was a need for a pastor to go there and live. So, we got a dear brother to go there and we immediately built a nice little parsonage and he was blessed and was used for a period of time, but the time did drift to a point, for some reason or another, he didn't feel like staying there any longer.

As far as the spiritual results, even to this present time, those that still remain around there never forgot those days whenever the Lord was answering prayer and directing us to minister to the people down in that area. The favor God gave us lasted to this present time among those who are still living in the area. So, we are thankful to share this with you.

Now, listen, stay on board. There's more from The Secret Place...and when I say from The Secret Place, that's exactly where it comes from. When Zion travailed, the Bible says she brought forth her children. When we seek the Lord and get His will He also provides the ability, the "go" signal, to accomplish what He has called us to do.

If you're not used to The Secret Place, why don't you walk into your bedroom and go ahead and start one there. That means just get alone with the Lord and pour your little heart out to Him. He's concerned and knows exactly what you have need of, but *you have to ask and you have to believe to receive*. It's just that simple, but the enemy doesn't want you to take time. Start today with a little talk with the Lord in The Secret Place.

**There's Nothing
Like Serving
The Lord...
That's More
Than Words.**

-J. E. Murdock

– 3 –

HEALING OF A SICK BODY OPENED THE DOOR FOR A CHURCH IN SWEETLAKE

We were pastoring there in Big Lake, Louisiana and the community of Sweetlake was about twelve miles away.

I didn't know anyone in that community, but one evening while I was working in the yard around the parsonage, a car drove up with about five people in it. I didn't know any of them. They got out and I could see they were nicely dressed people. They told me who they were and that they lived in Sweetlake.

The lady announced to me their purpose for being there, saying, "Brother, we've heard about your ministry here. Our mother is at the point of death. Would you come and pray for her?"

I said, "Yes." Immediately I got ready and followed them to her home. I saw immediately that certainly only the Lord could change the picture by healing her body. I prayed earnestly for the healing and then shared a few things from the Word to them and went back home.

About a week later, the same car drove up to the parsonage and the lady said, "I wonder if we could get you to go back and pray for our mother. It looks like she's not going to make it."

I said, "Sure."

I walked again into that home in Sweetlake and, really, it seemed to me like it was just almost too late to pray, if you've ever heard of that. But I went ahead and prayed earnestly and immediately something happened and she just began to come to herself. After a few more words shared with them, I went back home.

In just three or four days, they came again and said their mother was doing much better and wondered if we could have services in their home.

I said, "Oh, yes, we'll be glad to come and have a service one night a week."

So, we announced we would have services there on a Thursday night. It happened to be the wintertime then and they had an old heater in which they burned oil...it was a comfortable home. They were so happy to open up their home and that I would come and have services with them. They invited some of the neighbors and the French lady that had been healed, Mrs. Babineaux, was there. It certainly was easy to minister to them...they were hungry and they had seen a miracle of healing in Mrs. Babineaux's body. (Also, her grandson was in a prison camp and we prayed much for him and he was able to return home at a later time.)

Nevertheless, we went on with prayer services and our ministry there on Thursday nights and decided then that we would take steps to try to start a church there. We learned a lot from preaching at Mrs. Babineaux's home. We were not able to buy this lot, but used it to have an open-air revival. That allowed us to get better acquainted and prepared a better entrance to the people in the community. We had a good revival just out under the trees in Sweetlake...had stretched lights there near a grocery store and a filling station that were there on the highway that passed through the community. We began to enjoy our relationship with the people there.

We became more interested in building as three or four other families began to join in who had a great number of acres on which they farmed rice. They were what we called *rice farmers* and they became very interested in having a church there.

Then, the father of this family got sick and passed away and they wanted me to bury and preach the funeral of their father. That certainly gave us a closer relationship with the family. They said the family did have some grown boys, rice farmers, who had not married and who had favor with a man named Mr. Choakly, who owned the Choakly Farm. They asked him about a piece of ground right beside the highway to put the church on. Sure enough, they gave us a lot to build a church and it was no time until we had the lumber on the ground, the building up and had put a nice little brick front on it.

Needless to say, it's not hard to believe that surely the Lord did bless us. We had some wonderful services there with such a move of the Lord. Those folks that still remain today certainly remember the good old days of the pioneer work there in that little church in Sweetlake. It all stemmed from prayer for a person who was passing away. Now she was healed, her home was opened up for fellowship and she worked in the church to help get it going.

Whenever you begin to relate the hand of God, whether it was yesterday or years ago, there is something about the relationship with God that will still bless you...refresh you...encourage you.

That's why I enjoy telling you what happens in The Secret Place...in your soul...your heart...your life. It actually helps you and I to spread our lives out *to help someone else.* So we're grateful to share this beautiful experience, as you've heard the saying...as we were there when it happened.

How *good* the Lord is...remember The Secret Place.

The Secret Place Does Not Only Meet A Need, But It Points Out Where Your Needs Are.

-J. E. Murdock

– 4 –

OUR NEXT CALL: ORANGE FULL GOSPEL TEMPLE *STAYING IN THE SECRET PLACE KEEPS YOU MOVING WITH GOD*

There's nothing like serving the Lord...that's more than words.

It is actually proven that if you and I can be led by the Lord and stay in The Secret Place, and sit and wait upon the Lord, even when you grow weary and tired, it is a marvelous experience.

Now, we had spent seven and a half years in the Big Lake church and had seen some wonderful things. We'd had baptismal services right out in the lake at night and how beautiful the touch of God was. But the day came when the Lord desired to move us on to another church. This was a nice church at 1106 Park Street in Orange, Texas. The pastor felt led to go other places and he wanted us to come and try out the work there...we did. And we prayed and sought the Lord and the Lord laid it on our hearts to pastor that church.

We had great favor with the people and that church was certainly acquainted with The Secret Place. They had a nice church and an auditorium-like prayer room that was upstairs and they were very familiar with daily prayer and even all-night prayer meetings on Friday nights.

Going there didn't only give us a place to preach, to witness to a new group of people, but it also put another call, we might say, to do more there than just pastor. We had seen that the old church had been moved onto the back lot behind the new beautiful church building. This old church was in a rundown condition and really needed some repair work. The Lord had called me to do work like that when I had pastored different churches before so we decided, with the cooperation of the church, that I would do most everything myself because the men in the church were usually on the job somewhere. They had little time to help and the church didn't have the finances, especially in those days, to hire out much of the work done. But that didn't stop us so we got busy and tore down the old building and built a ten-room Sunday School building out of concrete blocks...it made a beautiful little building. You could come out of the large new church and go into this new Sunday School auditorium. It certainly was a blessing to the church and certainly gave us a little more favor with people in town.

And Friends, seeing God help us in different areas...to build and carry on when we certainly needed the Lord to touch the finances so as not to overload the congregation with a heavy bill and indebtedness, but to be able to pay along as we went, was most wonderful. We experienced wonderful things there in the all-night prayer meetings and saw God's work.

The Lord spoke to my heart after we had been in Orange for a period of time. It seemed to me there was a heavy load and a feeling of responsibility to see more done in the hearts of the people...see them *grow* in the Lord. To see them becoming more involved with earthly things and things that hindered their prayer life actually became a real concern of ours. Few were coming anymore to spend time in prayer during the Friday night prayer meetings.

One Friday night, another brother and I started to pray and no one else came. I was kneeling before the Lord and it was not the first time that I had felt burdened about the church. And as I bowed my head and waited before the Lord feeling pressured to try to do or minister to the people in such a way as to find favor so I would feel that we were accomplishing something for their souls, it seemed that the Lord brought a scripture to my mind. The scripture reads like this, "Can anyone taking thought add one cubic to their stature?" And I looked that scripture up and I answered that voice out loud. I said, "That's true, Lord, I can't do anything about it."

A light couldn't have come on any quicker, and immediately the heavy load that I felt I couldn't hold up under very much longer—the whole load (I called it "tons")—just seemed to roll off of me. *Then* everything was so clear, even the noise on the streets, (which was quite a bit for it was a popular street; the park was right there in town and the Dairy Queen was beside the church), even the walls of that tall auditorium...looked so peaceful and so pleasant. Would you believe just what God did in seconds there? The load had rolled off, I had admitted I could not do anything myself and everything became so peaceful.

Then another scripture came to mind, "This is the day that I have made and I will be glad and rejoice in it." The revelation that came to us while in prayer there has not died. It has become more real...helped me many times not to get under the load myself but to take my concern to the Lord in prayer and trust that He will have His way...*just work with the Lord instead of just work for the Lord. To be a co-worker with Him and be led by the Spirit will change your ministry almost from darkness to light.* And I said. "I don't want to forget that." I still have burdens, still have intercessory prayer, still have concerns, but God's way will not overload us or cause us to faint.

I went home after the prayer meeting that night, just a little ways to our house on 2605 North Tenth Street, and thought, *Well, this is so wonderful...that heavy load is gone and a revelation of a day that the Lord has made is before me and the peace...*it just looked to me like I was in a different world. Really it was. I wasn't shouting out loud, I was just drinking in a peace that I hadn't had and never experienced to that depth, and that was called, "*This* is the day the Lord has made." But I thought to myself, *Well, I'm going to wait until morning and if I still feel this revelation is real and alive, then I'm going to tell my wife* (who felt that I was under so much pressure). I was in my prayer room, a little office at our home, with my head between my knees so many times that she'd have felt much better if I'd have been in bed...comfortable and asleep.

But The Secret Place was the only place I could actually survive under the pressure and find out what to do.

The next morning I woke up and, honestly, the noise of the little children and even the things that were out of place, off of the table or on the floor that happens sometimes when your children are small, looked like they were all in place. The day the Lord had made was still there the next morning...how beautiful it was! Then on Sunday morning, I was sharing it with our little church congregation with a peace that I didn't know was possible.

Then I went to a fellowship meeting that they had every Sunday afternoon in Beaumont after which visitors that came a distance would say, "I went to that service." God was using a dear sister there that had been there but a very few days, using her and seemed to reveal to her things that He wanted her to tell other members of the church or other people that were in the services.

The thought just came to me as I started up on the tall platform there with the other ministers, *Well, this is so real I wonder if God would let her see that I'd had such a visitation.* Then immediately I ignored that voice and thought, *I'm not going to build myself up...that's the Lord's business.* So, I just dismissed it from my mind.

The services went on beautifully and the dear sister that was ministering was ready to turn the service over to the pastor when suddenly she cried out, "Oh, God has showed me that He has revealed and given someone a revelation and a visitation that's different than He's given any of us." Her back was turned to me because I was sitting on the row of chairs with other ministers there right behind the pulpit, but she swung her arm around and looked right at me and said, "And brother, it's **you**!"

Well, of course, I couldn't speak in English, then, for a

little bit the revelation was so real.

So, really, my Friends, The Secret Place doesn't just throw things out there and then walk off and leave you. But The Secret Place gives you and I something that will abide with us...something we can share with others...something that others can actually witness that God has given them a visitation.

It's just amazing how lasting the visitations are that God can give you. This same prayer meeting has not ceased to *continually contribute* to my heart and to my life...giving me strength and courage to look around and see if there's not a better way to minister for God...a better route to go, even in our prayer life.

Then I'd run across the scripture that says, "My yoke is easy and my burden is light," and I'll tell you what, Friends, I have looked into that a few times because these pressures, these trials, will come back again to see how well we have learned...to embrace what God has given us in other times of trials...until we *can* learn to be content with whatever state within because we're resting on the promise or the visitation that God has given us.

Last year a minister said, "Why don't you find out what God wants you to focus your heart and your mind or your ministry upon in the coming year?"

I wrote that down immediately during the service, *"Focus on finding the yoke that's easy and the burden that's light."*

And, of course, I had to explain myself feeling that some people thought I was trying to be lazy on the job, but I thought, *No, I'm actually accepting the fact that if I can find the yoke and the burden that He has for me, I'm going to find a different feel in the Christian life,* for God said it. *It is actually doing things that God tells you to do and the second step was to do it the way He told you to do it.*

The Word says, "We should always pray and never to faint." So, before fainting or before letting the load get too heavy, we find ourselves in The Secret Place, sometimes praying quietly, sometimes crying out to God, but above all enjoying the authority of the Holy Spirit that you and I will experience if we'll stay in The Secret Place long enough. God has a yoke that's easy and a burden that's light.

So, Friends, be encouraged. The next time you walk in The Secret Place...don't let it be next week but let it be the *first* thing in the morning.

God has more for those who will seek Him in secret.

He still has the key to our lives that will give us peace and victory.

He'll help us to know *how to run* the race...*fight* the battle, and most of all *how to lean* on God and *trust* in Him. Amen.

— 5 —

Highway And Hedge Evangelism Born In The Secret Place

At this point, we were pastoring a church in Waco, Texas — the Waco Gospel Tabernacle.

I knew quite a few people from Cameron, Texas, on up through Waco. We had known the pastor there for a number of years. He wanted us to come there and the Lord gave us favor. Quite a few things happened there, however, we only stayed there about a year and a half and spent quite a bit of time in prayer, as always. That was the Christian life...communication with the Lord...hearing from God...taking your burdens to the Lord...finding out the will of the Lord.

A great desire came over me *to do more* for the Lord.

That wasn't unusual, but I did notice this: a unique experience began to come to me and at first I didn't quite understand it. I was out visiting and it seemed to me like about all that would cross my mind was the condition of our *country*. Now notice: not our church, but *our country*.

I was crushed to see how far away *our country* was going from truly serving God and I couldn't imagine why I was so troubled with it...*what could I do?*

I had just come back from visiting and went right on into the prayer room and started waiting on the Lord. When I got into the prayer room, I still saw those things and the conditions of our country, but I felt more peaceful. That happened for a whole week, every day, and even at night I would just sit up and *pray for our country.*

After I had such a revelation of that, it was like you could turn the knob for the next picture, or revelation. I saw the church world trusting in their own ability to win souls...to serve God, to work for God, instead of being moved by the Holy Ghost, led by the Spirit, seeking God for answers, praying through. It looked like it was a lost art from the church.

I thought, "Well, what can I do about it?"

I didn't understand what was going on.

Was I imagining these things?

Was I just thinking up this myself? Was I just allowing myself to get under such burdens about things that I couldn't do anything about anyway?

But all of a sudden, while in prayer, the Lord spoke to me about how He caused His Spirit to come upon Ezekiel and caused him to go out with a revelation of the valley of dry bones. And this valley of dry bones represented the house of Israel...their condition spiritually and away from God. He said, "I caused Ezekiel to view these dry bones and that's what I've done for you. My Spirit is upon you...I've caused you to view the condition of the nation and of the church."

Just like He asked Ezekiel, He went on while I was in prayer, He said, "What do you think about these bones?" And I said, "Ezekiel said they were very, very dry." And He asked Ezekiel, "Can they live?" And Ezekiel said, "Thou knowest, Lord." And then the Lord spoke to him and told him to prophesy to them the Word of the Lord. These bones that were just nothing but bones out there represented all the real life that was gone from Israel...their relationship with God was gone, but he said as he prophesied that those bones began to come together and stood up on their feet and new meat came upon their bones.

Then the Lord spoke to me that the reason I was having to pray was that it was the only way that I could find peace or even bear up under the revelation that I was getting concerning our country and the church...***in prayer was the only way I could rest.***

Then He gave me the revelation and the call to meet this need...to call the people to prayer.

Intercessory prayer would birth a ministry and a

life that would be pleasing to God.

He showed me so real that the church world was trying to *educate* people to be soul-winners when the Lord says, "Pray ye the Lord of the Harvest that He will send forth laborers in the vineyard." It was the Spirit that was causing me to see those things like when the Spirit came upon Ezekiel and caused him to view the dry bones. He was giving me a revelation.

That revelation was so strong that I immediately began to attend churches and go places that I'd never been before...preaching to them and giving them *"a call to prayer"*.

The purpose of the call was to pray that the Lord of the harvest would *revive the ministry and send forth laborers* into the vineyard. It was time to carry the Gospel into the highways and hedges.

The Lord made it very clear that it was the last call, that He sent the servants into the streets and the lanes of the city. Those who were bidden represented the church world. Then He sent them out into the streets of the lanes of the city to bring them in that their table would be filled with guests. The scripture says they went out and invited them that were in the streets and the lanes of the city and there was still room for more. The servants came back and said, "We did what you told us to do," and the Lord said, "But there's still room for more. Now go quickly into the highways and hedges and compel them to come in that there be guests at my table."

The revelation was so very real that I've never wavered.

The Holy Spirit had given me that visitation while in prayer, showing me the condition of our nation and of the church world, and showing me what we could do about it through prayer...*intercessory* prayer.

I'm still sold on the fact that if we don't stay in The Secret Place and find God's answer to the extent that we obey God *we are in trouble.*

God is going to try and test everything to see how we are built.

So let's look again at the revelation of the conditions that God has already given to many of us and again adopt ourselves to doing something about it the way God said to...to *pray ye that the Lord would send forth laborers* into the vineyard.

So, as we covered about forty or fifty churches and had taken pictures of different prayer groups there praying for that type of ministry, the Lord inspired my heart to get a tent and van. We got a tent and van and went into the highways and hedges and began to minister.

The first church that we built after the Highway and Hedge Ministry was birthed in the little town of Franklin, Louisiana. At different times churches had been tried to be built there but they never could get one started, *but God* helped us to build one there.

So, we're convinced that God knows what the need is...what to do about it and that His people are to be involved. So, let's be involved or else God will raise up someone else to do what He's called us to do.

The way we can carry it out is to *stay before the Lord in secret.*

As we find in the Scripture, whenever the trials and the tests came against the disciples who were working for God, they felt like they needed strength to continue on.

They went into a place there in Jerusalem where the saints were praying and they told them what they were facing...that an authority had sent word not to preach anymore in the name of the Lord. Instead of obeying they said to the praying saints, "Let's ask God to give us boldness to continue on." And the Bible puts it very clear: They lifted their hearts to the Lord for that need to be met and the Holy Ghost came upon them as in the beginning and they arose from that time of prayer and went forth in such a way that the people recognized that these people have been with Jesus.

Friends, there is a place in The Secret Place that God wants you and I to come to so He can minister to us...giving us the needed strength, boldness and courage to continue on in the work that the enemy is certainly coming against in our day.

Stay in The Secret Place until God speaks to us...until we get our direction.

ROAD TO PERFECTION

by

DR. J. E. MURDOCK

TABLE OF CONTENTS

———⟫⟩·◇·⟨⟪———

WHY I WROTE THIS BOOK

———➤◦◅———

I have felt stirred in my heart for some time at the *necessity of perfection* in the Christian walk.

I have a fear of being *lukewarm*.

It would be a terrible thing to meet the Lord some day and hear, "Who art thou? Depart from Me. I never knew you."

Yet thousands of souls will hear those words.

Several times I have been asked the question, "What's your book going to be about?" At my reply, "on perfection," eyebrows are raised.

Raising the standard of the Christian life is my full intention.

We, as God's children, need to walk in victory pressing toward the mark for the prize of the high calling of God in Christ Jesus (see Philippians 3:14).

——— FACT 1 ———
Perfection Is The Highest Degree Of Excellence.

It is what we expect from God.

It is what He expects from us. He has made it possible.

Why the call to *perfection?* God gave Isaiah a revelation of Israel. They had a lot of pride, but He had to tell them of their condition and give them a call to repentance. *"...the whole heart faint. From the sole of the foot even unto the head there is no soundness in it; but wounds, and bruises, and putrefying sores "* *(Isaiah 1:5-6).*

This reveals God's x-ray of our condition.

FACT 2

God Gives Us Direction For Perfection.

"...When every one shall know his own sore and his own grief, and shall spread forth his hands in this house: Then hear thou from heaven thy dwelling place, and forgive, and render unto every man according unto all his ways, whose heart thou knowest; (for thou only knowest the hearts of the children of men;) That they may fear thee, to walk in thy ways, so long as they live in the land which thou gavest unto our fathers" (2 Chronicles 6:29-31).

Everyone should examine himself, know of his own condition and repent. Remember when Lazarus was full of sores? But now he is comforted and is carried to Abraham's bosom.

True repentance will bring us to such a relationship.

When should we reach towards perfection?

FACT 3

When We Recognize Our Imperfection, We'll Automatically Reach For A Cure.

If you are not searching—you are blind to your need.

FACT 4

Without Perfection You Won't Be Able To Face The Obstacles Of Life And Be Victorious.

"...and upon this rock I will build My church;" *(Matthew 16:18).*

Take heed **how** you build.

We are not crowned unless we strive **lawfully** (see 2 Timothy 2:5).

FACT 5

You Move Toward Perfection By Moving Toward The Word Of God.

"The law of the LORD is perfect, converting the soul:" *(Psalm 19:7).*

"Howbeit when He, the Spirit of truth, is come, He will guide you into all truth:" (John 16:13).

FACT 6

The Rewards Of A Perfected Walk Is Eternal Life.

Jesus, the perfect sacrifice is coming back soon for a perfect bride, without spot or wrinkle. He won't be satisfied until we awaken in His likeness.

"I wouldn't have you ignorant..."

-Dr. J. E. Murdock

**People Want
What God Has
To Offer...
Without Knowing
Him.**

-J. E. Murdock

– 1 –

THE ROAD TO PERFECTION—REVEALED

"....Man shall not live by bread alone, but by every word that proceedeth out of the mouth of God" (Matthew 4:4). "Let us therefore fear, lest, a promise being left us of entering into his rest, any of you should seem to come short of it" (Hebrews 4:1).

What is the call given to man? *The whole duty of man is to fear God and keep His Word.*

Adam's first attempt to restore relationship failed (the covering of fig leaves). God stepped in and offered the skin of an animal as a covering for their sins.

God aimed for restoration of man to relationship with Himself through other covenants—and man *failed.* Once and for all, a *new* sacrifice was offered. Now the call to surrender to Him is given, and the promise is made: to as many as would receive Him, to them gave He the power to become the sons of God.

Let us awake now to hear what the Spirit saith and begin our walk back into fellowship with God Who made us for His pleasure, and find rest for our souls.

FACT 7

Imperfection Began With Adam.

"And the LORD God called unto Adam, and said unto him, Where art thou? and he said, I heard Thy voice in the garden, and I was afraid, because I was naked; and I hid myself. And He said, Who told thee that thou wast naked? Hast thou eaten of the tree, whereof I commanded thee that thou shouldest not eat?" (Genesis 3:9-11). No matter where we are, we will

face God again. We shall stand before the judgment seat of God.

Adam had never been afraid.

This was his first experience with Disobedience.

God had told Adam he would die if he ate of the tree of the knowledge of good and evil.

They ate. Imperfection had began—in us.

When God came into the garden, Adam's shame caused him to hide.

FACT 8

Sin Still Makes Us Look For A Hiding Place.

People will even join a church to cover their sin.

What was once perfect was now imperfect.

Man was now in need of a cure (Savior). *"For as by one man's disobedience many were made sinners"* (Romans 5:19). God's covenant had failed with man, leaving him in bondage to his sinful nature.

— 2 —

FROM FIG LEAVES TO CALVARY—MAN'S DISABILITY TO GOD'S ABILITY

First Adam brought in sin.

Light (God) *exposed* the darkness.

Fig leaves could not cover it.

The shedding of animal blood didn't take away the consciousness of sin.

So, He sent His Son, Jesus.

FACT 9

The Perfect Sacrifice Was Christ.

"So by the obedience of one shall many be made righteous" *(Romans 5:19).* *"...And without shedding of blood is no remission" (Hebrews 9:22).* There is now no more sacrifice for sin.

FACT 10

Perfection Begins With Christ.

"Be ye therefore perfect, even as your Father which is in heaven is perfect" (Matthew 5:48).

God Is Not
Looking For
Vessels
To Fill...
He's Looking For
Clean Vessels
To Fill.

-J. E. Murdock

~ 3 ~

Five Steps To Perfection—A Short And Sure Way

[Should it take forever to grow up?]

"Come now, and let us reason together, saith the LORD: though your sins be as scarlet, they shall be as white as snow; though they be red like crimson, they shall be as wool" (Isaiah 1:18).

Step 1 — Ye Must Be Born Again

"Jesus answered, Verily, verily, I say unto thee, Except a man be born of water and of the Spirit, he can not enter into the kingdom of God. That which is born of the flesh is flesh; and that which is born of the Spirit is spirit. Marvel not that I said unto thee, Ye must be born again" (John 3:5-7).

―――――――――― Fact 11 ――――――――――
Perfection Begins With Being Born Again.

Ye must be born again. The new creature in Christ arises with better promises, given to us through faith, lifting us to heavenly places in Christ Jesus.

▶ **Discern Imperfection**

―――――――――― Fact 12 ――――――――――
Imperfection Is Discerned By Pain.

Pain puts you in search for a cure.

If sin reigns in any area of your body, your *mind* will seek it out and bring you into captivity of the law of sin which is in your members (see Romans 7:23).

When your mind located the problem (sin), then all the attention is centered upon it.

Let me give you an example: If you had a toothache, you could not rest until that pain was taken care of. Although the pain is only in your tooth, *your whole body will get involved with it.* You'll take off work and seek a dentist.

That is how sin operates.

A *little* leaven leaveneth the whole lump.

Sin brings wretchedness.

Wretchedness seeks a cure.

If a cure isn't found, then sin in its completion brings death.

Death means separation from God, Who is your whole support for joy and peace.

Many times pain is described as...emptiness. Even *loneliness.*

We are made for a *relationship with God.* Out of all His creations, He created us in His own image (see Genesis 1:27).

If He needs us, how much more do we need Him?

Can you believe that He made us for His pleasure? *"...for Thou hast created all things, and for Thy pleasure they are and were created" (Revelation 4:11).*

▶ Recognize Your Own Wretchedness

"O wretched man that I am! who shall deliver me from the body of this death?" (Romans 7:24).

The Pharisee stood and prayed...God, I thank Thee, that I am not as other men...And the publican smote his breast, saying...God, be merciful to me a sinner (see Luke 18). The Pharisee was depending on his good works to represent him.

The Christian life in reality begins at *Calvary.*

Christ is our righteousness.

The publican was only aware of his *sins*.

▶ **A Call To True Repentance**

―――――――――― **FACT 13** ――――――――――

**Crying Out To God With Repentance Is Your First
Step Into Mercy...Forgiveness Without Cost.**

―――――――――― **FACT 14** ――――――――――

Salvation Puts You On The Pathway To Perfection.

―――――――――― **FACT 15** ――――――――――

A Truly Repentant Heart Brings True Results.

John preached the baptism of repentance before His
coming (see Acts 13:24). *"Bring forth therefore fruits worthy
of repentance" (Luke 3:8)*. There needs to be a turnaround in
your life.

When you repent of your sins, you're to dedicate yourself
to the Lord. *"I beseech you therefore, brethren, by the mercies
of God, that ye present your bodies a living sacrifice, holy,
acceptable unto God, which is your reasonable service. And be
not conformed to this world: but be ye transformed by the
renewing of your mind" (Romans 12:1-2)*.

―――――――――― **FACT 16** ――――――――――

**The Secret Of Progress Toward Perfection Is Total
Dedication Of Yourself To God.**

*"Therefore if any man be in Christ, he is a new creature:
old things are passed away; behold, all things are become new"
(2 Corinthians 5:17)*.

▶ **Separation**

Now take a look at the walk of the believer. The Bible says, evil communications corrupt good manners.

—————— FACT 17 ——————

God Can't Perfect You Unless He Can Control Your Communications.

"Wherefore come out from among them, and be ye separate, saith the Lord,...for ye are the temple of the living God; as God hath said, I will dwell in them, and walk in them; and I will be their God, and they shall be my people...for what fellowship hath righteousness with unrighteousness? and what communion hath light with darkness?" (2 Corinthians 6:17,16,14).

—————— FACT 18 ——————

Perfection Will Often Create Loss Of Friendship.

Be not surprised when your friendships with the world fall off. Be not affected by this. *"That he no longer should live the rest of his time in the flesh to the lusts of men, but to the will of God. Wherein they think it strange that ye run not with them to the same excess of riot" (1 Peter 4:2,4).* When we learn early in our Christian walk to flee from wrong things and pursue that which is right, we are getting direction for our walk with the Lord.

▶ **New Desires**

Now that we are born again, it is a natural thing to have new desires. *"As newborn babes, desire the sincere milk of the word, that ye may grown thereby:" (1 Peter 2:2). "Search the scriptures; for in them ye think ye have eternal life:" (John 5:39).* You are saved by grace through faith. The just live by faith.

"Blessed is the man that walketh not in the counsel of the ungodly...But his delight is in the law of the Lord; And he shall be like a tree planted by the rivers of water, that bringeth forth his fruit in his season;" (Psalm 1:1-3).

▶ **Hear the Word**

Even in the natural a baby is protected by its mother. The baby is kept in a sanitary place and is not left alone. When we are babes in Christ, we desire to fellowship in the Word.

Joseph and Mary kept Jesus and took Him to the temple. *"And the child grew, and waxed strong in spirit, filled with wisdom:" (Luke 2:40).* We are exhorted to assemble ourselves with other believers, much more as we see the day of His coming approaching.

Now we begin to see the old Adam removed and the second Adam arise with a sure promise to all who follow and come to know the Lord. From forgiveness of sin (see Romans 7) to freedom from condemnation (see Romans 8).

Salvation is unconditional...but to walk with Him is to agree with Him. The new birth calls for a life in Christ, and this life for every believer. *"If ye then be risen with Christ, seek those things which are above," (Colossians 3:1).*

"Set your affection on things above, not on things on the earth" (Colossians 3:2).

"For ye are dead, and your life is hid with Christ in God" (Colossians 3:3).

"Mortify therefore your members which are upon the earth;" (Colossians 3:5).

———————————— **FACT 19** ————————————

Perfection Will Require You To Put Off The Old Man.

What does the old man look like? *"But now ye also put off all these; anger, wrath, malice, blasphemy, filthy communication out of your mouth. Lie not one to another, seeing that ye have put off the old man with his deeds;" (Colossians 3:8-9).*

Fact 20

Perfection Requires Putting On The New Man.

"And have put on the new man, which is renewed in knowledge after the image of Him that created him:" (Colossians 3:10). Now the Son of God brings to light the great mystery of godliness. Christ in you...the hope of glory. He inhabits us by His Spirit, we have no hope without Him.

Hearing the gospel that we were going to meet God one day, caused me to join the church.

I was only thirteen years old.

I didn't really know how to be "born again."

All I knew was I needed a savior so I would be "ready."

I wanted to accept the Lord, but...*I didn't have any knowledge of faith.*

I got a little Testament. I was going to try to "live better".

That lasted about two weeks. The inspiration left me after revival was over! Many can relate to this in their first step toward God. Sometimes a lack of information is the cause. I didn't completely stop pursuing the Lord, there was still an interest.

"Blessed are they which do hunger and thirst after righteousness: for they shall be filled" (Matthew 5:6).

Step 2 — Be Filled With The Holy Spirit

Fact 21

The Holy Spirit Is Necessary For Perfection.

The *gift* of the Holy Spirit was the *promise* of the Father.

It was the next thing to happen after Jesus ascended into Heaven. He had given His first commandment. Go to the upper room and tarry until the promise of the Father is given. This they did, and as always, God was faithful to His promise.

"And when the day of Pentecost was fully come, they were

all with one accord in one place. And suddenly there came a sound from heaven as of a rushing mighty wind, and it filled all the house where they were sitting. And there appeared unto them cloven tongues like as of fire, and it sat upon each of them. And they were all filled with the Holy Ghost, and began to speak with other tongues, as the Spirit gave them utterance" (Acts 2:1-4). Peter explained to those who had gathered around: that which they were hearing and seeing was foretold by Joel, the prophet. There never had been a day like it.

▶ How Can We Be Filled?

Tarry ye until. Tarry until you receive the Holy Spirit. *"And behold, I send the promise of My Father upon you: but tarry ye...until ye be endued with power from on high"* (Luke 24:49). There's much controversy on how long it takes to receive the holy Spirit. He said tarry until.

———— Fact 22 ————

God Isn't Looking For Vessels To Fill, He's Looking For CLEAN Vessels To Fill.

Your heart must be *prepared*. The heart is prepared through obedience to the "drawing" of the Spirit. We often overlook the groundwork. First, we must be drawn to Him. In John 6:44, Jesus said, no man can come to Me except the Father "draw" him. You need good soil to produce a good "crop." The Seed (Word) falls on everyone, but good soil will produce fruit. *"The preparations of the heart in man...is from the LORD"* (Proverbs 16:1). *"For God maketh my heart soft, and the Almighty troubleth me:"* (Job 23:16). He can't work on a stony heart. *"...Thou makest it soft with showers"* (Psalm 65:10). *"Break up your fallow ground, and sow not among thorns"* (Jeremiah 4:3). *"...Break up your fallow ground: for it is time to seek the LORD, till He come and rain righteousness upon you"* (Hosea 10:12). He does this to bring in His life. The rain from Heaven is to bring grass in the field, literally as well as spiritually.

Why does He want our hearts? Our heart is desperately wicked and who can know it?

—————— FACT 23 ——————
The Law That Brings Perfection Must Reach The Heart.

God said, I will not write My law anymore on tables of stone, but on the fleshly tables of the heart (see 2 Corinthians 3:3).

—————— FACT 24 ——————
The Holy Spirit Will *Work* In An Unclean Temple, But He Will *Not Dwell There* Unless We Yield To Him.

Without the Spirit we are "lame". *"For what man knoweth the things of a man, save the spirit of man which is in him? even so the things of God knoweth no man, but the Spirit of God"* *(1 Corinthians 2:11).*

—————— FACT 25 ——————
The Holy Spirit Handles The Problems Of Imperfection.

It is the power of God that *works* in us to will and to do.

—————— FACT 26 ——————
The Holy Spirit Doesn't Only Reveal His Will, But Gives Us The Power To Perform It.

Only then will our relationship grow. That's why we need to be *filled* with the Holy Spirit.

▶ The New Life in the Spirit

"...for, behold, the kingdom of God is within you" (Luke 17:21). *"For the kingdom of God is not meat and drink; but righteousness, and peace, and joy in the Holy Ghost. For he that in these things serveth Christ is acceptable to God, and approved of men"* (Romans 14:17-18). *"When a man's ways please the LORD, He maketh even his enemies to be at peace with him"* (Proverbs 16:7).

"And be not drunk with wine, wherein is excess; but be filled with the Spirit;" (Ephesians 5:18). *"But ye shall receive power, after that the Holy Ghost is come upon you"* (Acts 1:8a).

People who drink wine experience a boldness and a "lift" out of themselves.

The Holy Spirit gives you boldness and a "lift" out of yourself. The Holy Spirit gives you boldness and *"lifts"* you to another realm—a *better* way of life.

———————— FACT 27 ————————

The Holy Spirit Enables You To Walk In Perfection.

This same Holy Spirit was given so that He could bring forth a people that He would not be ashamed to call brethren (see Hebrews 2:11). Now the Holy Spirit that was given began working in their heart mightily to will and to do of God's good pleasure.

In pursuit of His likeness...*"Blessed are they which do hunger and thirst after righteousness: for they shall be filled"* (Matthew 5:6). This qualifies you.

Back to my childhood days...

The revival was over, the inspiration was gone. But my three little sisters were just getting started. Their lives had changed. My aunt decided that the next prayer meeting would be at our home. I wanted to be there. I liked what I saw. Their countenances had changed. My sisters' countenances glowed. This was something new and I wanted it. That was a prayer meeting! Prayer meetings back then brought you face to face with the Lord.

Salvation was wonderful, but I wanted more. The "more" I wanted was the infilling of the Holy Spirit. I sought the Lord every day. It took me about three months before I received it. My sisters would exhort me to surrender all..."just give yourself totally to Him." I believed He would fill me, but the key was *full surrender.*

I received the Holy Spirit. Immediately, I became sensitive to wrong actions, wrong talking and wrong thinking. I became very conscious of the Lord. I can't blame others for my convictions. The Holy Spirit convicted me. Know your teachers by the Holy Spirit.

The Lord's return was preached about often.

His soon coming was, and still is, the strong motivation to live a perfected life (see 1 John 3:3).

The proper revelation will motivate you to reach toward perfection.

I immediately separated myself from unchristlike relationships. I wanted to build a relationship *with Him.* To know Him was the main focus. That is a different appetite.

We make much ado over the gift, but pay little attention to the Giver.

People want what He has to offer, without knowing Him. This is a reason for spiritual growth.

Step 3 — Be Led By The Spirit

"This I say then, Walk in the Spirit, and ye shall not fulfil the lust of the flesh" (Galatians 5:16). "But if ye be led of the Spirit, ye are not under the law" (Galatians 5:18). "For as many as are led by the Spirit of God, they are the sons of God" (Romans 8:14).

When Christ gets in your heart, the natural can be discerned. Then we know what is working within us. There's a war inside, but if we will yield to the Spirit, He will overcome the natural man.

We already have the Seed of Christ within us. It goes to work to produce after its kind. Christ works in us to will and to do. In the midst of the battle we'll have peace, love and joy. To grow spiritually is our goal so that the carnal man will be conquered.

When people receive the Word, many opportunities are opened up to them. Lack of commitment and disobedience will cause them to go their own way. People have had a touch of God and have fallen by the wayside. What happened? They allowed the truth to slip away, or didn't add to their Christian life. Many times they give in to the carnal nature.

God not only wants us to be in the Spirit, but to walk in the Spirit. The Spirit will bear witness with our spirit that we are the sons of God. If our spirit were to leave our body, we couldn't see, hear, walk or even talk. It is life.

If we have not the Holy Spirit, we would know nothing about God. Jesus said it is expedient that I go away so the Comforter will come.

"Then was Jesus led up of the Spirit into the wilderness to be tempted of the devil" (Matthew 4:1). *"Ye are they which have continued with Me in My temptations. And I appoint unto you a kingdom, as My Father hath appointed unto Me;"* (Luke 22:28-29). *"If we suffer, we shall also reign with Him: if we deny Him, He also will deny us:"* (2 Timothy 2:12).

In your pursuit of perfection, God may suggest to you to give up that which you hold dear. *"The young man saith unto Him, All these things have I kept from my youth up: what lack I yet? Jesus said unto him, If thou wilt be perfect, go and sell that thou hast, and give to the poor, and thou shalt have treasure in heaven: and come and follow Me"* (Matthew 19:20-21).

God has to bring us "out" before He can bring us "in." The Spirit-led life begins with leading us out of "self" and into Himself. The Lord brought Israel out of Egypt before He could bring them where He wanted them.

We should discern the dissatisfactions that were in us. It may be Christ working in us. It is a calling of the Spirit to bring us to a higher walk. It is natural to reach for a higher goal. When the Holy Spirit is within, He reaches for a higher goal—a perfected walk. *"If we live in the Spirit, let us also walk in the Spirit" (Galatians 5:25).* The maintenance of your salvation will require your abiding in Him. Abiding requires the Holy Spirit.

Step 4 — Quench Not The Spirit

Quench - to put out, to cause to cease (put out a fire).

"Quench not the Spirit" (1 Thessalonians 5:19). "Let no corrupt communication proceed out of your mouth, but that which is good to the use of edifying, that it may minister grace unto the hearers" (Ephesians 4:29). "For they that are after the flesh do mind the things of the flesh; For to be carnally minded is death; Because the carnal mind is enmity against God: So then they that are in the flesh cannot please God" (Romans 8:5-8). To walk in the Spirit is self-denial all the way.

Step 5 — Grieve Not The Spirit

To grieve is to offend or cause grief, or sorrow.

"And grieve not the Holy Spirit of God, whereby ye are sealed unto the day of redemption" (Ephesians 4:30). To grieve the Spirit is to do things contrary to His will. *"Let all bitterness, and wrath, and anger, and clamour, and evil speaking, be put away from you, with all malice: and be ye kind one to another, tenderhearted, forgiving one another, even as God for Christ's sake hath forgiven you" (Ephesians 4:31-32).*

"Know ye not, that to whom ye yield yourselves servants to obey, his servants ye are to whom ye obey whether of sin unto death, or of obedience unto righteousness?" (Romans 6:16). If we yield ourselves to the Spirit, we shall reap of the Spirit life everlasting. The spirit of the prophet is subject to the prophet, therefore it is up to us not to grieve the Spirit.

The Lord knew how frail we were from the beginning.

That's why He gave His Son for our sacrifice. The Spirit is grieved when we do anything that is displeasing to Him. Often if you are feeling sad inside, you can trace it back to having said something evil or unkind about someone. If you are conscious of the Holy Spirit in your life, He'll let you know when you have grieved Him. You won't have to go to a camp meeting to know what's wrong. The Holy Spirit is inside you and will guide you.

"Forty years long was I grieved with this generation, and said, It is a people that do err in their heart, and they have not known My ways:" (Psalm 95:10). They were looking for Jesus to set up His kingdom on the earth. They did not understand He was to set up His kingdom in their hearts. They would have made Him king. Many people accept the manifestation of a miracle, but His greatest miracle is in the heart.

The Lord grieved for the hardness of their hearts. They didn't think He should heal on the Sabbath day (see Mark 3:5). They were still under the law. For example, if the traffic light was red and a policeman waved you to go...you could go. Jesus wanted to release them and set them free from the law. He is Lord of the Sabbath.

Now watch the fruits of the Spirit be perfected—

What are the fruits of the Spirit? *"But the fruit of the Spirit is love, joy, peace, longsuffering, gentleness, goodness, faith, meekness, temperance: against such there is no law" (Galatians 5:22-23).* There is no excuse, because if we follow on, these fruits will develop.

"Herein is My Father glorified, that ye bear much fruit; so shall ye be My disciples" (John 15:8). "...being fruitful in every good work, and increasing in the knowledge of God;" (Colossians 1:10).

"...He that abideth in Me, and I in him, the same bringeth forth much fruit: for without Me ye can do nothing" (John 15:5). "Every branch in Me that beareth not fruit He taketh away: and every branch that beareth fruit, He purgeth it, that it may bring forth more fruit. Abide in Me, and I in you. As the branch cannot bear fruit of itself, except it abide in the vine; no

more can ye, except ye abide in Me" (John 15:2,4).

"(For the fruit of the Spirit is in all goodness and righteousness and truth;) Proving what is acceptable unto the Lord. And have no fellowship with the unfruitful works of darkness, but rather reprove them. For it is a shame even to speak of those things which are done of them in secret" (Ephesians 5:9-12).

I call it, "when death looked good." Eve looked at the tree and it looked good. Christians look and listen to things that they wouldn't dare partake of themselves. Don't be deceived. Evil communications corrupt good manners. *"And they that are Christ's have crucified the flesh with the affections and lusts. If we live in the Spirit, let us also walk in the Spirit. Let us not be desirous of vain glory, provoking one another, envying one another" (Galatians 5:24-26).*

We have the Seeds of peace, joy and love already, because we are in Christ. As we grow up in Christ, all this fruit comes to maturity.

The fruit of the Spirit is manifested *on the behalf of others.*

Let your light so shine before others.

– 4 –

THE PERFECTION OF THE BELIEVER

The Great Step Towards Perfection

"I beseech you therefore, brethren, by the mercies of God, that ye present your bodies a living sacrifice, holy, acceptable unto God, which is your reasonable service. And be not conformed to this world: but be ye transformed by the renewing of your mind, that ye may prove what is that good, and acceptable, and perfect, will of God" (Romans 12:1-2).

Let us take a look at Jesus' walk in the world. From the manger to standing at an open tomb with the keys of death, hell, and gave in His hand. Yes, our only hope. Many have already found, as Peter said, *"...to whom shall we go? Thou hast the words of eternal life" (John 6:68).* His walk from perfection to resurrection.

The Great Plan For The Believer

In John 17:1-26, Jesus prays for the believer...pointing out the toil and the walk of the believer. *"For I have given unto them the words which thou gavest Me;" (John 17:8).*

Jesus' Prayer:
- ▶ *"...and they have kept Thy word" (verse 6).*
- ▶ *"Now they have known that all things whatsoever Thou hast given Me are of Thee" (verse 7).*

Be persuaded.
- ▶ *"...they have received them (My word)" (verse 8).*
- ▶ *"...that I came out from Thee" (verse 8).*
- ▶ *"...that thou didst send Me" (verse 8).*

▶ *"...they are Thine. And all Mine are Thine and Thine are Mine;"* (verses 9-10).

▶ *"...that they may be as one, as We are"* (verse 11).

▶ *"...that they might have My joy fulfilled in themselves"* (verse 13).

▶ *"I have given them Thy word; and the world hath hated them, because they are not of the world, even as I am not of the world"* (verse 14).

▶ *"I pray not that Thou shouldest take them out of the world, but that Thou shouldest keep them from the evil"* (verse 15).

▶ *"Sanctify them through Thy truth: Thy word is truth"* (verse 17).

▶ *"...I sanctify Myself, that they also might be sanctified"* (verse 19).

▶ *"...that they also may be one in Us: that the world may believe that Thou hast sent Me"* (verse 21).

▶ *"that they be made perfect in one;"* (verse 23).

▶ *"...the love wherewith Thou hast loved Me may be in them, and I in them"* (verse 26).

His Instructions For Perfection

Perfection must have direction. At the marriage in Cana, Mary said, "Do what He says." They filled the water pots. He turned the water into wine. God created the heavens and the earth, but not in one day. Yet, He did it, and it was good. The loaves and fishes were put in His hand—the miracle began. *"If ye be willing and obedient, ye shall eat the good of the land:"* (Isaiah 1:19).

Begin to do what He says, and the miracle will be on its way.

When do we mature in Jesus? Maturity is when you are able to carry out His instructions on a daily basis. He brought them out of Egypt. They spent forty years in the wilderness... then died in the wilderness. Israel didn't grow. She always erred in her heart.

Many are like the man with one talent. He knew what

he could do with it, but he buried it. Where he could have heard, "Well done," he only heard, "Thou wicked servant," and was cast into outer darkness (see Matthew 25:14-30). He that knoweth to do right and doesn't do it; to him it is sin.

If we use what God has given us, more will be given. If we don't, that which we have will be taken away. If we obey what we know, we will grow. Grace is God's ability. If we use the grace God has given us, He will give us more grace, grace to pray, etc. Use it and get rich in God. He became poor so that we might be rich.

Obedience to God toward others. *"For I was an hungered, and ye gave Me meat: I was thirsty, and ye gave Me drink: I was a stranger , and ye took Me in: Naked, and ye clothed Me: I was sick, and ye visited Me: I was in prison, and ye came unto Me...Inasmuch as ye have done it unto one of the least of these My brethren, ye have done it unto Me...Come, ye blessed of My Father, inherit the kingdom prepared for you"* (Matthew 25:35-36,40,34).

Caution: *"For I was an hungered, and ye gave me no meat: I was thirsty, and ye gave me no drink: I was a stranger, and ye took me not in: naked, and ye clothed me not: sick and in prison, and ye visited me not...Inasmuch as ye did it not to one of the least of these, ye did it not to me. And these shall go away into everlasting punishment"* (Matthew 25:42-43,45-46).

Our relationship with God must be manifest toward others. *"Herein is our love made perfect, that we may have boldness in the day of judgment: because as He is, so are we in this world"* (1 John 4:17).

Let us find the promises of God that develop our lives to a well-pleasing place in Him.

How deep in the water (spiritual walk) are you? The Lord led Ezekiel out into the river one step at a time, revealing to him the abundance of His grace. But Ezekiel could only know or experience that grace as he walked in it. The river was uncrossable. God told Ezekiel wherever the water touched him, healing would occur. Whatever level you are, healing will flow (see Ezekiel 47:3-9).

A lot of people stop growing early in their relationship with the Lord. That is why the Lord gave five (5) ministries to the body of Christ; for the developing of the perfection of the saints.

We need to recognize how far out in the water we are. Ezekiel spoke of his depth in the water. He was ankle deep. Then the Spirit led him on out into the river. Where are you? Are you still on milk? The river was uncrossable. Eyes haven't seen, nor ears heard what God has prepared for his children.

Wherever your illness is, the Physician will locate it and heal you. The Holy Spirit will guide you to the promise that's right for you. Hold on to it by faith, and it will begin working.

Paul taught perfection to the church: *"This is a great mystery: but I speak concerning Christ and the church"* *(Ephesians 5:32) "...Christ is the head of the church: and He is the saviour of the body...Christ also loved the church, and gave Himself for it; That He might sanctify and cleanse it with the washing of water by the Word, That He might present it to Himself a glorious church, not having spot, or wrinkle, or any such thing; but that it should be holy and without blemish"* *(Ephesians 5:23,25-27).*

"He that hath an ear, let him hear what the Spirit saith unto the churches;" *(Revelation 2:7*; see Revelation 3 to the seven churches).

a) Thou hast a name that thou livest, and art dead. Hold fast that which thou hast, that no man take thy crown.

b) Thou art neither cold nor hot. Because thou are lukewarm, I will spue thee out of my mouth.

c) Thou sayest, I am rich, and have need of nothing: and knowest not that thou art wretched, and miserable...I counsel thee to anoint thine eyes with eyesalve that thou mayest see.

"For not he that commendeth himself is approved, but whom the Lord commendeth" *(2 Corinthians 10:18).*

The Great Steps Of Perfection Required

▶ Speak the same thing.
▶ That there be no divisions among you.

► Ye be perfectly joined together in the same mind and in the same judgment (1 Corinthians 1:10). Perfection of the unity of the body of Christ is important and possible.

The Lord added to the church daily (see Acts 2:47). We are to witness, but only the Lord can bring the increase.

Sincerity doesn't always speak of depth. "And he began to speak boldly in the synagogue: whom when Aquila and Priscilla had heard, they took him unto them, and expounded unto him the way of God more perfectly" (Acts 18:26). He was preaching what he knew, but they could tell he needed to be taught the ways of God more perfectly.

"And He gave some, apostles; and some, prophets; and some, evangelists; and some, pastors and teachers; For the perfecting of the saints, for the work of the ministry, for the edifying of the body of Christ: Till we all come in the unity of the faith, and of the knowledge of the Son of God, unto a perfect man, unto the measure of the stature of the fulness of Christ:" (Ephesians 4:11-13).

"...and this also we wish, even your perfection" (2 Corinthians 13:9).

The Bible states, *"...that man doth not live by bread only, but by every word that proceedeth out of the mouth of the Lord doth man live"* (Deuteronomy 8:3). *"Take heed therefore how ye hear"* (Luke 8:18).

Perfection Up Front (In Sight)

"Thou art snared with the words of thy mouth" (Proverbs 6:2).

"...for out of the abundance of the heart the mouth speaketh" (Matthew 12:34).

"Let these sayings sink down into your ears:" (Luke 9:44).

"A man shall be satisfied with good by the fruit of his mouth:" (Proverbs 12:14).

"...keep the doors of thy mouth" (Micah 7:5).

"...Out of thine own mouth will I judge thee," (Luke 19:22).

Perfect faith is possible. *"Night and day praying exceedingly that we might see your face, and might perfect that which is lacking in your faith?" (1 Thessalonians 3:10). "...labouring fervently for you in prayers, that ye may stand perfect and complete in all the will of God" (Colossians 4:12).*

Faith in perfection. *"That we henceforth be no more children, tossed to and fro, and carried about with every wind of doctrine, by the sleight of men, and cunning craftiness, whereby they lie in wait to deceive; But speaking the truth in love, may grow up into him in all things, which is the head, even Christ:" (Ephesians 4:14-15).*

My Page On Perfection

"For the law having a shadow of good things to come, and not the every image of the things, can never with those sacrifices which they offer year by year continually make the comers thereunto perfect. For then would they not have ceased to be offered? because that the worshippers once purged should have had no more conscience of sins" (Hebrews 10:1-2; read chapter 10).

"Therefore leaving the principles of the doctrine of Christ, let us go on unto perfection; not laying again the foundation of repentance from dead works, and of faith toward God," (Hebrews 6:1). "If therefore perfection were by the Levitical priesthood, (for under it the people received the law,) what further need was there that another priest should rise after the order of Melchisedec, and not be called after the order of Aaron? (Hebrews 7:11). Every time a priest would die, the laws would change, the law made nothing perfect. We needed a better covenant and an eternal priest.

"For by one offering He hath perfected for ever them that are sanctified" (Hebrews 10:14).

"And being found in fashion as a man, He humbled Himself, and became obedient unto death, even the death of the cross" (Philippians 2:8). "For it became him, for Whom are all things, and by Whom are all things, in bringing many sons unto glory, to make the captain of their salvation perfect through

sufferings" (Hebrews 2:10).

"And the glory which Thou gavest Me I have given them; that they may be one, even as We are one: I in them, and Thou in Me, that they may be made perfect in one" (John 17:22-23).

You are commanded to be perfect. *"Be ye therefore perfect, even as your Father which is in heaven is perfect" (Matthew 5:48).*

Caution: Ye did run well; who did hinder you that ye should not obey the truth?

"Thy word have I hid in mine heart, that I might not sin against Thee" (Psalm 119:11). "The law of the LORD is perfect, converting the soul" (Psalm 19:7).

"...and this also we wish, even your perfection" (2 Corinthians 13:9).

"Mark the perfect man, and behold the upright: for the end of that man is peace" (Psalm 37:37).

The Ingredient That Supplies Perfection Is The Word Of God

"All scripture is given by inspiration of God, and is profitable for doctrine, for reproof, for correction, for instruction in righteousness: That the man of God may be perfect, throughly furnished unto all good works" (2 Timothy 3:16-17). "...Man shall not live by bread alone, but by every word that proceedeth out of the mouth of God" (Matthew 4:4).

He is coming for a bride; one without spot or wrinkle. *"...and they that were ready went in with Him to the marriage: and the door was shut" (Matthew 25:10).*

**Self Denial Plays
A Big Part
In The Road
To Perfection.**

-J. E. Murdock

—5—

HINDRANCES TO THE BELIEVER

The Self Life/Self Denial

The self life is a manifestation of the carnal nature, meaning pertaining to flesh, as opposed to the spirit. *"For they that are after the flesh do mind the things of the flesh;... For to be carnally minded is death; Because the carnal mind is enmity against God: ...So then they that are in the flesh cannot please God"* *(Romans 8:5-8).*

The self life is the will of man operating instead of the will of God. *"But the natural man receiveth not the things of the Spirit of God: for they are foolishness unto him: neither can he know them, because they are spiritually discerned"* *(1 Corinthians 2:14).*

The self life will cause imperfections to surface. Many times we slam the door on satan only to leave the door handle on the outside. Satan gains entry through the self life. The natural man is selfish. He wants to glorify himself even if it is in the name of religion. The self life will put on a tie, go to church, sing, even preach..."just don't kill me." Your life is a show window to God...it displays what is on the inside of you.

Your self life will never produce righteousness. *"...all our righteousness are as filthy rags; (Isaiah 64:6).* But we are crucified with Christ. No more I, but Christ. He has all the right motives, but prayers can be hindered. "Self" may appear in our prayers. (Remember the prayer of the Pharisee?)

Your self life will try to handle what only God can handle. Our ways of handling problems are as far from God's ways as the fig leaves were from the blood of Jesus.

We're actually discovering where all our pain comes from.

Self doesn't run from God; it just tries to play God. Like the man who casts out devils in the name of Jesus "whom

Paul preacheth." He did everything the way Paul did, but he did not have Jesus in control. The evil spirit said, "I know Jesus and I know Paul, but who are you?" And the spirits jumped on him and overcame him. The greatest disappointment will come to many who tried to live Jesus...without Jesus.

The Lord seeks to perfect Christ in us. Everything in the Christ life is for the glory of God. *"For it is God which worketh in you both to will and to do of His good pleasure" (Philippians 2:13).* Jesus did nothing but what the Father wanted. The Holy Spirit in the believer will only do the will of the Father. The self life cannot be tamed...it (the natural man) must be crucified. Remember, Paul said, *"...I die daily" (1 Corinthians 15:31).*

You don't have to perfect the world to walk in perfection; you don't even have to perfect the home. It is necessary to reckon ourselves dead so that Christ can arise. We're not only to be in the Spirit, but to walk in the Spirit. You aren't perfect in the walk, only as you walk.

"And you hath He quickened, who were dead in trespasses and sins; fulfilling the desires of the flesh...even as others. For we are His workmanship, created in Christ Jesus unto good works, which God hath before ordained that we should walk in them" (Ephesians 2:1,3,10).

How will I know if the self life is operating in my life? The wretchedness that originates from self life will cause you to search for the problem. The self life breeds carnality.

How to get out of the self life. The self life originates from the heart. And the heart is given to God. This was where God writes His law on the fleshly tables of the heart. His Word is perfecting the soul. It sets in motion a power that works in us to will and to do His good pleasure. When we are doing His will we are leaving "self" behind. The will of the Lord is as different as day and night from the will of man.

"For as the heavens are higher than the earth, so are My ways higher than your ways, and My thoughts than your thoughts" (Isaiah 55:9).

There are crippling hindrances in the self life. Are we playing instead of praying? Are we spending more time in front of the television than in studying God's Word? Deny yourself good things—reach for better things!

Mortify The Deeds Of The Flesh

"Know ye not, that to whom ye yield yourselves servants to obey, his servants ye are to whom ye obey; whether of sin unto death, or of obedience unto righteousness?" (Romans 6:16).

The Holy Spirit wasn't given to you just to make you feel better, but to help you mortify the deeds of the flesh. Jesus holds the keys of death and hell. He has already triumphed. But satan doesn't give up—if we live after the flesh, we shall die. Make no provision for the flesh.

Self denial plays a big part in the road to perfection.

The Dos And Don'ts Of The Christian Life

When thou prayest, don't be as a hypocrite praying in the streets so that men can see thee; but enter the closet when thou prayest, and thy Father will reward thee openly.

When thou doest alms, don't sound a trumpet before thee like the hypocrites do, so that they may have the glory of man. When thou doest alms, let not thy right hand know what thy left hand is doing; and thy Father will reward thee openly.

The Only Thing That Makes You Different From Anyone Else Is... Your Faith In The Lord.

-J. E. Murdock

~6~

WHAT EVERY BELIEVER SHOULD KNOW

Faith

You must have faith.

Without faith, no man can please God. God gave to every man a measure of faith. That faith must be alive and working— a faith will move mountains and produce with a fear of God that brings obedience. This isn't usually an overnight process. It takes growing—abiding—following on.

What is faith? Faith is the evidence of things not seen. *"...to every man that is among you, not to think of himself more highly than he ought to think; but to think soberly, according as God hath dealt to every man the measure of faith"* (Romans 12:3).

"But without faith it is impossible to please Him: for He that cometh to God must believe that He is, and that He is a rewarder of them that diligently seek Him" (Hebrews 11:6).

There are different degrees of faith. Stay in the measure of faith that God has given you. If you do well in the foot race, then you'll run well in the horse race. *"Holding faith, and a good conscience; which some having put away concerning faith have made shipwreck:"* (1 Timothy 1:19). Faith without conscience will not work. Yes, God can do anything, but real faith works in good conscience.

Faith doesn't operate outside of God's will. How do I discern if my faith is under fire or not working? Is the answer to our prayer in God's promises? If there is a delay, then we need to examine our hearts. What is the motive for our request? If we ask in the will of God, and we do not see the answer, our faith is being tried. Faith is necessary for the perfect walk: *"...as it is written, The just shall live by faith"* (Romans 1:17).

You can learn to build unwavering faith. Why?

Wavering faith is unfruitful. *"But let him ask in faith, nothing wavering. For he that wavereth is like a wave of the sea driven with the wind and tossed. For let not that man think that he shall receive any thing of the Lord"* (James 1:6,7). *"So then faith cometh by hearing, and hearing by the word of God"* (Romans 10:17). This explains the importance of taking heed how you hear.

I was at church in Franklin, Louisiana. I felt I needed something from the Lord. I said, "Lord, bless me." The Lord said, "Have faith in Me." In my mind I thought, "I am believing You." The Lord gently spoke to me and said, "No, I have blessed you many times in spite of your faith. But the time will soon come, when you will have to have faith to receive."

Faith under fire.

Anytime you move toward God your faith is tried. God's Word promises,...*the trial of your faith, being much more precious than of God that perisheth, though it be tried with fire, might be found unto praise and honour and glory at the appearing of Jesus Christ:"* (1 Peter 1:7).

Our faith has to be able to withstand the obstacles on this road to perfection. To be out in the battle is not safe. We're exposed to the fiery darts of the enemy from every side. Satan tries to pull down our faith. Our faith is the shield against those fiery darts of the enemy (see Ephesians 6:16). *"Beloved, think it not strange concerning the fiery trial which is to try you, as though some strange thing happened unto you:"* (1 Peter 4:12). Faith under fire doesn't mean faith has failed. The exercising of your faith is actually for the perfecting of your faith.

You can support your faith with your prayers. Jesus prayed for Peter. He said, "Satan has desired to sift you, but I pray for you that your faith fail not." Our relationship with God sustains our faith when under fire. *"But ye, beloved, building up yourselves on your most holy faith, praying in the Holy Ghost,"* (Jude 1:20).

You can build your faith through praying in the Spirit.

Evil forces are real, and they will fight to destroy your faith. Don't run from the battles. Prepare for them. You don't run with faith—faith is your shield.

I asked the Lord to help me prepare for the evening service. I said, "Lord, let me turn to a scripture." This is what the Lord gave me. *"He that dasheth in pieces is come up before thy face: keep the munition, watch the way, make thy loins strong, fortify thy power mightily" (Nahum 2:1).*

The trial of your faith isn't always moving mountains—it also sustains you in the valleys.

Commitment

There are decisions along the Christian pathway. It takes a commitment all the way, staying submissive before the Lord. There are times in the Christian walk when nothing seems to be happening. Stay committed. Trust has to be in operation. Just turn everything over to the Lord.

The mother of Moses made a basket to keep baby Moses in. She did all she could do to protect him, and then she put his little basket in the river. She had to trust God. God takes over at the blind spots in our commitment.

"Commit thy way unto the LORD; trust also in Him; and He shall bring it to pass" (Psalm 37:5).

One plants, one waters, but the Lord gives the increase. When you have done all you can in the will of God, commit it to the Lord. Then stand. He's the one who has the last say-so anyway. Do what He tells you to do, then commit the rest.

At the marriage of Cana, they were out of wine. He said, "Fill the water pots with water and bring them in." They did what He said to do. They could do no more. Then He took over and turned the water into wine. The Lord gives the increase.

One of the most outstanding times, I recall, was when I had to learn to submit. I had been hitch hiking. We had our little trailer parked in a peach orchard in Cameron, Texas. Our lights and water were hooked up to the neighbor's. I had already done all I knew to do to get an open door into ministry.

I had ceased to strive within myself, but I gave myself to prayer. Peace came over me. There still weren't any open doors. I just gave it over to the Lord. I caught a ride to Orange, Texas and went to the services at an Assembly of God church. A lady came up to me and asked if I was looking for a revival. I said, "Yes, if the Lord opens the door." She told me about a church I could preach at. I didn't worry. Commitment from God brings total peace. I got that revival. I've had to learn to commit all along the way.

When the Israelites got to the Red Sea, God told Moses, "The battle is not yours. Stand still, and see the salvation of the Lord." Up until that point, God had instructed Moses all the way. God was the instructor, and Moses carried out all instructions. Both of them were involved. Now Moses was to turn it over to the Lord. They crossed the sea, and when they looked back they saw the salvation of the Lord. His sister danced before the Lord. Obedience turns into rejoicing. Total commitment brings joy.

We're gripped with anxiety until God is able to develop total commitment to Him in us. You're not indifferent to God's plan, just submissive to it. It comes from learning to do it God's way.

"Rest in the LORD, and wait patiently for Him:" (Psalm 37:7).

Abiding In Him

"He that dwelleth in the secret place of the most High shall abide under the shadow of the Almighty" (Psalm 91:1). The Secret Place of the Most High is called the sanctuary of the Lord. His way is in the great sanctuary. As David looked at the prosperity of the wicked, he was troubled. He said, "I almost lost my place until I went into His sanctuary and there I understood." So he stayed connected in the secret place.

"If ye keep My commandments, ye shall abide in My love;" (John 15:10). The fulfillment of the demands God has for us calls for a relationship with Him.

You must continue removing things as well as adding things if we are to abide in Him. We shed the old man and put on the new (see Ephesians 4:24).

The abiding life offers support in every phase of the Christian walk. It makes us more than conquerors. Afflictions will not "move" us, if we are continually abiding. We can then finish our course with joy. Even in the lion's den, or in prison, it'll give us a song in the night.

The abiding life is to continue in His will and abide in His love. If we will hold fast to His truths, His promises will follow through. *"But seek ye first the kingdom of God, and His righteousness; and all these things shall be added unto you" (Matthew 6:33).* When you come to the word "if," the main message lies to the right. *"...If ye continue in My Word, then are ye My disciples indeed;" (John 8:31).*

Holiness

Holiness—quality of being holy; sacred. *"Follow peace with all men, and holiness, without which no man shall see the Lord:" (Hebrews 12:14).* We can't worship God without holiness. *"Having therefore these promises, dearly beloved, let us cleanse ourselves from all filthiness of the flesh and spirit, perfecting holiness in the fear of God" (2 Corinthians 7:1).*

God's goal for us is to be in His likeness. *"For I am the Lord your God: ye shall therefore sanctify yourselves, and ye shall be holy; for I am holy:" (Leviticus 11:44).*

Jesus did not want the church to have any spots. *"That he might present it to himself a glorious church, not having spot, or wrinkle, or any such thing; but that it should be holy and without blemish" (Ephesians 5:27).* (See 2 Peter 3:14).

"Blessed are the pure in heart: for they shall see God" (Matthew 5:8).

The Fear Of The Lord

"The fear of the Lord is a fountain of life, to depart from

the snares of death" (Proverbs 14:27). It is the unfailing force of God. People who have the fear of the Lord don't usually backslide.

The Bible says, *"The fear of the Lord is the beginning of knowledge:" (Proverbs 1:7).* You have to choose the fear of the Lord. *"For that they hated knowledge, and did not choose the fear of the Lord:" (Proverbs 1:29).*

The fear of the Lord is to hate evil and depart from it.

What are some of the benefits of the fear of the Lord? The fear of the Lord...

- ▶ *"...prolongeth days:" (Proverbs 10:27).*
- ▶ *"...is clean, enduring for ever:"*
  (Psalm 19:9).
- ▶ *"...is strong confidence:...place of refuge"*
  (Proverbs 14:26).

"The fear of the Lord tendeth to life: and he that hath it shall abide satisfied; he shall not be visited with evil" (Proverbs 19:23).

The fear of God is a product of the Holy Spirit. Behold the goodness and severity of God (see Romans 11:22)! Severity toward those that fell. Israel rejected the Lord. He cut them off. The goodness was to those who accepted Him and continued to abide. Otherwise, they too would be cut off. Example: fire is used to warm you, or it can burn you. The fear of God is not tormenting, but is the Christian's saving power.

Faith and fear of the Lord work together. We ask God to give us our daily bread. Why not ask for daily perfection? Let's do what He says on a daily basis. Noah didn't build the ark of protection in one day. God withheld destruction until it was built. Noah didn't fool around. If he would have, he would not have been saved. Noah believed by faith. He built the ark because he feared the Lord. He was saved by his obedience.

So then by faith we believe;
by fear we move;
by obedience we are saved.

Perfect Love/God's Love

"For God so loved the world, that he gave his only begotten Son, that whosoever believeth in him should not perish, but have everlasting life" *(John 3:16).*

"Hereby perceive we the love of God, because He laid down His life for us: and we ought to lay down our lives for the brethren" *(1 John 3:16).*

"He that loveth not knoweth not God; for God is love" *(1 John 4:8).*

Perfect love out in the open. *"For if ye love them which love you, what thank have ye? for sinners also love those that love them"* *(Luke 6:32).* If we say we love God and hate our brother, we are liars. How can we love God Whom we have not seen, if we can't love people we have seen (see 1 John 4:20)?

"And this commandment have we from Him, That he who loveth God love his brother also" *(1 John 4:21).* *"He that loveth his brother abideth in the light, and there is none occasion of stumbling in him"* *(1 John 2:10).*

God's love brings satisfaction. Everything God's love produces is profitable. This is impossible within ourselves. The spirit and the flesh are at war. But know in Him, you can. It is the Spirit that does the work. He works in us to will and to do. He makes us willing and then He does the work.

"There is no fear in love; but perfect love casteth out fear: because fear hath torment. He that feareth is not made perfect in love" *(1 John 4:18).*

How do we get perfect love? *"...because the love of God is shed abroad in our hearts by the Holy Ghost which is given unto us"* *(Romans 5:5).* Our love must come from the Holy Spirit to be honored by God.

"Herein is our love made perfect, that we may have boldness in the day of judgment: because as He is, so are we in this world" *(1 John 4:17).*

"...If we love one another, God dwelleth in us, and His love is perfected in us. Hereby know we that we dwell in Him, and He in us, because He hath given us of His Spirit" *(1 John 4:12-13).*

Perfecting Your Prayers

Your prayer life is your channel of receiving.
Your prayer life must be **perfected.**
Prayer is used as an exit to get out of trouble.
You can actually avoid trouble through prayer.
Prayer is an entrance which brings the life of Christ into us.

"Ask, and it shall be given you" (Luke 11:9). Many times we ask and nothing seems to happen. James said we ask amiss. *"Ye ask, and receive not, because ye ask amiss, that ye may consume it upon your lusts"* (James 4:3).

Many people think if they go to church the Lord should give them a package to take home with them. We often feel ready for the answers, but we are not prepared to receive them. Romans 10:2,3 says, "they have a zeal for God, but not according to knowledge. They go about to establish their own righteousness, have not submitted themselves unto the righteousness of God." The Lord looks upon the heart.

The younger son asked the father to give him all that belonged to him. Then he spent it all in riotous living. He wasn't prepared for it. Just because we ask doesn't mean we are prepared to receive. Though we are sons, we differ not from the servant. We have to grow from the milk of the Word to the meat (see Galatians 4:1-2). Then we can discern our motives. If we don't receive, then there is a reason. It could be a defect in our prayer life.

The Holy Spirit prayer life is as important for the believer as salvation is for the sinner. The Holy Spirit is important in our prayer life. *"...for we know not what we should pray for as we ought: but the Spirit itself maketh intercession"* (Romans 8:26).

Prayers with hindrances—husbands and wives should dwell together according to God's knowledge and not according to feelings. Not rendering evil for evil; that your prayers be not hindered, and that ye should inherit a blessing (see 1 Peter 3:7-9).

Prayers with sacrifices hindered: *"Therefore if thou bring thy gift to the altar, and there rememberest that thy brother hath ought against thee; Leave there thy gift before the altar, and go thy way; first be reconciled to thy brother, and then come and offer thy gift"* *(Matthew 5:23-24).*

Sometimes it's the trial of our faith. *"And the Lord said, Hear what the unjust judge saith. And shall not God avenge His own elect, which cry day and night unto Him, though He bear long with them? I tell you that He will avenge them speedily"* *(Luke 18:6-8).* Though God may tarry, He will hear our cry and answer.

The Secret Of Tarrying

Tarry ye until. Tarrying covers a lot of areas. It doesn't just bring answers, but conditions us for the answers.

When Elijah prayed for fire, he prayed according to the Lord's Word and *the fire fell.*

But when he prayed for rain, he stayed on his knees. *It took seven times.*

Tarrying is actually staying in His presence until you receive. It is waiting on the Lord until the answer comes. God can do anything, but the *way* He does it *confuses the natural man.* We understand if He answers the first time;.

But if we have to pray seven times, God has a different setting in mind.

He teaches us something new *with each setting.*

Tarry with *purpose.*

Waiting can make the difference between fainting and "mounting up."

Quality tarrying is putting your whole heart and faith into it.

Tarrying can iron out the wrinkles of anxiety and fear. It will bring on a still night, not a windy one.

That is the importance of being still and knowing He is God.

My Boyhood Experience

When I was a teenage boy, I got lost in the woods. I wasn't upset until I discovered I really was lost. Then I began to churn inside with fear. Being saved, I took off running as I prayed—only to find myself running in circles. I lost all direction of north, south, east and west. My anxiety clouded my thinking and I lost focus. I would holler out. Oh, if I could have heard a rooster crow, I would have started towards it. Often when one finds he is lost, he will run in circles and end up in the same shape he was in when he first began his search.

I knelt down with one knee on the ground and one up ready to run. I got up before I received any direction or any peace of mind. My search began again. I was still walking in circles! Occasionally I would see my tracks, so I knew I had to be going in circles. I hollered out again. If only I could have heard a train or a car, I would have walked toward it, but no sounds. As I walked I said, "Lord, You know where I'm at— You know the way—And You can lead me out." But I said all of that in the midst of my anxieties and fears.

The Lord says, "Be still and know..." Now I sought a better way to receive. This time I put both knees on the ground. I said quietly, "Lord, I'm lost. I cannot get out of these woods without You." My running, praying, and one knee kneeling still had not subsided my fears. So don't faint when "one knee down" doesn't get you through. You may have to come to a place where both knees are going to have to drop to the ground. Surrendering *all*.

Suddenly, I noticed all fear and anxiety were gone. It seemed I had forgotten I was lost. I stood up and looked every direction. Everything was calm. It was a still day. Such peace came over me. Then in a moment, I said aloud, "I feel peace to turn to my right." And I began to walk.

I came upon a tree trunk that had fallen across the path. It didn't completely destroy my view of the path. Opposition will come to hinder you from following the path of peace. I thought I would go around the tree and come to the path on the other side. Never detour in opposition. Right off to the side of the tree, I saw a tin building. I thought, "That is why I got lost." I had walked around looking at the old building. So I thought, "No, I'm not going around the tree. I'm going under it." I hugged close to that path. I was still lost, but I kept walking.

My mind was at *peace*. It was still a ways to my house, but I didn't know that. I just followed the peace. Stay with the peace at any cost. I had to stop and bow my head a few times more. I didn't look to the right or left. I said aloud, "I feel peace to go on." Suddenly, I saw my house across the highway from my path in the woods.

Let the peace of God rule in your heart.

Tarry *until you are free* from anxiety. Be anxious for nothing.

Tarry until your heart mounts up with praise. Your prayers should be supported in praise. In the upper room they were tarrying in one accord, with praise, when the Holy Ghost came upon them.

Perfecting Forgiveness

Perfect forgiveness is from the heart. *"For if ye forgive men their trespasses, your heavenly Father will also forgive you: But if ye forgive not men their trespasses, neither will your Father forgive your trespasses" (Matthew 6:14,15).*

Forgiveness is a must. Perfect forgiveness can be when we have really been forgiven. We must be forgiven and then forgive ourselves. Then we are debtors to forgive others. Remember when the man received forgiveness for all of his debt? When he refused to forgive another who owed him, his lord (who had forgiven him) was wroth and delivered him to the tormentors till he should pay all that was due him (see Matthew 18).

"So likewise shall My heavenly Father do also unto you, if ye from your hearts forgive not every one his brother their trespasses?" (Matthew 18:35). Forgiveness is two ways. You must forgive your fellow man and you must forgive yourself.

How many times must we forgive? *"...Until seventy times seven" (Matthew 18:22).* There is no limit.

Forgive everyone his trespasses. If from the heart you haven't forgiven, your joy and peace will not be full.

You will never be happy if your relationship with others is not right.

You can loose your prayer life with forgiveness. *"And when ye stand praying, forgive, if ye have ought against any: that your Father also which is in heaven may forgive you your trespasses" (Mark 11:25).* Confess your sins. *"If we confess our sins, He is faithful and just to forgive us our sins, and to cleanse us from all unrighteousness" (1 John 1:9).* A relationship with the Lord will handle unforgiveness in its early stages. Let the Holy Spirit handle it on a daily basis. If it takes root, it will get bigger than you.

Let not the sun go down upon your wrath.

Perfecting Your Asking Ability With Obedience

Obedience gives your prayers ability. Be obedient to God. *"And this is the confidence that we have in Him, that, if we ask any thing according to His will, He heareth us: And if we know that He hear us, whatsoever we ask, we know that we have the petitions that we desired of Him" (1 John 5:14-15).*

"...for I do always those things that please Him" (John 8:29).

Perfecting Your Relationship With Him

"And He that sent me is with me: the Father hath not left me alone; for I do always those things that please Him" (John 8:29).

Perfecting Your Time Spent With Him

"But they that wait upon the LORD shall renew their

strength; they shall mount up with wings as eagles; they shall run, and not be weary; and they shall walk, and not faint" (Isaiah 40:31).

Jesus commanded the apostles that they should not depart from Jerusalem, but wait for the promise of the Father (see Acts 1:4). Pray until the answer comes. What is His will? Tarry ye until...

Elijah had to pray seven times before the rain came.

If he had prayed six times, what then?

If Naaman would have dipped only six times in the Jordan, he wouldn't have been healed.

God will honor *every* effort. He was in the first dip in the Jordan as well as the last one.

Completion comes with the answer.

Tarry ye until...

When you spend time with God, you shall come out with more than you had when you went in.

Perfecting—Following On

We need to be perfected enough to discern hindrances to our spiritual growth. If you are traveling a road and you take a wrong turn, you should discern this before going too far. The Holy Spirit is a guide and will give you a witness when you are right or wrong.

"...let us lay aside every weight, and the sin which doth so easily beset us, and let us run with patience the race that is set before us, Looking unto Jesus the Author and Finisher of our faith; Who for the joy that was set before Him endured the cross, despising the shame, and is set down at the right hand of the throne of God" (Hebrews 12:1-2).

Perfecting Your Ability

We are to mount up with wings as an eagle. In the beginning, a little bird leaves the nest and only hops to the branches close by; but with the exercise he begins to get stronger, until he is able to fly far away into the sky. We are to stay in the realm of our faith, and not try to operate outside of our faith.

If your strength isn't enough to believe for your needs, then exercise your faith in a promise of God. Then, wait upon the Lord.

We're to run and not grow weary. We're to walk and not faint. Teach us, Lord, to wait upon You. Sometimes it is easier to run than walk. Many times we want to run to the will of God. The enemy wants us to get ahead of God. This is a lack of patience. At the Red Sea, the miracle wasn't just opening the sea, but getting the Israelites to stand still and wait for God to move. Walking demands patience.

If we stay led of the Lord, then it is the Lord's battle.

Perfecting Your Thought Life

"For as he thinketh in his heart, so is he:" (Proverbs 23:7). Perfection in the heart produces right thinking. We have to bring every thought into captivity, because the devil works through our thought life.

Years ago, I heard a saying, "You can't keep the birds from flying overhead, but you can keep them from making a nest." The enemy will throw thoughts upon you. Those thoughts are not from the heart. Bring them under submission. Get rid of them, immediately.

"For the Word of God is quick, and powerful, and sharper than any two-edged sword, piercing even to the dividing asunder of soul and spirit, and of the joints and marrow, a discerner of the thoughts and intents of the heart" (Hebrews 4:12).

"Finally, brethren, whatsoever things are true, whatsoever things are honest, whatsoever things are just, whatsoever things are pure, whatsoever things are lovely, whatsoever things are of good report; if there be any virtue, and if here be any praise, think on these things" (Philippians 4:8).

Perfecting Your Tongue

When our heart gets right with God, it goes to work on perfecting our tongue. The Holy Spirit works to remove speaking. *"...for out of the abundance of the heart the mouth speaketh" (Matthew 12:34).* We can discover the condition of our heart by our words. Our words also reveal our thought life.

"Let no corrupt communication proceed out of your mouth, but that which is good to the use of edifying, that it may minister grace unto the hearers" (Ephesians 4:29).

"That ye put off concerning the former conversation the old man, which is corrupt...Wherefore putting away lying, speak every man truth with his neighbour:" (Ephesians 4:22,25). Our hope of perfecting our tongue really comes from a Spirit-led life; right reading, right thinking and right viewing. All comes from the heart. If God can get your heart, He can get the rest of you.

"Out of the same mouth proceedeth blessing and cursing. My brethren, these things ought not so to be. Doth a fountain send forth at the same place sweet water and bitter?" (James 3:10-11). If you continue in your former corrupt conversations the Holy Spirit will convict you. If the warning is ignored, and wrong talking is continued, the conviction will leave and so will the Holy Spirit.

"...If any man offend not in word, the same is a perfect man, and able also to bridle the whole body" (James 3:2). Many times we say things against our brother, neighbor, etc. When we say something wrong we damage ourselves on the inside. God's Word is not our burden. Our words are. Our words can free us up or overload us.

The psalmist wrote, *"Set a watch, O LORD, before my mouth; keep the door of my lips" (Psalm 141:3).* That should be every Christian's prayer.

Understanding That Leads To The Throne

And in all your getting get understanding. How do you get understanding? *"Through Thy precepts I get understanding: therefore I hate every false way. The entrance of Thy words giveth light; it giveth understanding unto the simple"* (Psalm 119:104,130). *"For the LORD giveth wisdom: out of His mouth cometh knowledge and understanding"* (Proverbs 2:6).

It's important to develop understanding. *"When any one heareth the word of the kingdom, and understandeth it not, then cometh the wicked one, and catcheth away that which was sown in his heart"* (Matthew 13:19).

Your understanding is developed by your relationship with God. Joseph had a dream. As he built his relationship with God, his dream unfolded. The closer you get to God, the more you will understand His plan for you. Although it was hard to understand at times, Joseph's obedience carried him to the throne. The road to the palace is not a popular one. Few choose it.

Daniel also knew the importance of a relationship with God. Not only did he leave the lion's den, he went to the palace.

Our understanding promotes us to higher ground.

Eyes And Ears Of Your Understanding

Look and live; or look and die.

Look and live. The Lord told Moses to make a serpent and put it on a pole. And every one who was bitten by the fiery serpents could come and look at the serpent on the pole and live (see Numbers 21:8). Jesus said, "If I be lifted up, I'll draw all men to Me." If we look to Jesus, He is life.

Look and die. God told Adam and Eve not to eat of the tree. He said if they did, they would die. The tree got much attention. It looked good. (I think of it like this: When death looked good.) The serpent said, go ahead and eat. You know the story. They ate. Death entered the picture. Wrong understanding can be a gateway to deceit.

"...the commandment of the LORD is pure, enlightening the eyes" (Psalm 19:8).

Understanding ears: *"Verily, verily, I say unto you, He that heareth My Word, and believeth on Him that sent Me, hath everlasting life, and shall not come into condemnation; but is passed from death unto life" (John 5:24).*

Stay Focused

"...mine eye affecteth mine heart" (Lamentations 3:51). Things that we see and hear put pressure on our faith in God. What motivated Peter to walk to Jesus on the water was his focus on the Lord. He only saw Jesus. He didn't see the waves. He was single minded. Failure did not come until he observed his surroundings.

Watch with great caution what you look at and listen to. Jesus stayed totally focused while He was on this earth. To do the will of His Father was not His main goal, but was His only goal.

When Daniel went to prayer, he had to wait 21 days to receive an answer. He purposed in his heart and waited until he received. *"...neither know we what to do: but our eyes are upon thee" (2 Chronicles 20:12).* Stay focused.

Perfection Is Your Desire

"One thing have I desired of the LORD, that will I seek after; that I may dwell in the house of the LORD all the days of my life, to behold the beauty of the Lord, and to enquire in His temple" (Psalm 27:4).

People want what Christ has to offer, but they don't really know Him. He rains on the just and the unjust, but to know Him is to desire Him. Paul says, I count all things as dung that I may win Christ. The better view you have of Jesus, the more you'll want to become like Him.

How To Discern The Good, The Acceptable, And The Perfect Will Of God

"For I say, through the grace given unto me, to every man that is among you, not to think of himself more highly than he ought to think; but to think soberly, according as God hath dealt to every man the measure of faith" (Romans 12:3). Just because a child in school makes an "A" doesn't make him ready for graduation. He must stay in school and go through each grade.

Understanding what God is talking about is not the same thing as abiding in it. We have to follow on...*"And be not conformed to this world: but be ye transformed by the renewing of your mind, that ye may prove what is that good, and acceptable, and perfect, will of God"* (Romans 12:2).

> ▶ What is the acceptable will of God? *"...Let every one that nameth the name of Christ depart from iniquity"* (2 Timothy 2:19).

> ▶ The perfect will of God? *"...but he that doeth the will of God abideth for ever"* (1 John 2:17).

─ 7 ─

WHAT EVERY BELIEVER SHOULD DO

You Can Discern The Signs Of Perfection

The Divine Nature. *"According as His divine power hath given unto us all things that pertain unto life and godliness, through the knowledge of Him that hath called us to glory and virtue: Whereby are given unto us exceeding great and precious promises: that by these ye might be partakers of the divine nature, having escaped the corruption that is in the world through lust. And beside this giving all diligence, add to your faith virtue; and to virtue knowledge; And to knowledge temperance; and to temperance patience; and to patience godliness; And to godliness brotherly kindness; and to brotherly kindness charity. For if these things be in you, and abound, they make you that ye shall neither be barren nor unfruitful in the knowledge of our Lord Jesus Christ"* (2 Peter 1:3-8). *"...and this also we wish, even your perfection"* (2 Corinthians 13:9).

All these features make up the character of the Christian life.

▶ Virtue—Moral Excellence

Virtue is everything that pertains to purity. We are to grow in purity in our walk, our talk and all other areas.

▶ Knowledge—Understanding

"For if after they have escaped the pollutions of the world through the knowledge of the Lord and Saviour Jesus Christ, they are again entangled therein, and overcome, the latter end is worse with them than the beginning" (2 Peter 2:20). The

Bible says, in all thy getting, get understanding. To obtain knowledge is to follow on, and ye shall know the Lord. Grace and peace are multiplied unto you through the knowledge of God.

▶ **Temperance—Moderation**

▶ **Patience—Ability to Endure Calmly**

"In your patience possess ye your souls" (Luke 21:19). "To them who by patient continuance in well doing seek for glory and honour and immortality, eternal life:" (Romans 2:7).

▶ **Godliness—Divine; Godlike**

▶ **Kindness—Gentleness; With Generosity**

▶ **Charity—Good Will**

"But he that lacketh these things is blind, and cannot see afar off, and hath forgotten that he was purged from his old sins" (2 Peter 1:9).

God wants us to grow up in Him in all things, so that we maketh increase of the body unto the edifying of itself in love (see Ephesians 4:14-16). It is important to bear our own burdens—but we are also to bear each other's burdens. It is our responsibility to be saved, filled with the Spirit, and led by the Spirit. As we develop, we can help others bear their burdens. That's why God wants us to grow up in Him. Our love for one another edifies the body of Christ (see 1 Thessalonians 5:9-11).

Growing up in the Lord helps us to be strong. Although our thumb is not as big as our arm, it grows at the same time. As we reach toward perfection, the Holy Spirit develops us in all of these areas. We need to be mature to do what God wants us to do. You don't have to be mature to be called to Africa— but you have to be mature to go. Many are called, but few are chosen. Everyone is called when they are born again. But we are chosen if we prepare. *"From henceforth let no man trouble me: for I bear in my body the marks of the Lord Jesus"* (Galatians 6:17). *"...for I have learned, in whatsoever state I am, therewith to be content"* (Philippians 4:11). *"That we henceforth be no more children, tossed to and fro"* (Ephesians 4:14).

We have grown to a perfected point.

Take Inventory

"If thou hast run with the footmen, and they have wearied thee, then how canst thou contend with horses? and if in the land of peace, wherein thou trustedst, they wearied thee, then how wilt thou do in the swelling of Jordan?" (Jeremiah 12:5).

"Examine yourselves, whether ye be in the faith; prove your own selves. Know ye not your own selves, how that Jesus Christ is in you, except ye be reprobates?" (2 Corinthians 13:5). *"For if our heart condemn us, God is greater than our heart, and knoweth all things. Beloved, if our heart condemn us not, then have we confidence toward God"* (1 John 3:20-21).

Caution: It can happen to the best of families. Now His parents (Joseph and Mary) went to Jerusalem: and when they had fulfilled the days, as they returned, the child Jesus tarried behind in Jerusalem; and Joseph and His mother knew not of it...they turned back again...seeking Him...after three days they found Him in the temple (read Luke 2:41-50). Though you stand by faith, make sure you have Jesus with you.

Many have thought they were walking with Christ, and He wasn't there.

Overcome

"To him that overcometh will I grant to sit with Me in My throne, even as I also overcame, and am set down with My Father in His throne" (Revelation 3:21).

Who is the overcomer? *"...but he that believeth that Jesus is the Son of God?"* (1 John 5:5). *"Ye are of God, little children* and have overcome them: because greater is He that is in you, than he that is in the world" (1 John 4:4).

Perfection is not just to shine us up, but to make us strong. "Nay, in all these things we are more than conquerors through Him that loved us" (Romans 8:37).

Can there be anything less than perfection?

Caution: "For if after they have escaped the pollutions of the world through the knowledge of the Lord and Saviour Jesus Christ, they are again entangled therein, and overcome, the latter end is worse with them than the beginning" (2 Peter 2:20).

A truly perfected life is rewarded. "I have fought a good fight, I have finished my course, I have kept the faith: Henceforth there is laid up for me a crown of righteousness, which the Lord, the righteous judge, shall give me at that day: and not to me only, but unto all them also that love His appearing" (2 Timothy 4:7-8). True perfection is to love His appearing.

"For which cause we faint not; but though our outward man perish, yet the inward man is renewed day by day" (2 Corinthians 4:16). "For in this we groan, earnestly desiring to be clothed upon with our house which is from heaven:" (2 Corinthians 5:2).

"But we all, with open face beholding as in a glass the glory of the Lord, are changed into the same image from glory to glory, even as by the Spirit of the Lord" (2 Corinthians 3:18).

"Then shall we know, if we follow on to know the LORD:" (Hosea 6:3).

Abide in faith. Follow on.

STONES

FROM THE

SECRET PLACE

VOLUME 1

DR. J. E. MURDOCK

Table Of Contents

Introduction

Before we begin our walk together in my book called *Stones From The Secret Place*, I want to take you to a book in the Bible named *Joshua*.

I've read it many times and have always been blessed because we seem to get two sides of the picture of God's work with His people. God had brought Israel from the land of Egypt and His plans were to take them into the promised land, a land flowing with milk and honey. As we follow Moses' leadership with the children of Israel we find they had some beautiful experiences.

Because of their lack of faith during their trials and testings, they continued to murmur and complain, so God couldn't go too far with them. And Moses himself became weary in leading the children of Israel. And the Lord said, "Moses, for the sake of Israel, I'm not going to let you go into the promised land."

Then the call came to another man of God named Joshua. It's beautiful when we look to see how God has not given up on us, but He wants to lead us on and show His arm strong in behalf of His people. At the same time, He wants to get *inside* of our life and *inside* of our heart. So Joshua steps into the leadership and they have come to the river Jordan. Now when the river of Jordan flowed, the banks were filled with water all year; there was water flowing from the top of the banks at times. Now it was going to take *another* miracle. The Lord told Joshua and the priests of God that carried the ark of the Lord to make steps toward the river, and as they did the river parted.

They crossed over Jordan and were standing on the bank. God wanted that testimony. He wanted what He had done for Israel to live on for a future time in a future generation. So He said, "I want you to take twelve stones out of this river."

They had placed some stones in the river where the priests stood firm as the Israelites were crossing over the river. A clear path was before the Israelites as they crossed over. But He wanted this testimony to live on so that others would see the hand of God. So He said, "Take these twelve stones out of the river and place them on the bank." The Word says in Joshua chapter 4, verses 20 through 22, "And those twelve stones, which they took out of Jordan, did Joshua pitch in Gilgal. And he spake unto the children of Israel, saying, When your children shall ask their fathers in time to come, saying, What *mean* these stones? Then ye shall let your children know, saying, Israel came over this Jordan on *dry* land."

The purpose of these stones on the bank was to be a testimony of God's grace, God's ability and God's mindfulness to the generation to come. Israel said, *Had it not been the Lord, the waters would have overflowed us.*

The Lord loves for us to see the miraculous because He does things in such a way that really the natural man wouldn't even think of doing. There is no one who would think of crossing a river with a million people on *dry* land. He wants us to look back and recognize that if it had not been the Lord, these waters would have overflowed us.

So that's the purpose of *Stones From The Secret Place.*

It relates personal experiences and relationships with the Lord. May the Lord bless it to your heart as you read carefully from page to page.

~1~

I'VE NEVER BEEN THE SAME

I was thirteen...I had joined a certain church and I do not blame the church, but I didn't know how to take hold of the Lord by faith, and no one told me. All they asked me was, "Do you want to accept the Lord?" I said, "Yes." "Do you want to join the church?" "Yes." "And do you want to be baptized?" I said, "Yes." That was very clear teaching, and we need those questions given to us. But we need a *follow-up* of how to receive the Lord and to accept Him by faith.

So with this new desire to please God I felt it was all up to me to do the rest. I got a little New Testament and began to seek to be different, *but I did not know how.* In a few *short* weeks I had misplaced my New Testament. Because of the opposition that would rise up between my brother, sisters and I—they questioned why I still acted like I did since I had joined the church—and they'd say, "Ah, you joined the church, look at you now." I had lost my temper, you see. I had reacted in a way that they wondered if church meant anything to me.

So, I traveled that road for about two years *until...*

I was standing in the yard on a midsummer day when a car drove up in front of the house. I noticed that it was an aunt of mine who had been to the house to pick up my mother and two of my sisters. They had gone to a prayer meeting. We had never been to one at all and knew nothing about them. My aunt turned off the motor and reached in the back seat and picked up a little sister of mine who was only ten years old. When she picked her up and started in the house, I thought that something must be seriously wrong. In their prayer meeting, my sister had been saved and filled with the Spirit and was speaking in a heavenly language, and you may know how that attracted me! I had *never* heard of that.

As they went on into the house where we lived, my aunt said, "We are going to have prayer meeting here tomorrow afternoon." And I thought to myself, *I am going to be in that prayer meeting!* I looked forward to it. I saw something in the face of my little sister from that moment until the next evening. I heard her in prayer along with two of my other sisters...they were talking to the Lord just as if He was right there in the room. I had *never* heard anyone talk to the Lord as if He was right there with them. That *really* got my attention!

I could hardly wait until the next afternoon. Sure enough, about three o'clock in the afternoon, I stepped into that prayer meeting. Three or four others were kneeling down and talking quietly before the Lord, and I heard some of them begin to cry. Then I heard this little sister of mine begin to speak in a heavenly language. I looked around real quietly. And remember this was my very *first* time to get into a prayer meeting!

I believed in prayer. Many times you'll find people believe, but they don't ever pray. That's quite obvious everywhere you turn these days: There are a lot of people who believe in God, but they don't serve Him...*they don't seek after Him.* **Many have stepped into the presence of God and have never been the same**.

So, I just kneeled on the floor, then I crawled on my knees over to one of the others and listened. Then I found something happening in my own heart and I began to cry a little. I began to tell the Lord, *"Oh help me, help me."* That's all I could say, *"Help me, Lord. Help me, Lord. Save me, Lord."* Every now and then I would hear others in prayer speaking very softly, not boisterous but with a broken spirit saying, "Lord, You're coming back again. You're soon to return."

Somewhere or another I'd heard the message that Jesus would return again. And that really got a hold of me...He was coming soon. Before I realized it eight hours had passed and here I was, a little 15-year-old teenage boy to whom my mother had once said, "Son, if you don't change, you are going to the pen before you get grown."

I certainly believed in God, but I didn't know how to reach for Him. I didn't know how to *lay hold* upon God.

So that evening something happened that has lived on and on. How helpful it has been because we've come to some rivers to cross. We've walked through some valleys...had mountains to climb. We've met opposition just like when Israel came to the Red Sea and then she came to the Jordan. We often face different obstacles. I trust that these *Stones* will relate to you and will be helpful, for that was the purpose of putting the stones on the bank of the river.

That evening, my twin sister, who had been filled with the Spirit, had a vision of Heaven and was called into the ministry. It wasn't long until she was preaching the Gospel and young people were filling the little altar full...turning to the Lord.

There is power in the presence of the Lord. But to help us recognize His presence is the *real* purpose of writing about these wonderful experiences in the years that have gone by...how the Lord has been faithful...and how He teaches us more each day how to come before Him.

But that evening as I observed these things, something was planted into my heart that I was not able to get away from. I really didn't want to get away from it. I felt, *tasted* and witnessed something real...very precious. I like to relate it this way. There was a little lady at the well that the Bible tells us about in the book of John. She went to get water and met a Person there, Who was named Jesus, but she didn't know who He was. While she was there, He asked her to give Him water. She couldn't understand her being a Gentile and this man being an Israelite why He would even talk to her, because they had nothing to do with each other. Then the mystery began to come forth as the Lord began to talk to her. He related something to her that really got her attention. He asked her about the condition of her life. She thought immediately that He must be a prophet for He began to get into her life in areas that she thought were secret, but He told her *everything* that she had ever done.

Back in the prayer meeting, I thought of a lot of things. **Every wrong thought and action is uncovered in The Secret Place.** It was the presence of the Lord no doubt that had brought these things to my attention. So when Jesus sometimes comes to you, you may hear things about yourself that are necessary for you to be reminded of. There is One Who knows *all* about you, Who is *interested* in you and is offering you *living* water.

So when the little lady got through talking to Jesus, she left her water pot and went into the city. She said, "Come and see a Man that told me everything that I did. Is not this the Christ?"

That's what the Lord wants us to see: *He knows all about us whether we tell Him or not.*

She told people in the city of Samaria and they arose and went out to the well. They stood there and listened to Him. They insisted that He spend more time with them, and He spent two or three days talking to them. And then they said to her, *"Now we believe, not because you have told us, but **we have seen Him ourselves.**"*

That is *exactly* what we desire to relate to you. It is not altogether what others have said, but what we have heard from the Lord, too. That's the purpose of His patience and longsuffering today. He wants us *all* to hear the voice of the Lord.

One visit in the presence of the Lord and my heart was changed. I was amazed to end that day with a hunger and thirst for God. I began to seek the Lord. We didn't have a church to go to so we took *everything* to the Lord in prayer. **That's why The Secret Place means so much to me today.**

Because that's where I really was born again and my sins were forgiven. My relationship with the Lord gave me a peace and a hunger for more of God in such a way that I began to *pursue* the Lord. I went day and night on my knees when I'd come in from school. The three that had been saved and filled with the Spirit in our home were continuing their relationship and that certainly helped me to pray and seek the Lord. After we got saved and turned our hearts over to the Lord, we were aware very quickly that there was more yet for us from the Lord. I wanted to be filled with the Spirit like my sisters.

So, I began to seek the Lord so that He would fill me. My sister would say, "John, just surrender all." Whatever that meant, you know. "John, just surrender all." That was the first time I had ever heard anybody say that. And, "John, just seek Him with all your heart. He loves you. He wants to help you. Keep your mind on the Lord."

I call those words of exhortation, back then, my ABC's. I really had learned to say my ABC's before I went to school. I felt proud of my education, but I felt like there was more yet to learn whenever the spelling teacher asked us to spell words—then to have to reach into that ABC alphabet and pick out the right letter to spell that word. That's when I saw the need of more studying.

I am sitting here with a know-so that God has yet more in store for me, and we shall have that as we follow on. So let's enjoy together wonderful experiences, changes that take place, strengths that come, encouragement that comes even along with tears and hardships.

I've found His way is in The Secret Place.

The Answer Arrives Quicker When The Anxiety Leaves.

-J. E. Murdock

~2~

EXAMINE YOURSELF

The most important thing that happened in my first visit to The Secret Place was that I really examined myself. A new life had begun that made me aware of myself. I found a scripture that said to examine yourself to see whether you really are in the faith or not (see 2 Corinthians 13:5).

The Secret Place does not only meet a need, but it points out where your needs are. It's like eating a meal. The meal that we eat doesn't just support one member of our body, but it works to supply the need for every member. The presence of the Lord doesn't just touch us in one point, but it actually ministers to *every area of our life.*

So, I was seeking the Lord to be filled with the Spirit. Some had already been filled with the Spirit in the first prayer meeting they were in. But for some reason or another I didn't get filled that quick, but I was hungry and thirsting...working hard to see what hindered me from being filled. Then again the words of exhortation would come, "Just surrender all." Matthew 5:6 reads, "Blessed are they which do hunger and thirst after righteousness: for they shall be filled."

If we get before the Lord, it's like going before a mirror—you just see things that you never saw before. You see changes that you want to come into your life.

The motivation for prayer/salvation came from watching the lives of my sisters. There was such a change in their lives and they were reaching for God (like the woman at the well).

I didn't get *filled* for three months. I kept seeking. I had found the well and was reaching.

Our whole motivation was built on this fact—*He's coming again.* That revelation will make you purify yourself...seek to please Him. **If you have no revelation of meeting God,**

you don't have much to work with. "And every man that hath this hope in him purifieth himself, even as He is pure" (1 John 3:3).

One of my prayers in The Secret Place was: *"Lord, move out everything that is not of You. And even forgive me of some little remarks that I have made since I was saved."*

You'll seek the path that gives a *personal* relationship with the Lord. One of the writers in the Bible said he counted everything as dung, that he may know Him and be in right standing before the Lord. Get hid away in God.

– 3 –

FLEE FOR THE LIFE OF JESUS

Don't go back the way you came.

This is more or less a strange message, but we find out that we play a great part in *keeping what we have received* from The Secret Place. Our scripture is found in Matthew 2, verse 13, "And when they were departed, behold, the angel of Lord appeareth to Joseph in a dream, saying, Arise, and take the young Child and His mother, and *flee* into Egypt, and be thou there until I bring thee word: for Herod will seek the young child to destroy Him." This refers to a definite experience that came to Joseph and Mary after Jesus was born.

The Wise Men had talked to Herod concerning the star they had seen. A child had been born. Now the prophets had talked about it: Jesus, the Christ...the babe in the manger that would be born. ·And it had happened.

Herod the King said, "You go and bring me word. Tell me where He is and I'll go and worship Him." That sounded good if you just didn't know the inside of it. But the Lord appeared unto the Wise Men, after they had found Jesus and worshipped Him, and said to them, "Don't go back the way that you have come because Herod seeks to destroy the child." In Psalm 2:11, we read, "Rejoice with trembling." Even in the celebration of the Child, they were warned because they were ignorant of the danger.

So, the Word says the Wise Men didn't obey the King, but went back another way. And after they had gone, the Lord appeared to Joseph and said, "Joseph, I want you to arise and take the Child and His mother and *flee* into Egypt for Herod seeks to destroy the Child."

What we learned shortly after our first trip into The Secret

Place was how to *keep* what we received from the Lord...how to *maintain* our relationship with Him. Let's you and I do as Joseph did. Let's do as the Wise Men did. **Let's obey. Don't go back the same way that you came.**

That's what The Secret Place is about...to change you and me. And not only to change us, but also to *give us direction to walk in that change.* As the Word says, we're not to hide, but have the grace of God and the revelation of God working in our lives in such a way that we can hold onto what we have received from the Lord and not lose it.

Protect your relationship with the Father. In the Scripture there was a younger son and an older son. But the younger son said to his father, "Father, give me what you have promised me...what belongs to me." So the father gave it to him. And the Word says that, by and by, this younger son left home. And when he left home he got away from the close bond and influence that was at his father's house. So he began to spend what he had in wrong living...doing the wrong things. And first thing you know he had it all spent, and there he was a long way from home.

So, you can tell from the story in the Bible that our walk *out* from The Secret Place is going to be just that important. *The purpose of waiting before the Lord is to get direction and the ability to obey.*

This younger son ended up at the hog pen because the people of that country wouldn't give him anything to eat and he was hungry. The Word says that when he was working feeding the swine they didn't give him as much as the husk from the corn. So *he cried out.* He came to himself to find out that he had sinned against God. All he had left was...*he remembered*...back home the servants had plenty. *(Remember The Secret Place.)*

This Stone is for you and me to learn how to maintain the relationship out there in the world after we leave The Secret Place. For He says to *go home and tell your friends what great things the Lord has done for you.* We should stay before the Lord until we have received something that has changed us and a desire for our loved ones to know about it.

Fleeing for the life of Jesus is actually holding on...protecting what the Lord has given unto us. The Word says we are temples of God. If the Lord comes into our lives, we are to follow His direction or we'll lose it. Now a lot of people don't seem to understand that you've got to protect Jesus, but listen, Friends, it's very clear throughout the Word that there are two people living inside of the believer and that's the self (the natural) and the spiritual. We are to get enough of Christ to ignore, put down, lay aside, even *mortify* the deeds of ourselves and the desires for wrong things in order to keep our relationship with the Lord. We've got to learn to agree with God or we can't walk with God. We've got to learn to obey the Lord. **Obedience is the only thing that will make a difference**. To receive Him, we have to follow Him...*to keep Him, we have to obey Him.*

There are many precious people that have had great refreshings and great blessings from the Lord and died without Him...actually lost their way. And we want you to recognize the necessity of protecting your relationship with God with a true commitment to the Lord. For the Word says this, "Whoever we yield ourselves to, we will become a servant to." It is up to the believer to hold on to what God has given.

Adam and Eve lost it. They were deceived and thought they would become even greater if they would eat of the tree that God told them not to. And when they did, something gripped their hearts that they had never had before and *then* they were afraid when they heard the voice of God. *Live close enough to the Lord that you can enjoy the comfort that is in Him,* *knowing* that when temptation, trials and testings come, you'll be able to turn away and shun the very appearance of evil.

I've used this illustration a lot of times. Think of a person driving a car. He knows how to drive a car...he has a license. Yet all it takes is a little distraction and he will end up in a ditch. Think about how much time we have to devote ourselves to being able to stay on the road while we're driving a car.

There is no time at all for us to get over in the back seat and go to sleep while we're driving. The highway won't move for you—you have to stay on the highway. And the Word also says to *take heed; it's just a little ways from losing out with God.*

The Scripture tells us about Lot's wife whenever they had to flee from Sodom. God said, "I'm going to destroy it." They had a command not only to get out, but also not to look back. And whenever Lot's wife looked back, she became a pillar of salt. He warns us to remember Lot's wife. *Many have lost their relationship with God by looking the wrong direction.*

The Lord warns you and me to flee from things that distract us from God. *Your reading material, things that you look at, if they do not embrace the Lord and they do not please God, you'd better turn them loose.* If it happened in the Garden of Eden, it can happen in the TV room and it can happen with wrong relationships. **To hold on to Jesus, you'll have to forsake all to follow Him**. In fact, He says, pick up your cross and deny yourself and follow Him and you'll have great riches in Heaven.

We have many personal testimonies of how our conduct had to be in order to keep our relationship with the Lord. God looks upon the heart. He's looking for a place to abide. And do you know where He wants to abide? The Bible says He wants to abide in your heart. He want us to get that relationship in our heart and then keep Him there by keeping our heart right with God. *Flee for the life of Jesus.* **Every moment of the day calls for watching and praying**.

Jesus said to the disciples at the Garden of Gethsemane where He was in prayer, "Sit you here and watch." Then He came back and He found them asleep and said, "Oh, watch and pray, couldn't you watch with me one hour?" And they went to sleep again. And it wasn't long until the test came and everyone that knew Him seemed to deny Him.

So, Friends, find out what it takes to keep *your* relationship with the Lord. I've lost it in my lifetime and I'll tell you what, no one had to tell me. I *knew* I had lost it. When

He had slipped from my life, was when I stopped praying. I stopped reading the Word, and I spent time doing things that didn't seem any harm yet these things kept me from praying. And *anything* that keeps you from praying—I don't care if it's sitting in a chair and just going to sleep when you ought to be awake—will create a flaw in your relationship with God. It is time for you and I to *flee from evil and protect the things that God has given unto us.*

Sometimes it's not what we do that defeats us, but what we don't do. Neglect is dangerous (see Hebrews 2:3).

Listen, Friends, the enemy will go all out to get the relationship that you have with Jesus. Have faith in God when you go into The Secret Place...when you cry out to God.

I had rather have Jesus than anything in this world. I stayed long enough with Him to find out how to get it—how to keep it—and that's to stay in The Secret Place with God.

We always want God to reach for us, but *we must reach for God. The Word says everyone that comes to Him must believe.*

Protect your relationship with the Lord.

Always Add Faith To Your Prayers In The Secret Place.

-J. E. Murdock

– 4 –

I Do This According To Your Word

"And it came to pass at *the time of* the offering of the *evening* sacrifice, that Elijah the prophet came near, and said, Lord God of Abraham, Isaac, and of Israel, let it be known this day that Thou *art* God in Israel, and *that* I *am* Thy servant, and *that* I have done all these things **at Thy word**" (1 Kings 18:36).

Elijah was praying fire down in front of the prophets, but his motive was to reveal God's glory.

How many times we have readjusted our purpose, our motive for praying! We've had to become more sincere. I remember times when I'd say, *"Lord, bless me."* And the Spirit of the Lord seemed to whisper so gently, "Why do you want Me to bless you?" I got the message immediately. (And I was where when that happened? In The Secret Place.)

"Why do you want Me to bless you? Do you want Me to bless you where others will brag on you, where others will esteem you? Or do you want Me to bless you for *My* glory?" There's a different picture there.

You and I would be surprised to know how many times the good old self life will walk into prayer in The Secret Place with such motives. Stay before God. It will help you to straighten out.

I began to say, *"Oh, dear Jesus, if I have a wrong motive to become a big preacher, to become world-known, or to just be blessed for my glory, You know about it. And I understand that that kind of prayer will not go through. Help me to pray in the right way."* When right praying strikes your heart and mind, there is a confidence and a faith that begins to take over because **God wants you to have what you need**. He wants you to have what it takes to fulfill His will. *It's easier to believe when you're seeking God His way according to His Word.*

The Shepherd of the flock still leads us into green pastures. **If we're not finding any green pastures, that means the Lord is not leading**. What a new life the Lord will give you as you follow on.

Never build independent of Him. He will build His work in you and me in a way that we'll have to stay in contact with Him in order to abide in the confidence that all will be well.

I've prayed a lot of times when I seemed to get nowhere, like when I was lost in the woods. I had caught a ride to a prayer meeting at my uncle's house. When it was time to go home, there was not much traffic so I decided to cut through the woods. My uncle told me there was a trail about a mile down from his house. He said, "You will see an old sawmill on your right. The trail is right past the sawmill. *Do not* turn to the left."

When I saw the building, I decided to walk around and look at it. But then I could not find the trail. *I was lost!* I dropped to my knees and prayed, but still couldn't find my way out. I said, *"Uh, oh, I'm going to have to get an answer."* So the second time I knelt down and prayed, I felt peace. I couldn't see my way out yet, but I followed the peace of my heart. I saw a little trail, but a tree was lying across it. I thought, *"I will go around that tree to the other side."* And then I said to myself, *"No, that's how I got lost."* So I got on my knees and crawled under the branches so that I could stay on the trail. A voice inside said, *"You're still lost!"* I said aloud, *"I feel at peace to go on."* Soon I came out of the woods across the highway from my house.

Don't get distracted from the way. *Stay in The Secret Place until the question you have is answered.* Stay before the Lord until you mount up as with wings of eagles. When the Lord addressed the disciples to go to the upper room, He didn't say if He doesn't come in two days, stay the third day. He just says stay there until the Holy Spirit descends. *So tarry until...*

I do not know the different moods that group of believers went through at that time. I know we all go through things, especially when we have to wait a while...we get restless. But He said, "Go there to the upper room." *He even tells us where to go*, "Just stay right there until the Comforter comes." **The answer arrives quicker when anxiety leaves.** Why, I think a lot of times the Lord just stands there patiently until we lose the frustration, and *then* we learn patience...and patience is important in our Christian walk.

We have learned a little measure of wisdom from God. Don't be discouraged if the answer doesn't come immediately. If you're unable to actually spend sufficient time in The Secret Place, you can still arise from there and your relationship with God will go with you. I've had some strong praying and strong revelation come to me *after* I had left The Secret Place. It's because in that *place* of prayer the Lord takes a hold of our heart so we can learn to pray without ceasing.

Pray even as you work; say a word...*worship*. Different kinds of prayers will begin when you are in a relationship with the Lord. As you worship the Lord, it's almost like the children of Israel going according to His Word as they marched around the walls of Jericho every day for seven days, the last day seven times. And then after all of that He said, "Shout!" *I'll tell you that The Secret Place can come to that—a shout.* And when they shouted, the walls fell. *There are steps that we're still unaware of that God has for us to make if we'll just stay a little longer in The Secret Place.*

You know you don't expect a child to leave the cradle and immediately run a race around the house. You expect him to learn to stand alone...to walk gradually. And the Lord doesn't expect the wholeness of worship to be mastered at once, but *He does expect us to walk in the light that we have* and then He'll give us more light. So don't let delays discourage you. *Just stay there until...*

There's More In The Loaf When You Let The Lord Break It.

-J. E. Murdock

STONES

FROM THE

SECRET PLACE

VOLUME 2

DR. J. E. MURDOCK

TABLE OF CONTENTS

– 1 –

JESUS TAKES GIANT STEPS WITH US

What does God really expect out of us? To love people that don't love you. Be kind to your enemies; pray for them that speak evil against you. I knew that that was the right way. But now how to do it, that was another thing. The whole purpose of Jesus' coming into the world and sending the Comforter was to have a people on earth that could be like He Himself, who would care for those that had no care; who would love those that couldn't love.

We are to grow in the Lord. We are to actually come to the place where we can be more of what He wants us to be. And I believe if we see the importance of it, we will be more ready to accept it.

The verses we want to read to you are about Jesus taking giant steps with us. These things had never lit up until I got in The Secret Place with the Lord. You know if we will really take time, *God will put the emphasis on what we need.* A lot of times our mothers and fathers, in the days when they paddled us, said if it didn't go over properly, they had another way of impressing us. But we don't have to wait until then. *If* we'll be willing—and we've been saved and filled with the Spirit—we need to buckle down and say, "Lord, *You* make the difference in our life. You are shaping us and You are helping us make giant steps."

Verse 43 of Matthew 5 says, "Ye have heard that it hath been said, Thou shalt love thy neighbour and, hate thine enemy." When you really pay attention to those words, you can tell they don't sound just right. And it says *you've heard it*. You didn't hear it from Me, the Lord says, but you've heard it said "Thou shalt love thy neighbor, and hate thine enemy."

Isn't it strange how you can hear a partial truth and the very next words just seem to offset us from reaping the blessing by detouring us—causing us to fall short of being what God wants us to be?

In the Old Testament, God used many different sacrifices to change our life. If these had brought the change, another way would not have been sought. We would be surprised to know how far off we have been. And that's why He came into the world Himself and has offered us the Holy Spirit that will shed love abroad in our heart. And this love will be the real love, the right kind of love. Not a love that condones sin, but *a love that becomes patient and long-suffering and becomes a light to those that are in darkness* until they can see that you and I, the believer, have something. What is that something? It is the peace of God and the love of God that helps us to love people that don't love us.

All right, the Bible says *you've* heard it said, but that's not really the way it is. *"But I say* unto you, *Love your enemies, bless them that curse you, do good to them that hate you, and pray for them which despitefully use you, and persecute you,"* (Matthew 5:44). He has also shown us the way to qualify or have the strength to be what He has called us to be. Think of having to love your enemies. Who told us to do that? Jesus did. Who told us to hate our enemies? Somebody did. They didn't call any names, but it says, "Thou hast heard that it has been said."

Don't make any excuses for it. It's just a little ways to The Secret Place to call on the Lord and say, *"Lord, make a change in my life. Don't let me be so foolish as to miss Your will concerning others, even my enemies."*

Let me say this: Bless them that curse you. I don't think we have to take it in our own hand as to how to bless them—how much to bless them or what to give them—just do good to them that hate you. You know you can render a lot of things and still be a hypocrite with how you treat others. The Lord doesn't want us to be hypocritical and make out like we love one another when we don't. In fact, He told the disciples, "Beware ye of the life of the Pharisees, which was hypocrisy."

But listen, if we let Christ come into our life and begin to move in the direction of the Lord, our relationship can build something in our heart, and then we will be what the Lord wants us to be.

And Jesus said then, "*Pray* for them, which despitefully use you." I can't say I've followed in these tracks all of the way everyday. But I can say this: that I'm sure making a special effort to do it because I know enough of God's will in this area to know there is an unbelievable peace *and* faith *and* courage in God when I'm able to fulfill this kind of attitude and service towards those who despitefully use and persecute me.

First of all, Jesus, being the great example for us, whenever He went to the cross—He did it willingly. He said to them, "Don't weep for Me, weep for yourself." He's en route back to the Father even by the way of the cross. And He did not murmur nor complain.

Then there's Stephen, just as common a man as you'll find in this life. Whenever he was being persecuted, he had reached a place to be able to pray for those that were persecuting Him and despitefully using Him, and he said, "Father, forgive them for they don't know what they do."

So, there it is Friends. I hope you take this very seriously for I'll tell you if man had said it, then that's something else, *but Jesus said it.* He has promised to give us strength and grace to take these kind of *giant* steps. You and I won't have to take them many days until we'll *want* to take them because God will so reward us and our relationship with God will become richer. You'll have more faith and confidence, more care for others and *your prayers for others will be more effective.*

So, let's just pick up on these two or three verses and say, "Lord, that looks to me like that is a giant step." *It is!*

I shall never forget illustrating that one time in a church service. And the church didn't know what I had in mind, but I asked a CPA brother to come down to the front and take some little, short steps. He was embarrassed in a way and even the congregation wondered what it was all about, but I didn't tell them until he had taken the little, short steps. And when he had taken them, he ended up on the other side of the auditorium at the church, and I said, "Now, brother, take some giant steps." And he turned and, oh, he was truly relaxed when he had taken those giant steps. He took some long ones. He was tall and slender. We all had to smile and laugh. His short steps looked so funny compared to his giant steps.

Then I gave them the little message on giant steps. The Lord takes giant steps. I asked the congregation, "How many of you can take little, short steps like our brother has taken?" Some of them grunted a little bit and said, "Hmm, anybody can do that." I said, *How many of you can take giant steps?* I can take pretty good steps, but this brother just did it in such a big way. But everybody wondered, "Can I?"

I said, *Now, you remember the little, short steps?* "Yes." I said, *That means you love them that love you.* That's easy to do, isn't it? They caught on quickly. I really didn't have to go any further. *Anybody can make those kinds of steps, loving those that love you, but the giant steps are loving those that don't love you...*praying for them that persecute you and all who despitefully use you.

That certainly could be a big part of the cross that Jesus said, "If any man come after Me, let him deny himself and pick up his cross." That's a pretty heavy load to have to humble yourself and come to the place where you can love them who are not friends. Verse 45 says do this so, "That ye may be the children of your Father which is in heaven: for He maketh His sun to rise on the evil and on the good, and sendeth rain on the just and on the unjust."

We're really on our way if we can overcome what our enemies say about us. So the Lord says you and I are called upon to be in this world as Jesus was. Let's go for making giant steps. "If ye love them which love you, what reward have ye? do not even the publicans the same? And if ye salute your brethren only, what do ye more than others? do not even the publicans so?" *A call from religion to reality: "Be ye therefore perfect, even as your Father which is in heaven is perfect"* (Matthew 5:46-48).

–2–

HE TELLS YOU HOW TO BUILD

⟫·•·⟪

There's nothing more interesting than to read God's Word for He touches every area of life that we actually live in this world. His words concerning our building in this world or for eternity—why, He uses things that you'd hardly have to go to school to recognize the importance of it!

Jesus showed what it would mean to *not* build according to what He has to say. I really have been obsessed with the feeling in my heart that we must do things according to what Jesus said. Look at what happened in the beginning of creation just from eating the fruit of a tree that the Lord said not to eat from or you will die.

Reading in Matthew chapter 7, verse 21, "Not every one that saith unto Me, Lord, Lord, shall enter into the kingdom of heaven; but he that doeth the will of My Father which is in heaven." What plainer statement could the Lord begin with to clear our understanding of the importance of doing things like God wants us to do? He said, "Many will say to Me in that day, Lord, Lord, have we not prophesied in Thy name? and in Thy name have cast out devils? and in Thy name done many wonderful works? And then will I profess unto them, I never knew you: depart from Me, ye that work iniquity" (Matthew 7:22-23).

One of the first thoughts that comes to my mind in reading the words of Jesus was...did they really do what they professed to do? How could they do as much as they confess to do if they do not know God and they're not living for God? But that's very simple today. There will be many who *think* they're doing the will of God and the works of God, but *it's truly impossible to do the works of God without the proper relationship with the Lord.* That's why we're told to not let anyone deceive us and that there will be many false christs that will say they are Christ, but He said don't go after them. He takes a few words to clarify who the real Christ is, and if we're hungry to know Him, we ought to read the Word of the Lord and meditate upon His Word.

He said, "Depart from Me," to that group who professed unto Him that they knew Him. They were doing some wonderful works. Why, He professed to them in verse 23, "...depart from Me, ye that work iniquity." Now He's going to give us the real true instructions. One thing about the Lord in His Word is that *He doesn't just reprove us about the way we do things when we do it wrong, but He gives us plain instructions of how to do it right.*

Verse 24, "Therefore, whosoever heareth these sayings of Mine, and doeth them, I will liken him unto a wise man, which built his house upon a rock: And the rain descended, and the floods came, and the winds blew, and beat upon that house; and it fell not: for it was founded upon a rock." We are told to take heed how we build if we expect the house to stand.

God alone can build and direct us the way to build where we can stand in the face of the tests and trials that come against us in life. Verses 26-29, "And every one that heareth these sayings of Mine, and doeth them not, shall be likened unto a foolish man, which built his house upon the sand: And the rain descended, and the floods came, and the winds blew, and beat upon that house; and it fell: and great was the fall of it. And it came to pass, when Jesus had ended these sayings, the people were astonished at His doctrine: For He taught them as *one* having authority, and not as the scribes." In other words, they heard Jesus a little differently and His deliverance message registered a little differently than the Pharisees. He tells us plainly which house will stand and the house that will not stand.

That's the importance for you and I today...to find out *how* to build because the winds are going to blow, and the rain is going to beat upon the house. There are going to be testings and trials and it's going to be the kind that you and I are not familiar with. And the Lord said this is going to test your house.

I'll tell you what, for God to put the test on us, it's going to be something else. And I don't mean He's just going to make it so hard, but it's going to prove the very simple teachings of Jesus...you didn't build it right, you didn't build according to My Word. You read My Word, *but* you didn't dig down and actually put your house upon the rock. But it speaks of the wise man who builds, "He will dig down deep and he will put his house upon the rock. And when the winds come and blow and the rains beat, it won't fall, *it will stand the test.*" That is one thing we have experienced...as long as we're in this life, we're going to have tests. They are going to prove us one way or the other—are we still building right...are we able to face the storm?

Now, Jesus brings it out in the apostles' writings: *Life is like a foot race, then it's like a horse race, then it's like actually facing the rising of Jordan.* Being a young boy at one time, I enjoyed running, racing and playing ball. Then I learned the importance of keeping myself in shape, that I could last and run successfully until the game was up. And I found out this: that you just can't wait until the game starts and expect to be prepared to run the race. You must practice and give yourself to the race in order to prepare for the ballgame that you're going to enter into. *There's nothing more encouraging than to find yourself with the ability to play until the game is up.*

The Bible speaks of this: that there will be times that people will plant and build in such a way that, by and by, they will become offended. We're living in that day. They are hurt about something or something has been said that discouraged them. They have fainted and moved back out of the worship of God.

I never will forget a precious man...a car salesman in the church where we pastored in Texas. He had gotten saved and filled with the Spirit. His presence coming into the service meant a lot to us. It was so good for me as the pastor to look out and see a man so strong in the faith who appeared to be completely sold out to God. But his test day came while I was pastoring there.

I didn't know what was taking place because he and his little wife had been sitting on the front seats when they came in, and they always got there in time to spend a bit of time in prayer. And when the time came to testify for what the Lord had done, why, they were ready. Their testimony was very real to me.

But, one day I saw them drifting. They drifted back a few seats, then a little *farther* back. It wasn't but a few services until I noticed they were sitting on second to the last seat from the door that leads to the outside. I was a little disturbed about that. I had never told people where to sit in church, but I did wonder why such a move had been made.

Would you believe that a wind had blown? Something had been said and they were offended. I found out that this dear brother in the Lord was up testifying and somebody behind him had said in a loud voice, "Well, this man says the same thing every time he gets up." And he was offended at that, and had drifted towards the back of the church.

I was preaching one day in the service and they were seated in the back, which was a ways from the pulpit because it was a long church, a nice church. I was wondering what was the matter. When I was preaching, I could feel something worse yet to come. I wasn't necessarily preaching to them, but I was hoping to say something that might get their attention, show them that I cared. I said, *"Anything that will take you off the front seat of the church where you worship and enjoy the Lord and sits you on the back seat is not through moving you. The next move you make will make you stay home and not even go to church."* I actually wanted to weep. Knowing this man, I would have thought he was able to stand a test of any kind. That man was the type—*I'm for God, regardless.* But whenever the wind blew and the words of criticism came, *which they will do,* he was offended.

And sure enough the time came; they left the church, hurt and wounded, all because of what somebody said. We'd all say, "Well, of course that would hurt." That's right. I feel that it would hurt me, too. I've been hurt, but that's why *before* the winds blew, I tried to *prepare* for them.

Jesus teaches us how to build so that when trials come, we can stand the test. Now we are not the first ones who testified the worst winds...*the hardest and the most beating rains can come from those who go to the house of God with you.* According to the statement that David said in the Psalm, "If it would have been an enemy that had done this, I could have hid myself. If it would have been a stranger, I could have made my way around." But he said, "Where my wounds came was from someone who went to the House of God with me that actually said some things that were more than I could bear."

But think of this, Friends, and do not faint. Jesus Himself was asked the question, "Where did you get those nail scars? Where did you get those bruises?" And He said, "I got these in the house of my friends, some that were supposed to have believed in Me, trusted in Me."

Now what I'm trying to say under the title of this word...He tells you how to build. This is not to put you and I down if we are rocking under the pressures of what somebody said. What I'm trying to say is this: let's find out how to build where we will not be affected and will stand. For we do have examples of people in the Bible, and somewhere down the street you'll find someone whose gone through the same kind of trial, but *they're standing.* Find out how they stood the test. The hour is upon us where you can never tell from where the test may come.

The apostle Paul, who had great care for the church, was interested in knowing if they were still doing well and were they standing the test. There is one thing Paul desired, and that is that the people who began in the race would be able to go through. So he said, "I didn't withhold anything from you that would be profitable to help you to build and be prepared for whatever kind of wind that blows."

The Bible says that Paul did glance back at the people he had persecuted in the church. He said now since he's been converted, he sees his mistakes...sees where he failed. He said, "I did it ignorantly. I really thought I was doing the right thing."

And there are souls today that feel they are building right. They are going to church and they may read their Bible, but they're really not doing what God said.

So the apostle Paul emptied out his feelings and care with these words, "I look at my people now and my heart is filled with continuous sorrow for my people, Israel." He said, "I know them. They have a zeal for God." Think of that. They have a zeal for God. They work for God. They do things for God, but *not* according to knowledge. They're not doing it the right way.

So now the Lord is calling upon you and me to *double check* again and see that we do what God wants and do it the way He wants. If we do that, it *will* stand the test.

There's no greater example than to look back through the beginning of time when the Lord said, "The wickedness of the world has come up before Me." He was actually repenting that He had made man. But, He did find a man who feared God and his name was Noah.

He said, "Noah, I'm going to destroy every living thing upon the earth for the wickedness of the people is great and it has come up before Me. But I'm going to show you favor because you fear Me. You believe in Me and you fear Me. This is what I want you to do. I want you to build an ark for the saving of your household. And this is the way I want you to build it, and hear it clearly." He said, "I want you to build it and use certain kinds of measurements, a certain width and height and breadth. I want you to put a certain covering on the outside and I want you to put a certain covering on the inside. I want you to build it just like I tell you because, Noah, you've never seen a rain and a flood like I'm going to send. But if you'll do it this way, you'll be safe."

There was just *one* thing Noah had to do and that was to *build according to the pattern.* Now he has the pattern and don't ever think that it didn't cross his mind to cut corners on building of the ark, to do it a little different. I'd say he wouldn't be the first one that had built something that had different ideas come to him while he was building. No doubt something occurred to Noah, *I don't think it's necessary to build and to put it just this way. We can cut corners. It will answer for the same thing.*

That's the way many people worship God, and they expect God to accept any kind of worship. It's not so, Friends, and don't ever think that God hasn't told us about it. He has. But the Bible tells us that Noah moved with fear to the building of the ark. What was he afraid of? He was afraid that he might miss the pattern of how to build and he would be destroyed.

Friends, that's one thing that I have felt disturbed about all along the way because I feel definitely the winds are blowing. Contrary rains are falling and trials are coming from all sources. At times you could almost faint if you didn't remember to get alone with God and seek Him in The Secret Place. We're not the first ones that have been tempted to pull aside. In the early church, there were those whose lives were beaten and who actually became martyrs instead of giving up their faith and their obedience to God. But the Word says they counted it a pleasure to obey God and to go through tests and trials to please the Lord. The Lord said that even in their trials they rejoiced...they were counted worthy to suffer for His name.

Jesus tells you how to build, not the friends down the street, not someone across town, not false teachers or leaders. And there's no one that stood tests greater than Jesus. He stayed true to the Father's will in spite of everything that came His way. God will support you and I if we'll obey Him. How are we going to do it? Stay in The Secret Place until the presence of God takes control of our life and we can *gladly* build according to the pattern.

Take The Pressure Off Of Your Faith With Patience.

-J. E. Murdock

– 3 –

"THESE THINGS WILL PASS AWAY"

In one week's time, I was in the Lord's work.

Every step the Lord makes with us is profitable.

But with love and patience and long-sufferings, He will gently work with us. I would encourage you to keep a daily relationship with the Lord, even if you're just praying about things around your home or on the job, whatever your concern, just stay available for God to talk to you and direct your step. I've prayed this prayer more than once, "Lord, if I can't hear Your voice, just *cause* me to make the right choice."

Moses saw the burning bush and went over to it. The Lord called him to be a deliverer and placed a time on it. The calling had been in his heart so he was being prepared all along, not just for a short time, but, he had no idea how God would do it.

I was on the side of the hill praying. I just turned and looked back towards the house. Everything was trimmed up...the shadows of the trees looked beautiful in the moonlight. The Lord spoke these words, "These things shall pass away." "...and they that turn many to righteousness as the stars for ever and ever" (Daniel 12:3).

I immediately came from my prayer time and began to prepare to go into the Lord's work. I had gotten a replacement for my job (my sister and her husband.) I told my uncle, *"I'm going out in the Lord's work."* He said, "I'm not surprised."

We stored our furniture, sold a few things I had (cows, etc.) and paid off my '31 one-seater Model Ford. I had fifteen dollars left. I knew of an old building with a sawdust floor; my twin sister had held a revival there way back in the piney woods of east Texas. They called it Possum Walk.

We planned to go by my mama's and say goodbye and drive on to the community to see if we could get that building. We kissed mama goodbye...walked down the steps to the car and suddenly my brother-in-law, who took over my job at the dairy, handed me a letter that had come to my box where I used to live (they now had moved in). I opened the letter and it was from the Cameron Full Gospel Tabernacle in Cameron, Texas.

The pastor wrote:

Dear Brother Murdock,
Since you all were here in the early spring, I talked to the church about getting you all to move here and work with our young people and help me in the church. We have decided if you all can come that we will come and get you with a truck and move you here. We've decided we can give you eight dollars a week. We would love to have you. Let us hear from you.

I just happened to visit that church in a time of fellowship one day because they were about 150 miles away from where we lived, and in those days people didn't travel like they do today. So with a trip like that, why, you could almost call it a foreign country to be that far away from home.

Just think how quickly the Lord opened this door! But did He do it all in a week's time? No. I have a feeling that those times of prayer and waiting on the Lord, building a relationship with God, were preparing me for the answer to come.

My prayer time on the side of the hill at my house was to me like the burning bush to Moses. I had felt the call, but no direction. When I think of the feelings that came over me before this experience on the side of the hill and see how quickly God can do *anything*, then I really feel like the bottom line for

God's people is to just *stay available* to God. *Then* He will bring things about and you will find yourself in the center of His will.

And it makes no difference of the opposition that wars against you while abiding in His will; it can be taken care of in prayer. Get still; get quiet.

I'll tell you, it's been a beautiful experience to see what can happen in such a short time. If I would have known He was going to work it out just like that, why I might have been in an easy chair. If I'd have gotten comfortable, I would have felt satisfied right where we were. But those feelings kept working in us and kept us on our way to The Secret Place just seeking the Lord and a relationship with Him. And we've used a little statement: *Take the pressure off of your faith with patience.*

And that trip from my "burning bush" has lasted over one-half of a century.

It's a beautiful thing, if a believer can get a hold of the fact *earlier* of just what a relationship with the Lord means...*to sit* in His presence...to *think* upon His Word...*meditate* in His law. You don't have to go there and wait until you are just snowed under with needs. Learn to enjoy His presence and give God time to bring you to the place where you can have the assurance that you are doing His will in every way.

Listen, Friends, *you may not be but one week away from the answer to the greatest prayer that you've ever put before the Lord!* And the Bible does say it this way, "You will reap in due season if you faint not." I don't cease to marvel of what God did. It has lasted about 57 years in the work of the Lord, and every time that it would strike us to get a little weary and pull aside, why, pull aside to what? To these things that will pass away? It doesn't mean that God doesn't bless us with things, but He wants to prepare us for the blessing.

Listen, Folks, the whole purpose of this true experience is to make you hungry and build your confidence in what can happen in The Secret Place. *Your next step can place you in the center of your calling.*

**Let God Do It
The Way He
Wants To,
Then You Will
See The Hand
Of The Lord.**

-J. E. Murdock

– 4 –

SIX WORDS THAT SHOOK TWELVE DISCIPLES

One of you shall betray Me. I cannot forget how the Lord brought this statement across to me and showed me the importance of examining yourself. And that has been mentioned more than once in the Scriptures...to examine yourself and see whether you are in the faith or not.

This was the brief, little message the Lord gave the twelve disciples as they sat at the table for the Last Supper...before Jesus was ready to be led away and be crucified. Jesus made a statement that, most of the time, wouldn't arouse people at all: "One of you shall betray Me."

A disciple responded, "There are twelve of us; if it's just one of us, there's no use to be upset. It's just one of us. The message certainly isn't for me so why should I be disturbed?" The Lord *let me see this importance...*if we see somebody fail, we need to take heed. If it happened to someone, it could happen to me. And that really struck home. And I began to seek truth and the importance of being cautious ourselves, lest we happen to be the one.

The 26th chapter of Matthew says, "And the disciples did as Jesus had appointed them and they made ready the Passover." Now when the evening had come, He sat down with the twelve, and as they did eat, He said, "Verily I say unto you, that one of you shall betray Me." The Spirit of the Lord caused me to pick up that little phrase that we have used in the ministry on this subject. And I counted those words, *One of you shall betray Me*, and the Lord emphasized, then, the importance of, *"Lord, is it I?"* And the scripture reads on, "They were exceeding sorrowful, and began every one of them to say unto Him, 'Lord, is it I?'"

We use that statement sometimes a little too lightly. But I have said wouldn't it be nice if you could shake twelve preachers today; cause them to think, to take heed of what's happening around them, to be sure that it's not happening within us? That is one reason that we feel very pressed of the Lord to forewarn each of us of what can happen. *If it can happen anywhere, it can happen in us.* If it can happen in the garden where Adam and Eve were and where the Lord had placed them, it can sure happen in the TV parlor of today. Lord, is it I?

Many times things are put before us to try us, to test us, to see what we're really made of. He lays things before us to see if we can stand it; not to cause us to fail, but to cause us to find the way to keep from failing. The Lord said, "In the last days," and Paul especially drove that home to Timothy, a young minister that was going to be carrying the Gospel, "the day will come they will not endure sound doctrine, but will heap to themselves teachers having itching ears." *They want to hear it like they love to hear it said, and they will find someone that can say it like they like it.* Lord, is it I?

Jesus said, "The time will come there will be a great falling away." And then I said it sincerely, *Lord, is it I?* It doesn't hurt for you and I to double check our life, and there's no better place to hear it said right and to prepare to receive it than to stay before the Lord in prayer. *Prepare to receive reproof if necessary.* Be prepared to receive and to embrace truth. "The day *will* come when there will be a great falling away." "Lord, is it I?" Let's take those statements seriously.

The whole message Jesus gave that shook the twelve apostles, you and I can follow it through every caution and warning that God gives us in the Word. As the Father says, (I think He includes all of us in this statement), "Though you stand by faith, don't be haughty or high-minded, but fear. For if God spared not the angels that sinned and the natural branches were cut off, He won't spare you."

So listen, Friends, one of the most important things in

The Secret Place, is to get alone and let God *search* your heart. Don't take for granted that what the other fellow says is right, his remarks about you. Now it was not true of every one of the twelve apostles, but it was true of one. But they were all stirred; now which one? So we are cautioned in the Word to take heed and to save ourselves from this untoward generation.

One of the apostles said, "Lord, what is John going to do?" Now you can take that statement as if he was impressed to be concerned about John. *Don't be so overly concerned about someone else that you forget your own need.* For the scripture does say, "They made me a keeper of other vineyards, but my own I haven't kept." We used to call them the *fruit inspectors*...they inspected the lives of others and overlooked the need of searching their own life.

Jesus said to the man who asked, "What's John going to do?" He said, "What is that to you? Follow Me." He's not sowing indifferent attitudes that we're to have toward others. He is saying the thing for us to do is to follow Him, and then we can, when necessary and when our opportunity comes, help the other. *But when we follow man, we soon position ourselves to a place where we have nothing to give to the other from the Lord.*

Go before the Lord. Don't take anything for granted. You may be standing good today, but be sure to check again to see if you're in the faith "lest you become a reprobate." *Lord, is it I?*

Don't Be A "Fruit Inspector"...
Inspecting The
Lives Of Others
And Overlooking
The Need
Of Searching
Your Own Life.

-J. E. Murdock

Stones

From The

Secret Place

Volume 3

Dr. J. E. Murdock

TABLE OF CONTENTS

– 1 –

GOD HAS A PLAN

The Lord teaches: "Blessed are your eyes for they see. Some have eyes and do not see." Then He said to them, "And blessed are your ears for they hear. For some have ears and they do not hear."

The enemy deceived Adam and Eve through their pride. When the Lord called them, they answered, "We heard your voice and were afraid." And the Lord asked them, "What have you done? Why are you afraid? Have you eaten of the tree?" And immediately, it seemed like the Lord knew about their conversation and where it came from. They had disobeyed Him and had eaten of the tree. And they said that they had. (Adam and Eve did not confess. God had to *dig* it out of them.) Actually they sewed fig leaves together to try and cover their sin. "He that covereth his sins shall not prosper:" (Proverbs 28:13). They recognized they had a problem and now their pride caused them to try and cover it.

The enemy said, *You will be as God.* So there was a pride that came into their life, no doubt, that even works today; a pride that makes people want to feel like they are somebody. And they wanted to feel like they could handle their problems. *They wanted to feel that it was all right to want to feel that.*

But there's only one way to feel and that is to want to embrace God's plan and do it His way. It's marvelous to see the effort that God has made to bring us back into that relationship. It was not easy to get Adam and Eve away from the fig leaves, their own method of saving themselves and to face God and renew their relationship with Him. And whenever I see how many have lost their way and have never found their way back to God, it's really disheartening.

In Acts 9, verses 10-20, the apostle Paul, once named Saul, who was a strong leader of wrong teaching, said that he did what he did thinking he was doing God's service...thinking he was doing God's plan...only to find out he was persecuting God. He was actually doing things *against* the Lord. And when the Lord spoke to him, he recognized, hey, this is someone else with authority, because he fell to the ground and was blinded. And he heard a voice saying, "Saul," and he said, "Who are you, Lord?" And the Lord told him, "I'm Jesus Whom you are persecuting." In other words, **If you are persecuting My people you are doing it to Me**.

Saul was quickly aware the time had come that he'd better find out who that was that had struck him to the ground and left him there blind. And the voice said, "I'm Jesus, Whom thou persecutest." *The only way to begin to get into God's plan is to begin to recognize another voice...His voice.*

Someone else is talking now. It's not just the neighbor, it's somebody else that's talking. Saul recognized that. And he said, "Well, what would you have me do?" And the Lord told him exactly what to do to begin...where to go...and a word would be sent to him.

So, Saul was *led* to a certain place. In order to get into the depth of God's plan, I definitely believe we don't have to be struck blind...**But we've got to find His plan in order to have peace...to find joy...and happiness or contentment**.

He inquired and now he's at a certain place. The Lord spoke to a man of God and said, "Ananias, go over and pray for this man, Saul." He knew about Saul. He didn't want to go. But the Lord said, "He's a vessel. I've chosen him and he's ready for you to come to him. Don't be afraid. Go and pray for him so that he'll be filled with the Spirit." And so he went, and found Saul praying. He found him in The Secret Place.

Wherever you can touch God is a marvelous place. The way to touch God is to worship Him with all your heart and with a surrendered will to Him. He can hear you in a lot of places if you can pray right from the depths of your heart.

Then the plan of God was revealed to Saul. The scripture

speaking of God's plan is John 3:16-18, that says, "For God so loved the world, that He gave His only begotten Son, that whosoever believeth in Him should not perish, but have everlasting life. For God sent not His Son into the world to condemn the world; but that the world through Him might be saved. He that believeth on Him is not condemned: but he that believeth not is condemned already, because he hath not believed in the name of the only begotten Son of God." Did you really notice the plan there: how to come back to God...how to receive from God?

Just think how brief the message was to believe upon the Son of God. Believe in the Name...His name shall be called Jesus. He shall save His people from their sins. But did you notice the powerful word—*believe?*

Everyone that finds the plan can only put it to work through faith. How hard it is to have faith if we allow ourselves to look at many other plans...even God's plan that man has twisted in such a way. Only faith in the Son of God and in the bloodshed of Jesus can take away sin. But *if* we'll believe, we will begin to witness a comfort and assurance that He has heard our prayer...He has forgiven us of our sins.

As we follow on, we can get more in the plan of God. He says in one of the Old Testament scriptures, "Let us return unto the Lord, for He has smitten, He has torn, and He will bind us up." Now think about it, "He has smitten," in other words, *it is not what others do to us, it's where we stand in God.* And when we lose out with God, God has to humble us, God has to break us and bring us down. Oh, the blessings that follow those who *obey* Him. It's unbelievable what God will give to an obedient heart. But reading in Deuteronomy, if we fail God, what a dark night is before us.

It's so important to find the plan that gives us rest and gives us peace. God's plan gives both. *God has a plan and we, by faith, are to fulfill that plan, **not** change it.*

Jesus went into the Garden of Gethsemane. And He prayed a prayer that made an attempt to change God's plan, but it didn't change it.

Now think of that. Jesus prayed earnestly, "Father, if it beYour will, let this cup pass from Me. *Nevertheless, let not My will but Thine be done.*" And Jesus had to go right ahead and follow God's plan. He said He came not into the world to do His will, but the will of the Father.

Even Paul, in 2 Corinthians 12:8-9, sought the Lord three times to help him get rid of a thorn in the flesh. God said, "satan was sent to buffet you, but My grace is sufficient for you. I pray that your faith will not fail."

God's purpose, when He opens our eyes to see truth and our ears to hear truth, is that we may follow and obey that truth. So *find* His plan and don't try to change it, but walk in it.

I have found this to be true...in order to keep the plan real to our heart, we have to stay in The Secret Place before the Lord. We've got to be reminded of the plan, the purpose, and the importance of it. His Word will become a lamp unto our feet not only to show us the plan, but also to point the way and give us strength and ability to perform *that* plan. And listen, if you haven't gotten started, **stay in The Secret Place until the plan is revealed**.

～2～

IF IT'S HOLINESS, I'M UNDONE

In Isaiah the sixth chapter, I read something there that the Lord really made alive to my heart. I decided to teach it in a certain church and I will never forget. The revelation to Isaiah was, *In the year that King Uzziah died, I saw also the Lord sitting upon a throne, high and lifted up, and His train filled the temple.*

One of the most important things that stood out was how the Lord has to remove things from our natural eye, things that have our attention. Uzziah was a great king. Many were attracted and heard no voice but Uzziah's. But the scripture brings out that the year Uzziah died (the distraction was removed) Isaiah said he saw the Lord. "I saw also the Lord...high and lifted up," (Isaiah 6:1).

There are many things that distract us from the Lord that He sees fit to remove. It may be painful, but it's important that we see the Lord, *high and lifted up.*

Think of how many different pictures come to us through the lips of others, even across the pulpit...which actually keep the face of a Holy God *hid* from us. It's one thing to know God has all power. It's another thing to know what He expects out of you and me...what He wants to do...what He came in this world to do.

There was nothing wrong with God's plan, and the law was good. But nothing in man could blend into God's law. The only thing they detected about the law was that they couldn't keep it. It's like asking a child that's still in the cradle to drive a car. He cannot. Yet, driving a car can be done, but he can't.

We find that the covenants that the Lord made with the priest, offering sacrifices for their sins and for the sins of the people, were not enough. They were reminded year after year that they were sinners. The fallen nature of Adam and Eve was still there.

God looked down through it all and probably thought, *Sooner or later I'm going to have to do something else. I'm going to have to fix a way that I can come into the hearts of men and dwell in their lives and inhabit them so that they'll be able to do what I want them to do.* And that's when He promised to send a sacrifice that no one else could make. No one else's sacrifice counted because no one could bring them to the vision that He wanted them to have *except* Christ, the Son of God.

Reading in Isaiah, "Above it stood the seraphims: each one had six wings; with twain he covered his face, and with twain he covered his feet, and with twain he did fly. And one cried unto another, and said, Holy, Holy, Holy, *is* the Lord of hosts: the whole earth *is* full of His glory." Friends, this is truly the message God has wanted to bring to us since the fall of man. *He is a Holy God.*

So then we are going to have to recognize sooner or later *that we're undone*. Let's don't wait until life gets painful. God's Word can light up our pathway and let us know that it's Christ in us...the hope of glory; Christ in us...the hope of holiness; Christ in us...the holiness Himself. And that's Christ *in* us. He inhabits us by His Spirit. He said man doesn't know anything at all save the spirit that's in man.

The neighbor wouldn't have to tell you that you had a grass burr in your foot. *You'd* know. You wouldn't have to wait for someone to tell you. And man knows there's a need...something lacking. When he sinned the first time, he knew something was wrong and tried to cover his sin with fig leaves. It didn't work. **The presence of God reveals that man's covering is not sufficient**.

So to find our way back into God's good pleasure where we can have favor, we must have Christ *in* us. He cannot get into us if we do not believe. He cannot work through us if we are ignorant of His plan. So we must have faith in the Word of God so we can grow and the Christ life can come forth.

How beautiful it is to find that there were some who walked with God and who were taken, such as Enoch. And there were some in the upper room that went forth and their life was so inhabited by reality that it fought their battles whenever persecution came and they actually suffered for righteousness' sake *gladly*.

Holiness doesn't only speak of relationship, but it places us in a realm to receive. God opens a door to those who seek Him with a whole heart. *No good thing will God withhold from those who walk uprightly.*

So then we hear them in the third verse singing this song, *"Holy, Holy, Holy."* I never will forget I was meditating upon these things as I was driving down the road and all at once I went to singing the little chorus, crying, "Holy unto the Lord. Oh, if I could, I surely would stand on the rock where Moses stood, crying, Holy unto the Lord." Would you believe, while those thoughts were coming, the Lord impressed upon me that the raindrops that fell in the days of Noah had a song...they were singing, "Holy, Holy, Holy, Holy." I actually went to crying in the car to think *that's* the message God wants to get over to us.

They were sinning in those days and God wasn't asking them for this or that. *He wanted to teach them holiness, for that's what's going to count.* And really, I don't know if I've ever heard that statement made that those raindrops, as they hit the ground, were saying, "Holy, Holy, Holy, unto the Lord." We find that God delays His coming because He wants to get over to you and I the message "and holiness, without which no man shall see the Lord:" (Hebrews 12:14). *(We can be without a spot and be without blemish.)*

There was no use for the Son of God to come into this world and leave you and I suffering the same as it was when the high priest offered sacrifices. They did not escape though they rejected. And how much more will we, in this day of God's grace, fail to escape the judgment of God if we reject the Son of

God Who was given to not just sit on the throne but to *take over* in our life...to be *in* us what the Father was in Him.

We wouldn't know His holiness if God didn't open our eyes to it. The holiness of God isn't just doing things. The holiness of God is a personality...a person. "Even the mystery which hath been hid from ages and from generations, but now is made manifest to His saints: To whom God would make known what is the riches of the glory of this mystery among the Gentiles: which is **Christ in you, the hope of glory**:" (Colossians 1:26-27).

The message came so strongly in The Secret Place: that if what's needed is holiness, we're undone. My Friends, if you're seeking God with all of your heart, nobody has to tell you if you're ready or not. You can know for yourself. *Don't take your own advice...don't take the advice of others...***Take advice from God**. Cry out to Him.

In Luke 18:10-13, the Lord spoke of two men praying. One of them stood and prayed. He was called a Pharisee. He thanked God that he wasn't like other men. He was proud of his righteousness. He said, "I pray three times a day. I'm found in The Secret Place. And above all, I'm glad I'm not like that publican over there." The publican just fell on the ground. And the Lord said he prayed. So let's look at both prayers.

And the publican cried out, "Oh, God, have mercy on me, a sinner." That man arose and went away with peace and went away justified. He was forgiven. I'll tell you **if right praying can get a hold of us, right living is on its way**.

The man who was so glad he was good and prayed three times a day was full of his *own* righteousness. (Yet the Lord declared our righteousness is as filthy rags and no one is good.) That kind of praying stems from the lips and God's life comes from the *heart*. That's why He has so plainly said He'll write no more the law upon tables of stones...but He'll write it upon the fleshly tables of the heart; because if He doesn't get a hold of the reins of the heart, He can get nowhere with us. But with a touch of Him in the heart, we will do as Isaiah, "Lord, I am undone."

Reading in Isaiah 6:5, "Then said I, Woe *is* me! *For I am undone*; because I *am* a man of unclean lips." Alright notice, "...and I dwell in the midst of a people of unclean lips." How does he know that? That he is a man that has dwelled among people who don't talk right, people who talk sinful and say things that are displeasing? How did he know that's wrong company? Then how does he know that he dwells in the midst of a people with such unclean lips? He said, "This is the reason I know it. I've heard them singing, 'Holy, holy, holy'." Then, he said, "*I have seen the King*, the Lord of Hosts."

That's the place that The Secret Place must bring us to. We must see ourselves as God sees us. And when we see ourselves as God sees us, we're to cry out like Isaiah, "I'm a man of unclean lips."

And then we find in the seventh verse the Lord goes no further. He's ready to help us. He's ready to change the picture of our life. We need messengers that believe in the message Isaiah was talking about: Holy, holy. These seraphims were singing that song, "Holy, holy, holy, the Lord God of Hosts." And the results of that message were His train filled the temple and the presence of the Lord came down. *Then* Isaiah saw his condition. Don't we need it again? Lord help us find our way into a place where God can talk to us!

A lot of people believe in holiness, but do not know what it takes to be holy...do not know what steps it takes to become clean and pure and enjoy right living. But the seraphims knew the purpose of God. And they came down with a live coal in their hand, which He had taken with tongs from off the altar. He laid it upon my mouth and said, "*Lo, lo, this hath touched thy lips. Thy lips and thine iniquity is taken away and thy sin purged.*" **If you're not living holy, you're undone**.

God didn't just come to preach to us, He came to inhabit us. He didn't come just to show us the way, but to help us to *live* for Him and we've just got a little while to do it. Don't wait like the foolish virgins did in the 25th chapter of Matthew. They knew this truth, but they paid no attention to it. *There will be many who will hear the message from The Secret Place that will overlook the importance of hearkening to it.*

Don't let the revelation of holiness slip from you. It can be made known *now* or it *will be* made known on the Day of Judgment forever *(too late)* that we're unclean in our heart. And listen, there's no way to find holiness clearer than to read and follow the footsteps of Jesus' teachings in Matthew chapters 5 and 6. *He tells us how to get to places and the difference between places.*

And know this: **It's not what *others* say about you; it's not what you say about you; it's what *God* says about you.** But there will be some on that day who will say, "Lord, we have eaten in Your presence, we have ministered in Your presence, we have been in Your presence." He will say, "Depart from Me, I never knew you."

Stay in The Secret Place until not only you find God, but stay there until God finds you. He'll say, "Here's the way. Walk in it." *Don't lean too heavily on any source like you lean upon Him.*

Seek Him in secret; He'll reward you openly. Those are the words of Jesus.

– 3 –

IT CAN HAPPEN TO THE BEST OF FAMILIES

The second chapter of the book of Luke relates to us that when Jesus was twelve years old He went with His parents to Jerusalem. Verse 42 says, "And when He was twelve years old, they went up to Jerusalem after the custom of the feast. And when they had fulfilled the days, as they returned, the child Jesus tarried behind in Jerusalem; and Joseph and His mother knew not of *it*."

Verse 44 brings out an astonishing thought that attracted us to this particular subject. "But they, supposing Him to have been in the company, went a day's journey; and they sought Him among *their* kinsfolk and acquaintance. And when they found Him not, they turned back again to Jerusalem, seeking Him. And it came to pass, that after three days [think of that], they found Him in the temple, sitting in the midst of the doctors, both hearing them, and asking them questions. And all that heard Him were astonished at His understanding and answers" (Luke 2:44-47).

Let's look and see what an upset Joseph and Jesus' mother were in when they found Him there in the temple where they had actually left Him. "And when they saw Him, they were amazed, and His mother said unto Him, Son, why hast Thou thus dealt with us? Behold, Thy father and I have sought thee sorrowing. And He said unto them, How is it that ye sought Me? wist ye not that I must be about My Father's business? And they understood not the saying which He spake unto them. And He went down with them, and came to Nazareth, and was subject unto them: but His mother kept all these sayings in her heart. And Jesus increased in wisdom and stature, and in favour with God and man" (Luke 2:48-52).

Joseph and Mary were human beings as you and I. Now their attitude toward Jesus is very common but Jesus, no doubt, had already caused Mary especially to wonder, *There's something very special about my Son.* They left Jerusalem to return home *supposing* that Jesus was with them.

If we look at that from one angle, why certainly it would go well in our day, wouldn't it? Jesus, the Son of God, even at just twelve years old, is now about the Father's business. Now don't you know that they did wonder about that...and that Joseph hadn't even told Jesus to do what He was doing? So He got His call from the Father, even at twelve.

But the emphasis the Lord seemed to have put on that was to caution the believer today, to be sure that he's in step with the Lord and with His will. *Don't just guess at it.* Don't just hope at it. But you and I can know the will of the Lord, and *we can know where and how to stay in touch with the Lord.*

But here this mother and father have walked all day, and whenever the night and the shadows began to come, they looked around. No doubt the group of people that were walking along with them and talking, when the evening came...they looked around, too. It seems like when shadows come...when the close of day comes, we get in search for different things. And now the day was ending and they're thinking, "Say, have you seen Jesus in the last few minutes?" *And they, to their surprise, looked around and found Him nowhere.* My, what an experience for a mother.

Whenever you put that in a spiritual sense, you find that there will be many who will go to the judgment day supposing that they're ready, only to find that they're not; *supposing that the Lord is with them to find that He isn't.* (There are a lot of people that are going to hear the words, "I never knew you.")

Be sure that you are in touch with Jesus. For the Bible says it this way: "Christ *in* you is the hope of glory." Not just around us, but Christ must be *in* us. Now the only way for Christ to be with us is for us to be with Him.

The Bible says that Jesus was in step with the Father's will, "I must be about the Father's business." Now He became subject to His mother and they went home, but the message that God wants us to see is this: If it can happen to Joseph and Mary, it can happen to you and I. **Don't just suppose... make sure Jesus is with you**.

How easy it is for a person today to travel to the end of life's journey...supposing He's with us. Many people don't see the seriousness of it until the end of the day. There are people that don't seek the Lord until the day has come to an end, and that seemed to be even for Joseph and Mary. It is easy to get involved with other relationships. It was at the end of that day that they had noticed; *He's not with us.* It can happen even in the best of families.

Are we willing for God to show us if we are out of step with the Lord?

You Won't
Journey Far
Until You've
Run Short...
If You Haven't
Heard From God.

-*J. E. Murdock*

– 4 –

THERE'S MORE IN THE LOAF WHEN YOU LET THE LORD BREAK IT

There's no better way to get God involved in our life than to stay before the Lord and to meditate in His Word. He'll tell us what to do.

Now just think of the words and the power that is in the statement that Jesus made to those disciples who said, "We've got a multitude of people here and the day is spent. We need to send them away where they can buy themselves something to eat." But the words that come to us from verse 16 in the 14th chapter of Matthew, "They need not depart; give ye them to eat."

The disciples were truly involved. Their first thought was to send them away. And now they are addressed by the Lord Himself, they don't need to depart, *"give ye them to eat."* And here that the disciples claimed to have five loaves and two fishes. Maybe they were going to divide it among themselves. *"You* give them something to eat."

And I'd like to address our reader today to think it over. If you have got something very real from the Lord and He has comforted your heart and your life in some way, you're going to face somebody, maybe today or tomorrow, that needs a word of encouragement, that needs some advice. You may not feel it's enough to help the multitude, but listen, you will be surprised what God can do with your experience...your visitation from God.

Our experiences are our "loaves and fishes." This thought comes to me about little David going into the camp of

Israel. He finds that Goliath is out there begging the Israelite leaders to send someone out to fight him. With the courage that stemmed from the visitation that David had...he was ready to go and face the giant.

If we will stay in touch with God and hear His Word, we'll find ourselves to be complete to meet whatever opposition comes our way. But we must stay in touch; we must stay in His hand. And, if nothing else, tell Him about the need and then get His Word from there, and begin to follow it through.

Can you believe that a word from you could calm a troubled family...your children...or can turn pressure away from the door if you and I will just share what God has provided for us? God chose the loaves and the fishes to shew himself strong: "But God hath chosen the foolish things of the world to confound the wise; and God hath chosen the weak things of the world to confound the things which are mighty; That no flesh should glory in His presence" (1 Corinthians 1:27,29).

Now those disciples wouldn't have dared to step out on their own and feed five thousand people from their little loaves and fishes. "...for when I am weak, then I am strong" (2 Corinthians 12:10). But God wants to shew Himself in the miracle, and He said, "Listen, go right ahead and feed them yourself." And they had them all to sit down and get ready...be *still*, where they could serve them. One scripture speaks how they set them forth in fifties, in hundreds, where they could get around and serve them easier.

Oh, listen Friends, it doesn't always take a revival to bring the answers to the needs of the people...just a message from God's Word and a *step of obedience*. And that is what is happening here. They would have sent them away because they didn't feel like they were able to help the situation, just let them buy for themselves...and Jesus said, "Feed them yourselves. What do you have?"

The scripture relates to us there was a lad out to the side somebody had seen that only had some little loaves and little fishes. Jesus said, "Bring them here." And they brought them to Him. And there's where we get the thought: *There's more in the loaf when we let the Lord break it.* He had taken that and began to break it and they began to pass it around. They fed that multitude and twelve baskets were left over.

These scriptures speak about the material side, but the spiritual light of God came on the scene. *When we do things like the Lord says, we're going to find we do not have to switch from here to there...too far...or too much to find the answer.* You may think you have to read a whole book in the Bible to find inspiration; but I have found out that when I meditate in *His law*, not their bookshelf, *but* His law, it is almost unbelievable to see what He can do with a little truth. God can take, that one line in the Bible, and build it and bring in other truths. And that's where we saw, there's more in the loaf, more in the truth, more in the Word when we let the Lord tell us.

We find the disciples had run short of supplies. And then found that the Lord could just speak a word and change the whole pressure of opposition and fear of lack. This helps us to know we can see the answer and be satisfied with just a touch from God.

I've seen times that I've tried many ways to *sweep* away those moments of despair. Many will take a vacation; I'm not talking against vacations, I'm not talking against taking a break from your work; but I am saying this: don't leave out moments with God...in secret before Him.

You won't journey far until you've run short *if* you haven't heard from God. Now many people don't learn that in a lifetime. Some learn it early. I'm so glad I began to learn earlier in life: a few minutes in His presence can take care of what I thought would take weeks or months...or would I ever be rid of it?

As the Word says, "Be still and know that I am God." Just think about it, He could have said, "Fill up your library with many books," and I'm not against that. But any way the enemy can detour us from God's most common and simple way...he'll do it. *The more we will sit in His presence and meditate in His law, the quicker the problem can be solved.*

Think of how many are spending hours before the entertainment world and still have not got their need met! The Bible says in Psalm chapter 1, "Blessed is the man whose delight is in the law of the Lord; and in His law doth he meditate day and night. He'll be like a tree that is planted by the water, whose leaf shall not wither, and whatsoever he doeth shall prosper."

The Law of the Lord...one line can solve a problem.

Jesus asked Peter, "You're around quite a bit, you know the crowd, you know what's being said about Me. Who do people say that I am?" Peter said, "Well, Jesus, some of them think You are John the Baptist and some of them think that You are one of the prophets, maybe Isaiah or Jeremias. Well that's not true, but that's what they're saying." Jesus said this, "Well, Peter, who do you *say* that I am." Peter said, "Well, You are the Son of God." And Jesus said, "Peter, flesh and blood hath not revealed this unto you, but My Father hath revealed it unto you."

And the Holy Spirit can make the Word of God alive. So there is more in the loaf when we let the Holy Spirit open our eyes and help us to see. *Let's reach our highest potential in God by waiting upon the Lord.* "Even the youths shall faint and be weary, and the young men shall utterly fall: But they that wait upon the Lord shall renew their strength; they shall mount up with wings as eagles; they shall run, and not be weary; and they shall walk, and not faint" (Isaiah 40:30,31).

In any area of your life God can show up and do the impossible.

STONES

FROM THE

SECRET PLACE

VOLUME 4

DR. J. E. MURDOCK

TABLE OF CONTENTS

— 1 —

USE THE KEY "IF"

When this message came to me, I was shocked to see how very few people really read the entire verse of a scripture! It's very easy to miss the real answer from the Lord by just failing to get the full message. The Word tells us, "Take heed how we hear," but we're so quick to get something in a few words and run with it. Sometimes it works; sometimes it doesn't work. But this message, "Use The Key *If*" is pretty strong.

Church people have missed the blessing of the Lord and they never even knew it. I've often wondered how many church people have missed the wonderful experience of the baptism of the Holy Spirit, and all because one or two little things just threw them off, never noticing the emphasis that God puts upon reading His Word. In one place it tells us, "In all of our getting, get understanding."

"IF" suggests a command on our part.

In Franklin, Louisiana, several workers in another denomination were going here and there to invite people to their church. When they came to me, I made a remark and said, *"There's a whole lot of things between the lines if we could discover it."* And this person, who was sold on the Word, said, "We don't read between the lines. We read on the line." And, of course, I understood what these two brothers meant by that.

I remembered reading a scripture that Isaiah, the prophet, spoke of. He was foretelling the death of Jesus, but there was no name called in that particular verse. He just said, "He was as a lamb that was led to the slaughter, and He opened not His mouth." So I used this verse of scripture to reveal to them there are some things between the lines that God wants us to see and there are other places that can reveal to us what's between those lines. If it's not said there on that particular line, it might be necessary to read a little farther so we can find out what it's saying.

I also referred to Philip, the evangelist. The Lord had told him to go out into a desert place and join himself with a chariot carrying an Ethiopian coming from Jerusalem. Philip was having a great revival in Samaria when the Lord just spoke to him and directed him to do that. When he got to the place, he saw the man coming and joined him. He saw that the man was reading Isaiah's prophecy concerning Jesus. And he asked the Ethiopian, "Do you understand what you're reading?" The Ethiopian said, "Well, how can I unless some man shows me and tells me?"

So Philip read it and then the man said, "Who is he talking about?" It didn't call any names...just said he was as a lamb and he was led to the slaughter. And the Word says from that very scripture, Philip told him about Jesus; and that's really what the message is: *Read on to the right of the if.* It has a very important message for us. When Philip got through explaining to him about Jesus...where His name was not mentioned, he went right on and explained to him the *purpose* of Jesus.

And would you believe from that little discovery there in reading just a little farther, the Ethiopian began to look to see if there was a place he could be baptized? And as they were riding along, they passed by some water, and the Ethiopian said to Philip, "You said we're to repent and be baptized. Here is some water. Can I be baptized now? What hinders me from being baptized?" And Philip said, "Well, *if* you believe, you may be baptized."

And that's where the word *if* was used again, but how important was it for him to believe? I think there are a lot of times there are some who will go as far as being baptized, but they didn't get that, *If they believe,* and didn't put the emphasis that was needed on believing that the Lord required of them.

So we are putting a *lot* of emphasis upon reading just a little farther on, and that's what this little tract is about, *If.* The Word speaks of it this way, "Search the scriptures; for in them ye think ye have eternal life: and they are they which testify of Me" (John 5:39). The Bible tells us about the early church, how they had received the Word of the Lord with all-readiness of mind, "And [they] searched the scriptures daily, whether those things were so" (Acts 17:11). And someone told me many years ago, in preaching a sermon—before we take a scripture—that we should read *before* that scripture and *after* that particular scripture before we try to explain it. Make the promise *sure* that God has made sure for us by using the *Key of If...going on a little farther.*

The Lord said that anyone that comes after Him *must* have faith. You can run after Him all day or you can pray, but the Bible says *if* you believe, you can receive. So, *study* the Word and *search* the Scriptures. You won't find the whole truth many times in just one particular phrase, and you certainly can't understand it very well unless you read on.

We have another word about a new commandment. Jesus says, "I say unto you that ye love one another as I have loved you; that ye also love one another. By this, shall all men know that ye are My disciples." How? *If* ye have love one for another. Now that is a beautiful phrase concerning love. We should love one another. What are we getting out of it?

Well, the Bible says *if* we love one another, that's a sure sign that we're one of His disciples. And also, "Giving all diligence add to your faith, virtue, and knowledge and temperance and patience, Godliness, brotherly kindness and charity." Then here comes the reward, "*If* these things be in you and abound, they make you that ye shall neither be barren nor unfruitful in the knowledge of our Lord, Jesus Christ." Think of that. You could read about those qualities all day...virtue, faith, knowledge, temperance and patience, but it would do no good for it says, "*If these things be in you.*" So we've got to have them *in* us.

I've often said you can be in a grocery store and starve to death; you've got to eat the groceries to live. You can quote it all day, but you've got to have *faith* in God's Word. It says that we're saved by His grace if we believe. Then the Word says the just that are living...seeking to follow on, why, they must have faith in God. And I have had the Lord to almost twist my arm to get me to go on a little farther to where the promise of God was fulfilled. Go on until faith begins to arise.

"Wherefore, brethren give diligence to make your calling and your election sure; for *if*" (that little key *if* is back again) "ye do these things, ye shall never fall." Think how easy it is to overlook that phrase that we've read just above the *if* there, and then not know the payoff that we get by storing away and getting these things down on the inside of us. *If* you do these things, He says, "...ye shall never fall."

I'll tell you what, if you and I will stay before the Lord and meditate in His Word, we will find *if* we will do things like God says, we're going to make it; we can't miss it.

– 2 –

WARS IN CANAAN

We are a blessed people in spite of the warfare because we really don't have to enter this battlefield ignorantly. The Lord protected us before we were even converted. God has looked out for us to give us a chance at becoming a conqueror over these foes. And like I've mentioned, when I first got saved, I read the Word in the ditch, at the little altars that we'd built around my dad's farm and down on the creek. I found out that there was a race in this Christian walk...there's a race to run and a battle to fight.

I became acquainted and am still becoming more acquainted with the warfare that takes place in Canaan. It's not to defeat us, but it's to help us to learn not to trust in ourselves but to trust in God. To trust in God we have to build a relationship with Him. We have to take time with Him.

I remember that whenever I played on the basketball team we practiced every afternoon. Sometimes we practiced at least a couple or more hours getting ready for the real game. The real game wouldn't last all that long, but we had to practice and prepare for that game because we had just as much against us as we had for us. And the only way we could ever expect the team to win was to practice and learn how to get by the opposite team. It's a marvelous thing whenever you can bypass someone who is able to run as fast as you can, but somehow or another you have learned to dodge. The Bible calls it in a spiritual sense, *dodge* or *shun* the very appearance of evil; *learning to stay out of the reach of the enemy.* Ah, it means something. So I saw immediately that if I intended to last until the game was over when all the odds out there were against me, I was going to have to obey the coach. And I was going to have to practice and learn how to get the second wind.

When you first start on the field, the first hundred yards you run you feel like you are just about to give out, but I learned if I just stayed a little longer I got a second wind. And when we got our second wind, I actually believe we could have run all day.

And my Friends, it's a marvelous thing when you can turn that around and compare it with the Christian walk; there are times that, actually, the dread of facing it would almost turn you around. But if you press on through, you'll find God gives grace and, oh, how you can sing a song of victory if you'll just learn how to conquer those oppositions.

I've used this simple illustration and you might want to laugh a little bit. I never will forget my wife and I were acquainted with married life and we had seen the lives of other married loved ones and friends and decided we didn't have such a rough life. God blessed us abundantly because we knew the Lord. But we had a little daughter, our first daughter. We were to give her away in marriage. She had decided to marry and so I started walking her down the aisle, and I couldn't help but think, *Well, now my little daughter doesn't know about the warfare, you know...when the toast is burnt or when something hasn't gone just right.* And so I, in fun really, whispered to her as we walked down this long aisle in the auditorium in Orange, Texas, "Barbara, it's not too late to back out." And she smiled at me, but we walked on. I was saying it's not all a honeymoon; there are other things that go with it.

So we have learned this through the years that many precious people have recognized it's more than a honeymoon. And that's why the Lord binds people together with love, and that's why He offers you and me The Secret Place where we can pray for one another and we can talk to God. Because it makes no difference how good the marriage is, there's going to be warfare somewhere or another, and how wonderful it is to prepare for it by knowing God.

We had been so blessed with our marriage of sixty-three years together with how God had helped us and with what each of us meant to each other. In our day, the enemy is warring against what God's order is, and that's for people to get married and to become one together even as the church and Lord become one...*it's possible*. A short time back, one particular pastor wanted me to talk on marriage. I felt like he wanted me to bring out some good points...how to make us winners in our marriage. And I wanted to, for I was gravely concerned...there's nothing sadder than to find couples who have taken each other for life and then the enemy has come in to destroy the relationship. So I opened up the Scriptures. About the second scripture that I read was where Jesus said, "I have not come to bring peace, but a division where I will, where the father will be against the son and the son against the father; the mother against the daughter; the daughter-in-law against the mother-in-law." I looked at that again. I was looking for something that could erase that. But oh, if God came against it, how could I?

I wondered how I could explain that when suddenly the Spirit of the Lord brought to my mind the tower of Babel (see Genesis 11). The people all spoke the same language...had one mind. No doubt they had in their mind the flood that had come, back in the days of Noah, and they decided they'd get together and build a tower in case they had to escape high water. So they started building and they were being successful.

They were going right on up. Why not just leave them alone? They were able to work together. The Lord went down to examine the tower. When He looked at it, He saw something He didn't like. The people had left Him out and they were going to build and seek to save themselves; and they were in unity. And the Lord confused their language. And it seemed to me that the Lord was saying: *The reason these homes are falling apart is that they left Him out.*

We only have confusion when we try to build without Him.

And we're taught in the early scriptures and teachings of Jesus that in order to build a house, it must be built right. It must be built on a solid foundation. *It must be built according to His plan.* So that solved the problem there and it wasn't hard.

I don't think it was hard at all to get the point over as to why homes are falling apart. It's actually because we're missing God's order, God's plan for our life. We think, *Well, that's awfully cruel.* Not really. We'll actually find out any kind of a storm or trial that helps awaken us to the fact that we are failures without God and causes us to seek the Lord is good! He's ready to help. And you'll find Him with an outstretched hand.

The only way we can expect to make it is to do things God's way, then we will appreciate it. In fact, I read a phrase that was written like this, *"Blessed is the gale or the storm that brings us to Christ." Because we're prone to try to make it on our own and live by ourselves and live to ourselves, when God, through the Scriptures, has made us for His pleasure.* He's going to be seeking for that pleasure. And if He finds that we've become a displeasure...rather than to destroy us, He will seek ways and offer His help and strength to make the difference.

So Friends, don't let the wars in Canaan throw you off. *You're going to battle something so why not battle for the right thing.* The Lord pointed out that to win in the battlefield, you must go into The Secret Place and seek Him in secret and He will reward you openly. Don't forget it. *God's for you.* Do it His way. Remember The Secret Place.

— 3 —

WATCH THOSE SCISSORS

I just wonder; have you ever heard a title like that? You've had warnings of different things, but this is unique, yet it's very, very real. And those scissors are very powerful. I believe you will be blessed; and the way to be blessed is to let the Lord make truth real to your heart.

We have plenty of scriptures that we can call the *dos* and the *don'ts*...they started in the garden. In First Thessalonians the fifth chapter, verses 21-24, it says, "Prove all things; hold fast that which is good. Abstain from all appearance of evil. And the very God of peace sanctify you wholly; and *I pray God* your whole spirit and soul and body be preserved blameless unto the coming of our Lord Jesus Christ. Faithful *is* He that calleth you, Who also will do *it*." Verse 25 says, "Brethren, pray for us." The Word says that Jesus taught and pointed out very clearly the things that He wanted us to do. He also pointed out the things He did not want us to do, and if we did them, He told us of the death trap that would be there.

God has just created it that way. Where there is no law, there is no sin and no wrong. But the Lord has said this is wrong. Don't do *that* and do *this*. And so all down through the dispensation of time, it has been necessary to find out and to *know* God's ways for you and me.

This strong message came to my heart because, as I went along, I have tasted of things that would distract me from the Lord. *Everything that interferes with your serving the Lord, lay it aside.* While I was really worshipping and seeking the Lord as a teenage boy...I was playing ball. (I loved playing ball, in fact, I loved it so well I, actually, didn't go into the schoolroom very often. And would you believe it, the coach must have liked it. *I've got to brag a little bit here I guess*, the coach must have liked it so well that he really didn't get after me and I played in every game). I was a left forward on the basketball team. I was a Christian and nothing was really wrong with it, but I really got so wrapped up in playing that I began to neglect prayer and reading the Word. It wasn't long until it came time to talk about the Lord and testify, and I seemed to be silent. And I began to miss the presence of the Lord. It wasn't long until I began to do little things that I didn't even do before I was saved. So I drifted fast, and then to look and see that my little sisters were still praying...still speaking to the Lord. He was still real. *But I had lost out.*

Got a glimpse of the scissors? I was cut lose from the presence of the Lord by spending too much time just playing ball at the end of school. So, after the ball season was up, I said to myself, *I'm going out to the little place where I prayed in the barn at my dad's house, and I'm going to pray through.* So I went out there and was praying, *Oh, God, help me to return to You. Help me to find You again in a real way.* And I had to go a couple or three times before I really got through, but I got through. And I said in my heart then, *I'm never going to play again. I'm going to take time to pray...to keep this relationship.*

Between that time and the next ball season, I began courtshipping my little bride-to-be and would ride the horse to see her, and then we got married. When the season for the next year came, the coach, Mr. Knight, came to me and said, "John, aren't you going to play ball with us this year?" And he went on to say, "You didn't go to school much last year, but get you some tennies and play with us until I can order your new ones." I was really glad to say, "Mr. Knight, I'm married now." Would you believe that he said, "That doesn't matter. I'm married, too, and I play. Come on back and play ball." Well, listen, there was nothing more entertaining to me than playing ball. I loved it from beginning to end. But I knew what had happened. And that's where we get the idea: *Watch those scissors.* We'll explain that a little farther down the page.

Rather than to tell him of my experience, I went ahead and got me some tennies. I went to the gymnasium and several of the boys were out there. School hours weren't over and as I played around I felt something they didn't feel. I thought *Uh, oh, I believe I'm getting in the wrong place.* Finally, the boys went into the study hall and I was still out there and I began to say, *"Oh, dear Lord, if You will just deliver me and help me to leave here, I'll never come back. "*

I knew everybody around there and they knew me. I went to the door of the gymnasium and looked out on the campus to see if anybody was on the outside. And I felt so bad over what they would say or think. I didn't want anybody to see me leaving. I went ahead and slipped off my tennies and left them (they were only fifty cents a pair back in those days). I walked to the door with a prayer, *"Lord, help me to get away and I'll never come back."* And sure enough, the campus was clear, and believe me I walked away. I *never* went back.

And my relationship with the Lord was kept, and through little hard places and things that come to everybody, I found help from the Lord, and also hope for His return.

A friend of mine, who had ridden his horse in our courtship days to court my wife's little sister, went to fight in the war. I found out later that he returned home with a few thousand dollars that he had saved. And I understood he had become a rich man. He had been building homes in Houston, Texas, and had bought a place back near our old home place where we grew up together. I already, at this time, was in the Lord's work. Years later, my friend and I came in contact with one another in the little town of Grapeland, Texas, and he wanted us to spend the night. We enjoyed talking with each other; we had been such close friends.

Three or four years passed...we were in a service in Baytown and he came to hear my son speak. He told my son, the preacher boy, "Listen, your daddy could have been a millionaire." But my son spoke up and said, "Daddy has given us a heritage that money cannot buy. He's given us something worth more than a million dollars." He said that to this dear friend of mine on the outside of the church where he had preached that morning. It made me feel good that my son recognized that what I had done was worthwhile.

My friend said to me, "John, I've really been wanting to ask you a question for many years." He said, "Why did you stop playing ball?" I said, "I'm glad you asked me, Elton. Really, I don't think there was much harm in playing ball. I thought it was all right, but it separated me from prayer. I lost out with the Lord and that's the reason I stopped playing ball and came back to Him." He just shook his head and said, "Well, I've often wondered why you stopped playing ball."

I had overcome the scissors that time. We went on preaching the gospel. Then, the television age came in. I try to be broad enough to take in things that would be helpful, but I've always seen the necessity of shunning the very appearance of evil. *Be careful*. Like I've said a lot of times, I don't even back my car out of the garage without being careful and watching, much less when I get on the highway. So I say it gently, but I want to say it in the fear of God; I wish our generation could get a hold of it before it's too late.

We picked out this scripture about Samson...a man with strength, a man that was not afraid of the enemy, a man that was not afraid to go against the Philistines. God was with him. But there was a person that was used to lure Samson...brag on him, talk to him, we might say, just pet him in little ways...her name was Delilah. He went over to her place again and again. And finally...he didn't realize it, but he had begun to miss God's will for his life. In the first place, he shouldn't have been over there. He was there because of a wrong influence. He might not have said that when he first went, but that's what it proved out to be.

So the enemy of Samson talked to Delilah and said, "I wish you'd find out what has made him so strong." So, Delilah began to move in a way and talk subtly to Samson and said, "I just wonder; you are a mighty strong man, you're not afraid of the Philistines or anyone. I want to know why or what makes you so strong." This would have been a good time for God to help raise His standard in Samson, but he didn't tell her. He could have just said, "It's the Lord, and if I lose Him I'm just like another person." But he didn't say that. He told her several different reasons at different times. And the Philistines would come in and fight him, but they could not win. *Some victories can mean deception to you and me.*

Finally, he told Delilah, "Really, this long hair of mine speaks of a dedication that my parents made to God for me. And the Lord has honored the dedication and His presence is with me. If you cut my hair off, then I will be like anybody else." He didn't plan on her doing that. But finally she got him to lie down in her lap and prepared to give him a haircut. He was asleep. *Many people think if God is with me at all, He's with me all the way.* But listen, He was not with Samson all the way. He was dealing with Samson; He was patient with Samson. *Watch those scissors, Samson.* But Delilah finally cut his hair.

When he awoke, the Philistines had been called in again upon him. And Delilah said, "Arise, Samson. The Philistines are coming in." The Word says he arose...shook himself and went out as before to go against the Philistines, not knowing that the presence of God had departed from him. And when he reached for the Philistines, they reached for him. They caught Samson, this strong man who had won many victories, and punched out his eyes and made sport out of him.

I don't condemn Samson. I felt really touched about it to think, *How?* But before I was overcome with too much pity, the Lord let me see something. *Samson didn't get this haircut while the Holy Spirit was off somewhere visiting.* The Holy Spirit talked to him *before* it ever happened. He just drifted to a point that he wasn't hearing the Holy Spirit. And it wasn't long until he, through pride and the flattery that Delilah was giving, fell for it. And now the strong man was down.

"Be not deceived; God is not mocked: for whatsoever a man soweth, that shall he also reap." He had won many victories, but sowed to the flesh. "For he that soweth to his flesh shall of the flesh reap corruption;" (Galatians 6:7-8).

Watch those scissors!

**Stay In *The Way*
And Stay There
With A *Thankful*
Heart!**

-J. E. Murdock

‒4‒

WHERE ARE YOU IN THE WALK?

I had just gotten through reading about the ten lepers who received their healing, went their way and **were healed as they went**—*and only one of them returned back and gave thanks.* I'm sure it was because the Holy Spirit wanted to emphasize that to me.

I saw a little church up off the road in a magazine, and I saw a little pathway leading up to it. And a phrase came to me, along with the scripture and a scene of ten lepers being healed, and only one of them returning back and giving thanks. I drew a little sign at the entrance of that little path that led up to the church. On that little sign I put, "Where Are You in the Walk?"

The little church represents a spiritual path that we learn, and grow by the teachings in the little church. But that became so real that I went ahead and made the little sign and emphasized that the Lord was interested in what happened to the other nine. *The other nine represent people that are blessed but never come to a place of thankfulness.*

I've often thought of how God blessed and delivered Israel. In fact, there was such a deliverance of Israel when they came out of Egypt, the Word said, there was not a feeble one among them...a *mighty*, and strong deliverance. And then, He was going to take them out in the wilderness by a way. Then He said, "I'm going to take you a way that you don't know...*it's a way that you'll have to trust Me.* I'm going to take you that way to *prove* you."

When He began the test, we read back and forth about the Lord working with Israel there. I don't recall at any time...after they were blessed...after their trials and testings came...even when Moses interceded and prevailed in prayer...I don't recall where they ever showed thanksgiving and appreciation. What a difference it would have made for them if each time that God blessed them, they'd have just offered real thanks unto God, but they didn't; *they died* and *didn't get into* the promised land.

But the real emphasis the Lord asked me was, "Where Are You in the Walk?" And the Bible says that they were really considering Paul. Some of these converts were beginning to doubt Paul. Some had even said they'd already decided Paul wasn't just all that he confessed to be. This touched Paul because he had a father's heart. And he said, "Well, I hope that I don't appear to you as a reprobate." But he said, "Examine yourselves to see whether you are in the faith lest you become a reprobate." So, the real point comes. *Everyone is straightened in his own bowels; everyone is to save himself.*

The point of the first few words of this, "Where Are You in the Walk?" is to encourage us to examine ourselves to see if we have a thankful heart. The Bible leads us on to say this...*We are to give thanks and to be thankful in whatever state we are in*. In other words, praise the Lord regardless of what's taking place because you know the way.

Stay in the way and stay there with a *thankful* heart! Have you reached that part in your Christian life that in everything you can give thanks unto the Lord? That's a place! God's not only concerned about the big congregation, or the small. He's concerned about you and me as individuals.

Where Are You In The Walk?

— 5 —

ABC's

The Saturday evening before I married, I was going to go to town and stand around on the streets. I was serving the Lord. I wasn't intending to go there to do anything wrong. But my dad always had a little work for us to do on Saturday morning; we'd do that work and when we were finished, why, we were free! So, there was no hassle and no one resented me going to town. I wasn't going there to do anything wrong. But I was filled with the Spirit and the Lord was very real to my heart.

The Holy Spirit seemed to say to me, "Had you rather go to town and stand around on the streets, or had you rather take My Word and go down into the woods (where I had been praying beside a little creek)?" Something in me wanted to go to town. As time went by, I learned more about that which wants to do your own thing...but something else in me wanted to go down and pray. And I went ahead and took my Bible and went down to pray.

I laid that Bible down on the ground beside the little creek there and I opened it up and started to read. I would read one or two lines and cry. I would cry so hard that I couldn't read any more. That was the first time I had ever experienced that. And then I would open my eyes and look again and read one or two more lines, then cry again. Weeping, I finally read a whole page of the Bible.

In later years, I look back to that and it seems to me like the Lord was saying, "Now, that was your ABC's." You know your ABC's...you never can do without them. You'll always have to have them to spell your words. You'll always have to have them to enjoy and know what the Word of the Lord means; you'll have to have a knowledge of its power. And the Lord let me see that instead of going to town that evening, I tasted the power of His Word.

Let's you and I seek to discover the power to *take* the power there is in the Word. It can *break* the vessel. It can *bless* the vessel. It can *build* the vessel. I call that my ABC's in my Christian walk concerning the Word of the Lord. It is sufficient. And that's why many people lack in their Christian life because they don't have knowledge of that Word. They don't have the knowledge of the truth that will set them free. But the Word says this, "We live not by bread alone but by every Word of the Lord." He wants us to *know* His Word and to *know* it like I saw it that evening...it's just not a problem to push away other reading material and go right back to the Word of God. There's nothing like it.

We're not against reading. We put out little reading materials ourselves, but oh, to acquaint yourself with "...thus saith the Lord" and the Holy Bible, then you're going some place. That's the starting point. And the Word says, "He that cometh to God must believe that He is God." Know that He is God. And the starting point, I'll tell you what, that particular afternoon when I was sixteen years old, made me know there's One in the Word of God to bless you.

–6–

PERFECTION

It was a Thursday evening...when such a revelation of perfection came. Every time you think of perfection in the Christian walk, you think, *Well, well, now, what more will I have to do?* But you know when we go to a job, we really study the wage we're going to be paid for our work quicker than we do the job. We're ready to promise the boss that we can do anything *if* the pay is right. If it sounds good...then good! I'll tell you of the pay that's going to come to the perfected heart and the heart that will walk uprightly with Him.

Honestly, I don't think Heaven could be any different. I know that, in this tabernacle, we're still absent from the Lord. But I'll tell you there is a joy...a peace, and it all comes through...that's the *payday for perfection.* And I thought to myself, *Oh, if I could just tell the little congregation at the church tonight and they could see that, there would be such rejoicing...oh, here we are, Lord, because we can see the pay.* You know, you wouldn't want to buy anything if you didn't see there was more value in it than what you're paying for it. And most people just look at what they have to pay...instead of what they're *getting.* But if we can even realize what we're going to pay *without* perfection, we wouldn't want to sleep another night without making an effort to be more like what He wants us to be.

I drew a little stairway one time on a tract and I called it, *The Stairway of Perfection.* And the thought came to me, *Well, are we going to have to be all of this now before we can get to Heaven?* The Lord seemed to impress me, "No, you can go to Heaven from the bottom step if you're born again." But to climb those steps, you're going to have to be perfected. If we could be saved like the thief on the cross, just saying, "Have mercy, remember me," okay. But if we're going to stay here and meet the world out there and the temptations of the flesh, we're going to have to climb the stairs...we're going to have to grow. Let's grow, shall we? And then we can go.

You Never Know
Just What May
Come Alive
In Your Spirit
And Mind
As You Give God
A Chance To
Talk To You.

-J. E. Murdock

STONES

FROM THE

SECRET PLACE

VOLUME 5

DR. J. E. MURDOCK

TABLE OF CONTENTS

~ 1 ~

HAVE YOU HEARD THE VOICE OF THE SPIRIT TODAY?

"Day unto day uttereth speech, and night unto night sheweth knowledge. There is no speech nor language, where their voice is not heard" (Psalm 19:2-3).

After receiving such an inspiration on the importance of hearing the voice of the Spirit, it seemed that the Lord impressed me to ask the congregation if they had heard the voice of the Spirit today. Again and again the Lord spake to the churches in Revelation, "He that hath an ear, let him hear what the Spirit saith unto the churches." I have heard beautiful remarks made about the Holy Spirit speaking a whole lot. I don't think that He actually breaks in on the conversation unless there's a special reason...but He does speak to your heart in such a way that after you hear His voice a few times it's easier to discern. We do have the voice of the Lord calling.

In the Old Testament, when Eli was a priest of God, little Samuel was working under this spiritual leader. Samuel was just a boy, but he was in the service of the priest and he heard a voice calling his name. He thought that the priest was calling him, so he went to the door and said to him, "Here am I," and told Eli that he heard his name called. And Eli himself, though being the priest of God, at first didn't detect that maybe God was talking to Samuel. He told him to go lie down, that he didn't call him. And the voice came again and called Samuel. So he got up and told Eli that he heard the voice again. Eli now perceived that the Lord had called Samuel (see 1 Samuel 3:3-10).

So that puts light on the fact *that we don't always detect the voice of the Lord.* Now whether Samuel was too young or not, I don't suppose he was, for God was calling him. So Eli said, "Well, Samuel, it may be the Lord talking to you. Go back and lie down and if you hear that voice again say, Speak Lord, *Thy servant heareth*." And it happened. The Lord was calling Samuel and He gave him a message for Eli that was very important.

The Word says, "My sheep *know* My voice and another they will not follow." So unmistakably, we are promised a place in Him that we can discern the voice of the Lord and how beautiful it is to be able to hear His voice.

There were certain Pharisees and Sadducees that were seeking to trap Jesus. So they asked some of the soldiers, "Just where is the group that went to see Jesus?" In John the seventh chapter, they were anxious to find fault and destroy the influence of Jesus so that they could put Him out of commission. Verses 45-46 say, "Then came the officers to the chief priests and Pharisees; and they said unto them, Why have ye not brought Him? The officers answered, *Never a man spake like this man*." There was some authority there in the voice of Jesus that could not be resisted.

The Lord made it possible for us to discern His voice.

The Lord doesn't have to say very much. *He spoke the world into existence and spoke light in the face of darkness...and can confound the wise with just a word.* Saul heard the voice on the road to Damascus but didn't fully recognize it. *A lot of people hear Him and don't discern Him.*

There are two groups that hear His voice. One answers, "Here am I. Thy servant heareth." Matthew 13:16 says, "Blessed are your eyes, for they see; and your ears, for they hear." The other group, the Lord says, have ears but don't hear. "He that being often reproved hardeneth his neck, shall suddenly be destroyed, and that without remedy." *The greatest tragedy is to hear His voice and not to obey it.* Take heed that you hear what the Spirit has to say.

∼ 2 ∼

I Will Set Before You Evil And Good

———————

Behold the goodness and the severity of God. The goodness of God is upon those that will turn to the Lord, and His severity is actually to teach us that wrong will end up bad *if* change doesn't come. God delights to shew goodness and mercy. We have to walk in a certain path with godly sorrow in order to receive the mercies of the Lord...not just sorrow from being caught, but sorry because we have *grieved* the Lord. After all, the Lord has gone all out to bless us and give us a future. If we overlook that, we are in a bad shape.

How long would we last if the Lord never put out any danger signs...cautions...and never told us about the punishment that comes with wrong-doing? Well, the Bible says *we perish*. His people perish for the lack of knowledge. God wants us to know these things and not wait too late. That's why *preparation is one of the greatest cries of our time;* to *prepare* for what's coming upon the earth.

Many things will come for the simple reason to *teach* us what happens if we don't lean on God...if we don't cast our cares on the Lord. The sad part would be to allow our trials and our testings to cause us to become bitter and resentful towards the things of God.

We should be glad to pray the prayer that David prayed. He said, "Oh, Lord, be not silent to me, lest if You be silent I would go down to the pit." I believe he learned the importance of being cautioned. He also prayed a prayer that would help us if we got in on the answer and that is, "Lord, help me to know how frail that I am, that I may apply my days unto wisdom."

It's the frailness of life that moves us toward a remedy. And surely it is well known to the generation on earth today that there's a lack, and it's because we are *not* turning to the Lord with *all* of our heart and having faith in God.

The day will come that storms will increase until the only people that will stand will be those who have hearkened unto God's directions to build. It just takes seconds to read what it means to build according to the Lord, because He speaks of these trials and things that are going to come.

The Bible relates one of the hardest trials to go through: David said, "If it would have been an enemy, I could have hid myself. If it had been a stranger, then I could have avoided him. But, it's one mine equal, we go to the house of the Lord together." Many bruises come from among the children of God. That's why the emphasis is placed on the importance of the believer to *have love* one for another. He said to the disciples, "By *this* shall the world know that you're My disciples...that you have love one for another."

We couldn't make it if it wasn't for the Lord. Israel said, "Had it not been for the Lord, the rivers would have overflowed us." We can't erase the fact that God cares because He's made a way. But how to find His instructions, the Word said, is in His sanctuary. *Come into His presence.*

The travail of David in Psalm...the desire of his soul was, "Oh, that I might see Him like I saw Him in the sanctuary." David felt his commitment hadn't paid off. "For I was envious at the foolish, when I saw the prosperity of the wicked. When I thought to know this, it was too painful for me; Until I went into the sanctuary of God; then understood I their end" (Psalm 73:3,16,17). David felt things that all believers have problems with. We are prone to compare ourselves with others. The Word says he that does that is not wise. We should take time to find God's way for *us*. The things that we could not bear, David found how to *bear* them, how to rid himself of unnecessary things *in the sanctuary*. Let's you and I begin, as never before, to meditate in the law of God. The Stones in the

Secret Place are actually true revelations from the voice of God that we get as we sit in His presence.

I remember reading and ministering about the day when Israel was doing pretty well in her route to the Promised Land. They came down to the Red Sea and there the hills were on both sides of the sea. Then Pharaoh and his army were behind them. They were about to panic and they didn't know what to do. Here we are with the sea before us, the enemy behind us, and the mountains on both sides of us. "Now then, Moses, why didn't you leave us in the land of Egypt? Weren't there any graves there? If we're going to die anyway, couldn't we have just died there?" It's hard to believe that Israel received as much attention as God gave them...not just bringing them out of the land, but how He blessed them and kept them even in their bondage there in Egypt. Nevertheless, fear had overtaken them. The Lord spoke to Moses and He told him, "Now, you don't need to fight in this battle. You just tell Israel to stand still and see the salvation of the Lord."

A few times we have waited on the Lord until that quietness and that calmness came to us. The Word says, *"Be still and know...*in quietness and confidence shall be your strength."

*When you have actually used up all of your energy and you feel like there's nothing left, God still has a way for you to win the battle...*if you'll just listen for His voice and *obey* Him. Let's press to the point that we will wait on the Lord and *shut out things that hinder* us from hearing God's voice.

I wish we could say when one victory is won that there'll be no more battles, but we're only told there will be no more *tears* in Heaven...no more sorrow, pain, nor death. But until then, it seems necessary that we have things that woo us to the realization of following the Lord with all of our heart, soul, mind and strength. You're not by yourself with your troubles and trials. The whole earth today groaneth. There are some who are able to declare unto you and me that our trials are just God's opportunity to make Himself real to us.

I look at how Goliath was in the valley and walking back

and forth talking to Israel from a distance on the hill. He was daring them to come and fight against him. And, believe it or not, they were all afraid to go. Then the Lord used one little boy who was watching over the sheep. David had some experiences that I doubt if anyone knew about up to this point. A bear came out to destroy little David's group of sheep and he, I don't guess, paid any attention to David, but David knew he was to watch over the sheep so he did. No doubt he prayed a prayer and went for the bear and also the lion that came out against him. And the Word says the Lord gave him victory over them.

I've often said this: *Don't forget the bear fight, don't forget the victory that God gave you yesterday*. You'll need another surge tomorrow against discouragement—or whatever way the enemy may approach you. God doesn't want to destroy you. He wants to get our attention and help us learn to *lean* on Him...to *trust* in Him...to *believe* in Him. We will see at the end that these testings and trials are working for our good. We'll even thank the Lord for the storms that come our way. For who knows how far we would have wandered.

Israel made a bad mistake when she murmured in her trials, because she couldn't say God had never done anything for them. God had done plenty. He made a difference between them and the Egyptians even when they were in the Land of Egypt. He blessed them in many ways, but when He got them out there in the wilderness to prove them, He actually found out what was in their hearts. He found them murmuring and complaining at *every* little test. God was ready to destroy them because they had murmured so much. They would go to Moses and he would intercede. So, if they had paid any attention, they would have seen that the Lord blessed them and answered their prayer. They never actually grew feeble in the wilderness, but the Bible says they did *always err* in their heart in unbelief (see Hebrews 3:10).

The next time you enter into The Secret Place, I don't think it would be unwise for you to say, "Lord, You said if we lacked faith to ask You and You would give us faith." For without it, it's impossible to please Him. And we need not come to Him unless we believe because, He said, everyone that cometh to the Lord *must* believe. *He has brought you through until now. He can keep you in the future.* Let the sanctuary of God build your faith like little David. He was prepared not only to go against Goliath, but also *to win.*

Saul decided to put his armor on David, and David said, "Oh, I haven't tried this." He pulled it off and went down to the creek and he picked out five stones and put them in the slingshot and loaded one of them and went toward Goliath. He had done that before. That's not easy, is it folks, to pull off the armor of another soldier?

God has a way for you to fight your battles. Find out *how* He wants you to win. He likes to talk to you personally. Enjoy hearing from God...then it won't be so hard to get back into The Secret Place.

Stay In
The Secret Place
Until
The Question
You Have
Is Answered.

-J. E. Murdock

~ 3 ~

I DO THIS ACCORDING TO YOUR WORD

"And it came to pass at *the time of* the offering of the *evening* sacrifice, that Elijah the prophet came near, and said, Lord God of Abraham, Isaac, and of Israel, let it be known this day that Thou *art* God in Israel, and *that* I *am* Thy servant, and *that* I have done all these things **at Thy word**" (1 Kings 18:36).

Elijah was praying fire down in front of the prophets, but his motive was to reveal God's glory.

How many times we have readjusted our purpose, our *motive* for praying! We've had to become more sincere. I remember times when I'd say, *Lord, bless me.* And the Spirit of the Lord seemed to whisper so gently, "Why do you want Me to bless you?" I got the message immediately. (And I was *where* when that happened? In The Secret Place.) "Why do you want Me to bless you? Do you want Me to bless you so others will brag on you, so others will esteem you? Or do you want Me to bless you for *My* glory?"

There's a different picture there. You and I would be surprised to know how many times the good old self life will walk into prayer in The Secret Place with such motives. Stay before God. It will help you to straighten out. I began to say, *"Oh, dear Jesus, if I have a wrong motive to become a big preacher, to become worldwide or just to be blessed for my glory, You know about it. And I understand that that kind of prayer will not go through. Help me to pray in the right way."*

When right praying strikes your heart and mind, there is a confidence and a faith that begins to take over because *God wants you to have what you need.* He wants you to have what it takes to fulfill His will. **It's easier to believe when you're seeking God according to His Word.**

The Shepherd of the flock still leads us into green pastures. **If we're not finding any green pastures, that means the Lord is not leading.** What a new life the Lord will give you as you follow Him.

Never build independent of Him. He will build His work in you and me in a way that we'll have to stay in contact with Him in order to abide in the confidence that all will be well.

I've prayed a lot of times when I seemed to get nowhere, like when I was lost in the woods. I had caught a ride to a prayer meeting at my uncle's house. When it was time to go home, there was not much traffic so I decided to cut through the woods. My uncle told me there was a trail about a mile down from his house. "You will see an old saw mill on your right. The trail is right past the sawmill. *Do not* turn to the left." When I saw the building, I decided to walk around and look at it. But then I could not find the trail. *I was lost!* I dropped to my knees and prayed, but still couldn't find my way out. I said, *"Uh, oh, I'm going to have to get an answer."*

The second time I knelt down and prayed, I felt peace. I couldn't see my way out yet, but I followed the peace of my heart. I saw a little trail, but a tree was lying across it. I thought, *I will go around that tree to the other side.* And then I said to myself, *"No, that's how I got lost."* So I got on my knees and crawled under the branches so that I could stay on the trail. A voice inside said, *You're still lost!* I said aloud, *I feel at peace to go on.* Soon I came out of the woods across the highway from my house.

Don't get distracted from the way. **Stay in The Secret Place until the question you have is answered.** Stay before the Lord until you mount up with wings as eagles. When the Lord addressed the disciples to go to the upper room, He didn't say if it doesn't come in two days, stay the third day. He just says stay there until the Holy Spirit descends. *So tarry until...*

I do not know the different moods that groups of believers went through at that time. I know we all go through things, especially when we have to wait a while...we get restless. But He said, "Go there to the upper room." *(He even tells us where to go.)* "Just stay right there until the Comforter comes." I noticed that when the anxiety left, it was amazing how quickly the answer came. Why, I think a lot of times the Lord just stands there patiently until we lose the frustration, and *then* we learn patience—and patience is important in our Christian walk.

We have learned a little measure of wisdom from God. Don't be discouraged if the answer doesn't come immediately. If you're unable to actually spend sufficient time in The Secret Place, you can still arise from there and your relationship with God will go with you. I've had some strong praying and strong revelation come to me *after* I have left The Secret Place. It's because in that *place* of prayer, the Lord takes a hold of our heart where we can learn to pray without ceasing. Pray even as you work; say a word...*worship*. Different kinds of prayers will begin when you are in a relationship with the Lord. As you worship the Lord, it's almost like the children of Israel going according to His Word as they marched around the walls of Jericho every day for seven days, the last day seven times. Then after all of that He said, "Shout!" *I'll tell you that The Secret Place can come to that—a shout.* And when they shouted, the walls fell. *There are steps that we're still unaware of that God has for us to make if we'll just stay a little longer in The Secret Place.*

You know you don't expect a child to leave the cradle and immediately run a race around the house. You expect him to learn to stand alone...to walk gradually. The Lord doesn't expect the wholeness of worship to be mastered at once, but *He does expect us to walk in the light that we have* and then He'll give us more light. So don't let delays discourage you. *Just stay there until...*

The Enemy Comes Against The People Who Call On The Lord. Expect It And Be Prepared.

-*J. E. Murdock*

⚊4⚊

THE MIXED MULTITUDE

When we first began to glance in the Bible, especially after being saved, we found the name of this group of people called the Mixed Multitude. The Mixed Multitude was made up of the Israelites, who were in Egypt, and another group who were not Israelites...all down there mixed together. We followed them in the Scriptures and watched their outcome.

We began to see where the problem was. According to the law of the Lord, there was a scripture given to us that this group of people was not supposed to be among the children of Israel. While Israel was in Egypt, the pressures got so heavy...everything seemed to be against them. You really wouldn't have wanted to have been an Israelite.

The Bible tells us that as they cried unto God to send a deliverer, Moses came to bring them out of Egypt. The prophesies concerning Israel were already given: After he brought them down into Egypt, the day would come that he would bring them out of Egypt and into the Promised Land. So we notice what favor God gave the Israelites with the Egyptians down in Egypt. Everything seemed to be good with them and they began to borrow things from the Egyptians in such a way that they would have plenty to offer sacrifices to the Lord in the wilderness en route to the land of Canaan.

This is where the Bible reveals to us that there was another group of people who were not Israelites. They went along with the children of Israel and the time came that they brought a lot of downfall upon them because the Israelites were *affected* by the Mixed Multitude. The Word says that this Mixed Multitude would sit down to eat in the wilderness and would rise up to play, idly, and Israel began to do the same thing.

It's really not God's plan for His people to be mixed up with people who do not love God, do not fear God or who will not cling to the Lord because they will influence one who's seeking to believe. And the scripture gives us a call—to come out from among them and be ye separate so that the Lord can bless us...touch us...lead us.

The day came that God was unable to get anywhere with them because of this evil influence. It would be worthwhile for us to stop for a moment and look at this evil influence from unbelievers. These people didn't really care to know God, or care about the damage they did to those who were seeking to find God's plan and purpose for their lives.

After being converted, my life was changed. I noticed that others who did not surrender to the Lord were what the Bible calls unbelievers or people who are still in darkness. Times come when you feel like reading the Bible, but you are among those who don't read the Bible. It doesn't mean that we're not to associate at all with those people, but it does mean that our relationship with the Lord must be strong enough that we are influential for God *instead* of being influenced by the wrong people...how easy that is.

Somebody said this years ago, "Whenever a little child is at home, even in the high chair, you've got him all to yourself...he's listening to mother and daddy and knows nothing but to obey what they have to say, for that's the only influence that he has around him. After a little child has left home and gone to school, in one week's time the child you once had all to yourself has been all yours for the last time. Now he's coming home talking of the stories his little friends are telling in school. You can see the impact of those playmates out on the school grounds influencing him so strongly that he can hardly hear what mother and dad have to say when he gets home from school. Children are actually taken up with the conversations of new friends.

That's just another way of saying that when we get saved and get into a new family of God, one thing that will put the pressure upon us and hinder us greatly is to be among those who talk about other things...those whose wishes, aims, desires and motives are after things other than what God has for us. That's why we're taught in the Scripture to come out from among those who do not serve God, who don't want to hear about God.

Be a witness? Yes. But live so in the Lord that you're not influenced by this Mixed Multitude. It's very important and the Bible speaks of it this way, "If I were to keep you from the evil or to take you away from sin and evil, I'd have to take you out of the world. But I am able to keep you from the evil that's in the world." I really think that's one of the bottom lines concerning the Mixed Multitude...to live so in the Lord that we can help them instead of them influencing us to talk of things that displease God and that bring us into a place where the Lord can't get on with our lives.

Often the things of God, and even what the minister has to say in church, doesn't go far in the hearts and minds of a lot people in church because they have friendships with people who influence them to go a direction other than that of serving the Lord. It's very important in your relationship with others that if you can't help them, the Bible says, just shake the dust off of your feet and go on. If they reject your testimony and your commitment to God and make light of it, have no interest in it, just go on and leave them to themselves. Be separate and, above all, do not be influenced or overcome or brought into their lifestyle. For, according to scripture, God could not get anywhere with Israel as long as they were yoked up with this Mixed Multitude.

Our generation today seems to run wild in a country that should be tame because they are influenced by others. *We need to disassociate ourselves from those whose lifestyles are displeasing to God before they influence us in such a way that we lose our relationship with the Lord.*

The Bible speaks of a young son that Jesus talked about who said to his father one day, "Father, give me all my inheritance." The father gave it to him and, by and by, he gathered it all together and went into a foreign country. Of course, soon the relationships that he had in that foreign country had taken everything that the father had given him. He talked differently now...he'd lost everything. He was in bondage, had no joy, no peace, no liberty, no freedom. Finally, the Bible goes on to say, he literally went hungry and came to himself and joined to the citizens of that country instead of turning back to his father's house. He joined with the citizens of that country, which you could very well say were a Mixed Multitude, but it wasn't long until he saw the leaness that had come to his soul and he said, "Oh, I have sinned against heaven. I have sinned against my father. I have taken the things that he has given unto me and I have spent it out here in riotous living." They didn't have anything to give him, not even a husk from the hog pen. He was out there hungry and he came to himself and *remembered* that back home the servants had plenty. He said, "I'll go back to them and I will confess to my father that I sinned against him, I sinned against heaven, and I'm no more worthy to be called his son. I will be a servant." There was nothing else to do but arise and go back home.

When you accommodate wrong relationships who care nothing of talking about God, it won't take long for them to drain everything from you. The saddest thing of all is that they have nothing to give you to bring you happiness and satisfaction.

Now speaking of the Mixed Multitude, the Bible relates to us that Israel journeyed on and many of them, the older group, died in the wilderness...never getting into the Promised Land of milk and honey. According to the scripture, it seems that the Mixed Multitude had such a great impact upon Israel that they never did get their freedom with God.

Now I've lived long enough myself to see the influences that can come to believers who associate themselves with non-believers. The Bible calls non-believers the Children of Darkness and it asks how a person who is walking in the light can have friendship with darkness. One thing about it: When light comes in, darkness has to scatter. In other words, with

God there's no fellowship between darkness and light. I think that the Mixed Multitude is actually the name of the people who don't want to hear the gospel...they close up their hearts. The Word says they reject it. So, shake the dust off of your feet and go on. Don't be overcome by the Mixed Multitude. No doubt this reading is crossing the minds of someone today who is really unhappy. The bottom line to this is that we are associating in bad relationships too much and now our relationship with God is dwindling. So, according to the scripture, He calls us again to come out from among them and be separate and He will receive us.

Glance quickly in the Word of the Lord in Nehemiah where they desired to build the walls of Jerusalem that had finally, over a period of time, fallen down and now the city needed a lot of repair. Nehemiah began to have a burden to see the walls of Jerusalem rebuilt. He looked in the Word of God and read about those who were to get involved in rebuilding the walls of Jerusalem and found out that this Mixed Multitude was a group of people that weren't supposed to be among the children of Israel. Would you believe that leadership, a concern to do things right, was strong enough in Nehemiah that he had this Mixed Multitude pulled out from among the Israelites and separated from them. When he did that, the favor of God was upon them and they rebuilt the walls.

You'll find many places in the Scripture where there were people who had drifted from things they originally had in God...their lives had become contaminated and hindered by wrong things. The Bible speaks of it like this: There was a time that you walked in the love of God, but now you've gone away and gotten other things in your life...you've lost that love...you've turned away...you're in bad shape. He said, "Listen, if you don't return back to that love, then you're going to be destroyed. The light is going to be taken completely away from you."

There have been people that have actually journeyed in religious circles a long time before they found out that their relationship with God was gone. They had worked and mixed with those who did not believe in God, who didn't want God, who thought they could serve the world and God at the same time, who thought they could live wrong and live right too, and now their lives were empty.

I believe with all my heart that there's never been a time in history, even in the churches back in the Old Testament, when our churches were more mixed up with wrong teachings and influences. The Apostle Paul related to us that there would be others who would come in and seek to destroy and to pull away those who actually were serving God and make disciples after themselves.

Recognize what caused the emptiness that you feel in your own heart and life. *The reason many Christians have lost their joy and the peace of God...lost faith...is because their relationship has been broken by a Mixed Multitude trying to serve two masters...trying to live on both sides of the fence.* And the Bible says their hearts are heavy.

Whenever I was a 15-year-old boy, I was saved and began to build a relationship with the Lord. I had become very sensitive to the will of the Lord for my life, not only for my actions, but even in my thoughts. Every angle that could influence or grieve the heart of the Lord, I sought to back off from. But there was one thing...I loved playing ball so much that it wasn't easy for me to turn it down because I felt there was really no harm in my playing ball. No, that wasn't the harm. The harm was that it caused me to neglect my time with God in prayer, reading His Word. I believed in prayer...believed in the Word, but I was neglecting it to play ball. It wasn't long until I began to notice my relationship and awareness of the Lord and His presence, and even His sweetness and His goodness and the hope that I'd been enjoying in the Lord was disappearing. In just a very short couple of months it seemed I could not reach the Lord at all, and I didn't like that.

So, I made up my mind one day when I got in from school that I was going to begin to pray and to seek the Lord. I wanted my relationship with the Lord so I began to take time for it, and the Lord began to make Himself real. But of course the day came that the ball season was over and that gave me time to really build up my relationship with the Lord...I loved the Lord and that relationship was very precious to me.

But the next year came around and, by this time, I had actually found myself a little wife, 14 years old, and we were married. At this point, I was now 17. The coach came to me and said, "Johnny, are you going to play ball with us?" I gladly said, "Mr. Knight, I am married." I didn't really want to tell him the real reason that I had pulled out from playing ball because he wouldn't understand anyway. But he said, "Well, that don't make any difference. Come on and get you a pair of tennies and play, and I'll get you some good ones. I play ball and I'm married. Come on back to school and play." Now real warning and caution began to come into my mind.

I bought myself some new tennies, which were very cheap in those days. But while I was inside the gym, school was still going on and my friends gathered around, then went inside to class. I was out there playing on the basketball court, but my conscience was hurting me. I was afraid that I would get so involved again playing ball that I would neglect prayer. So I just prayed out there by myself after all the boys had gone back into the study hall and I said, "Lord, if you will help me to get out of here, I'll never come back." I didn't want to tell any of them why I didn't want to play...they wouldn't understand. So I pulled off my tennies and dropped them inside the shower house and went to the front door of the gym. I looked both ways to see if I could see any of my friends coming out of the schoolroom or out onto the campus. There was no one moving, so I thought it was a good time for me to walk off. I wouldn't have to give an excuse...wouldn't have to explain. Would you believe the Lord helped me to walk off as a 17-year-old boy and I've *never* been back?

What I am trying to say, dear Friends, is that there are things that in themselves are not harmful, but those things can become harmful by affecting us to the point that we don't seek God's face...don't pray...don't read His Word. In other words, you can just sit in a swing or walk on the grounds or just sit in a rocker, and I'll even go as far as to say you can go in a room and shut the door, but you can still miss Heaven! You've got to *build* a relationship with the Lord.

I wanted a relationship with the Lord even if I had to give up playing ball. There are a lot of us who are aware of this, but there are few who have actually walked away from things that have stopped their prayer life...stopped the revelation of the Word. They're just trying to carry on because they think they're not doing anything bad. But we've often used this phrase: A lot of times *it's not what you do* that's going to keep you on the outside...*it's what you don't do.*

So the Lord wants us to put Him first. As the Word says, if we'll seek Him first, the Kingdom of God, and let that be a daily routine, a daily merging toward God, He'll give us what it takes to keep us away from things we call the Mixed Multitude...things that hinder us from gathering around God's table and His Word and getting alone with God.

Please overcome things that seem to be of no harm by doing the things that will build a relationship with the Lord. We'll find out that things that don't help us surely could harm us. In other words, you don't have to shoot somebody to be a murderer, all you have to do is hate him, the Bible says, in your heart and you're the same as a murderer. You don't have to go out and get drunk, all you've got to do is neglect your relationship with God and you'll wake up in the carnal nature.

I'll close with this thought found in Romans 8:13, "For if ye live after the flesh, ye shall die: but if ye through the Spirit do mortify the deeds of the body, ye shall live."

STONES

FROM THE

SECRET PLACE

VOLUME 6

DR. J. E. MURDOCK

TABLE OF CONTENTS

‑1‑
THE PRESENCE OF THE LORD

You know, speaking of the presence of the Lord, it's really terrible to think that somebody wants you to buy something sight unseen. Even if you wanted to buy a watermelon, you'd love to see the watermelon before you bought it. So the Lord lets you see things. He lets you witness things and then tells you, "Now then, you can have this *if* you'll follow on."

But this just came to me when I was plowing in the field one time. In fact, I had a little altar in every direction in the different fields that I went to work in...about three different fields. When I'd go to one field, why it was separated from the others. I had a little place to pray there, and then when I went to the other field, I'd have a little place to pray there. I had about three different places to pray. And I always went to prayer. I wasn't trying to be holier than thou; I was just trying to be ready when Jesus comes. And He may come before the day is up, you know. That was the focus.

If you really have that true focus, you'll try to do right just like you'll try to drive your car right when a police officer is following right behind you. Somehow or another, you'll look again, won't you, to see how fast or how slow you are going? And when you have a revelation of Jesus' coming, the Bible says, "He that hath that hope will purify himself." You won't have to stay in a camp meeting. You just have that hope that's wrought in there by the Holy Ghost. Well, that's the way it was. So, blessings on the way to the field and blessings even in the field.

And I shall never forget; that's why I want to share this right here. I actually had to stop the old mule, not stop the tractor (I didn't have a tractor to ride). I had to walk behind an old mule and hold on to the plow handles, but that's all I knew anyway, so I thought that was good enough. The presence of the Lord was so real that I actually had to stop and kneel down and say, "Lord, this is too wonderful...You will just have to lift part of it." And the Lord lifted it enough to where I could go on. Now, I know that's hard to grasp and understand. You've heard of things too painful to go on, but *His presence was too wonderful!*

You can hear about the wonderful things of God and the wonderful hope the believer has, and it may not move you, it may not affect you, and again it may work on you for a little bit. But whenever the Holy Spirit dwells within you, you don't know it by the letter. As Paul says, "We're not ministers of the letter, but of the Spirit." And I'll tell you, when the Spirit says it and speaks the letter, and you hear what the Spirit saith, you'll say with others, "There's no one who has spoken like this." No man spake like Jesus for He spoke with the anointing of the Spirit.

I'll tell you that's *every* believer's privilege...to have Christ dwelling in their hearts by the Spirit. Even when you're reading before you go to bed at night, or when you get up in the morning...if you and I will make ourselves available to God, the Spirit will help you hear His Word and you'll never hear it said like He says it. You know, while I was *kneeling*, the Holy Spirit made the Word real to me. And when the Holy Spirit makes the Word real to you, you'll hear it like no other.

For whenever Jesus spoke, they said, "Hmm, this man spoke like no other." In fact, the Pharisees sent a watchman there to go and bring Jesus to them. They wanted to do something with Jesus. So these guards went to where Jesus was and stood there while Jesus was talking and ministering, and they went back and were asked, "Didn't you bring Jesus with you?" They said, "Oh no, no man ever spake like that man. We've never heard anyone talk like that." And they said, "Well, are you deceived also?" Oh, I think when God gets ready, He can leave the enemy behind and the enemy won't know which way He went. Or, He can stand there and talk and the enemy can't make a move to destroy Him. *There's safety in the Lord.*

So the Lord wants to let His Word be real to us where we can truly say we can't resist it. No one spake like Him. How beautiful and how blessed you and I are to be able to receive the precious baptism of the Holy Spirit as we read the Word. Let's go for it.

— 2 —

WHEN WAS THE LAST TIME YOU SAW JOB?

That little phrase came to me along the way. And we ministered from that one time because about the only time you hear anything said about Job it's...oh, he was having such trials, such problems. And the next thing you hear is how he served God...was an upright man. Then, the next thing...why he's really in trouble like no other. And many people were put to a real test to think that if Job, living for God, got in that kind of condition, I think I'll choose another way.

The Lord said, "Have you considered the end of Job?" I'll tell you that when you get to the end of Job, it says it all. In other words, Job said, "I now see the Lord." The Lord spoke of the blessing that came upon his life at the end. Paul mentioned that even Jesus said for the joy that was set before Him, He endured the cross.

So don't think it's strange concerning fiery trials that come upon you. You might have just walked out of The Secret Place...might even have been in prayer. I've had some real battles right in the prayer meeting. But when we begin to follow on, we begin to understand the spiritual warfare that comes along; and the Lord says that we're not only called upon to *believe* in Him, but to *suffer* for Him. And it says if we suffer, we'll reign with Him. So really there's quite an important message there, and that is to discover what the reward is for those who serve the Lord.

Considering the end of Job moves you away and makes the former pictures of Job very rewarding to you. If anyone had a cross, it seemed like Job had one. But listen, at the end of Job, you're going to see the Lord. The Bible says you'll see the Lord if you'll just follow on to the end. So, don't faint in your trial. A revelation of Him is just ahead of you.

Go Home
To Where
The Problem Is...
It's In
Your Heart.

-J. E. Murdock

– 3 –

GO HOME TO YOUR PROBLEM

The Lord spoke it so plainly that it looked like I almost had to just stop my car and write the little phrase down whenever it came to me: "Go home to your problem." And the first thing that came to mind was how the seventh chapter of Romans relates what Paul was saying: When he would do good, evil was present, and that which he wanted to do, he couldn't do...that which he didn't want to do, that's what he did.

I said, *Now, you think what a miserable life that is...can't do what you want to do...do what you don't want to do. Isn't that rough?* And so he said, "It's no more I..." in other words, he has thoroughly searched out where the trouble was, and he couldn't find it. But somewhere or another, he just spoke out and said, "So it's no more me, but it's sin that's in me." Then he cried out, "Oh, wretched man that I am. Who shall deliver me?" Then he stepped right on into the eighth chapter of Romans and said, "Thank God, there is now no condemnation to them that are in Christ Jesus who walk not after the flesh but after the Spirit."

That one little revelation of truth began to come to me. The next thing that came to me: Two men Jesus spoke of were praying. One of them was standing off to the other side. He was really thanking God that he wasn't like that publican over there that was praying, and thankful for being the good person he was. It didn't seem like he had a problem. One thing to recognize...*you do have a problem*. The publican cried out, "Have mercy upon me, a sinner" and *went home having found his problem solved*.

And Jesus said, "Now the man who prayed standing up over there...that's like a self-righteous person that doesn't need to repent. He feels like he's been good all of his life. But the publican came immediately to where the problem was. That began to grow in my Spirit, and I wrote down several things that actually confirmed the fact that the problem isn't out at the neighbor's house. The problem is in your own heart and in your own life. And that gives us hope.

The Lord doesn't have to save the community to save you. All He had to do was get your permission. The Lord didn't have to keep the city to keep you. All He had to do was get your permission.

So today, if we can let the Lord get what He calls for...He didn't call for better walking or better talking...He called for, "Give me a chance at your heart. *Son, give me your heart.*" Then he'll write the laws upon the heart. If you'll notice, after all, everything that flows from us, even from our lips, comes from the heart. And so we've got to have something good there. The Bible says the sad part about it is that we don't know the heart. It says, "It's desperately wicked and who can know it?" Only God can know it.

So don't cross the street again to find the problem. Find it in your own heart. That's where the problem is and that's where the little saying comes from, "Go home to where the problem is...It's in your heart."

– 4 –

Stay On The Ship Of Love

Everything that we draw from love seems to just come out full of inspiration and light. But, as we've traveled along, I haven't found anything really that's more difficult to understand than love. Actually, it really takes the Lord to help us to understand love.

I have written a little tract and put a little ship on the tract named "Love" illustrating what Paul and the prisoners were on when they were en route to Rome. On the way they sailed close to the island of Crete. The Lord seemed to reveal to Paul that they should stay at the island of Crete, but the captain of the ship paid no attention to what Paul had to say. He said it just wasn't a commodious place to stay. So, they went on.

As we follow on through the scriptures, we call that: "From Bad to Worse." You know, God's way may seem very difficult at times, but it's the best way to go, regardless.

So they went on and, sure enough, the storm got worse. The Word says that they didn't see the sun or the stars for many days and nights. It's bad enough to be in that condition on land, but to be out on the sea in complete darkness...what a terrible feeling they must have had! But Paul got alone with the Lord, and as he was waiting on Him, the Lord spoke to him and said, "Tell the men who are sailing with you that unless they abide in the ship, they will not be saved!" In other words, they didn't pay any attention to the warning over there at the island of Crete, but this time there's only one way out, and that's to stay where God told them to stay...and that was to stay on the ship.

As the ship sailed on, they came to a place where two seas met and ran the ship aground. The waves began to whip the ship around and it began to come apart. Paul told the men on the ship who could swim to cast themselves into the sea and get to land. They were close enough to swim to shore. The men who couldn't swim got to land on boards and broken pieces of the ship. And they all escaped safely to land (see Acts 27).

So in putting this together, what really stood out was that they must stay on the ship...and yet it was coming apart. The thought that came to us that was very real and important was this: **Love doesn't promise a smooth ride, but it does promise a sure landing.** And if we'll follow that through, why we'll do our best to stay on the Ship of Love. The love of God **never** faileth. It doesn't mean that everything is going to go smoothly, but it doesn't fail.

We've often thought about the highways today...they didn't move the highway for us, but they've put the highway down and we're to travel that highway. Just a few steps over is the ditch or a tree. It doesn't take long when you leave the highway until you can tell you've missed it. If we ever get used to the love of God in our hearts and in our lives, and stay in it, we can sure tell when we've missed it...very easy. No one has to tell you when you've stepped out of love if you've ever gotten a real taste of it.

Stay in the love of God *at any cost.* In fact, you're to stay in the love of God even among your enemies. You're to stay in the love of God when everything else seems to go wrong. Stay in the love of God. And I guess one of the most beautiful and encouraging things to know is that we don't have to create that love ourselves. We just have to *abide* in the Lord and the love of God, then, is shed abroad in our hearts. We will begin to experience what the scripture says..."Love never faileth."

May the Lord help us to stay on the Ship of Love at any cost. Love not only those who love you, but love those who don't love you. What a privilege we have to find the Lord in such a way that we can make our calling and our election sure by staying on the Ship of Love.

–5–

TRUTH OUT IN THE OPEN

I love that statement because really I saw something in the spiritual realm there as well as in the natural realm. Truth out in the open is just like taking something that's hidden and bringing it out to where you can see it. And it's a marvelous thing, my Friends, to not only hear truth, but to understand truth. So that's what we really have in mind about *truth out in the open.*

The Word speaks of, "There are some who have ears, but can't hear—some who have eyes and can't see." Jesus asked His disciples, "Whom do men say that I the Son of man am?" That's a great question. That's in Matthew 16:13. "And they said, Some *say that Thou art* John the Baptist: some, Elias; and others, Jeremias, or one of the prophets." Then verse 15 says, "He saith unto them," "But whom say ye that I am?" Verse 16, "And Simon Peter answered and said, Thou are the Christ, the Son of the living God." Then verse 17, "And Jesus answered and said unto him, Blessed art thou, Simon Bar-jona: for flesh and blood hath not revealed *it* unto thee, but My Father which is in heaven."

That's where it becomes so real in our hearts. *Truth out in the open.* Some thought Jesus was John the Baptist who had been martyred, and now he was raised. Some said he may be Elias or Jeremias. But He asked Peter, "Who do *you* say that I am?" And Peter said, "Thou art the Christ, the Son of the living God." The scripture explains to us how he got in on that truth...how that truth was hidden to everybody else around now was understood by Peter. How did he get it?... "for flesh and blood hath not revealed *it* unto thee, but My Father which is in heaven." How beautiful.

Seekers came to John in John 1:19, "Jews sent priests

and Levites from Jerusalem to ask him, Who art thou? And he confessed, and denied not; but confessed, I am not the Christ." Others, you see, came to John and asked him if he was the Christ. They didn't know for sure. The seekers became desperate. "And they asked him, What then? Art thou Elias? And he saith, I am not. Art thou that prophet? And he answered, No."

Now we have another scripture in Isaiah 40:3 that's come out in the open. Isaiah tells us that John was, "the voice of one crying in the wilderness...make straight in the desert a highway for our God." Many people believed in Esaias, the prophet, but they hadn't caught onto the fact that John was going to be a forerunner of Christ. It was prophesied in Isaiah, but *now* it's out in the open. They were asking John who he really was. Was he not the Messiah? Was he the Christ? He said, "I'm not."

"And I knew Him not: but He that sent me to baptize with water, the same said unto me, Upon Whom thou shalt see the Spirit descending, and remaining on Him, the same is He which baptizeth with the Holy Ghost."

In John 1:33, something else great came out into the open to John. He explains that the One who had anointed him to go and preach repentance and baptism said, "Whenever you baptize someone that's going to come your way, the Spirit is going to descend from heaven like a dove upon this particular *one* that you baptize. Now this is the way that you're going to know who is the one that's going to baptize with the Holy Ghost and with fire." And sure enough, this very prophecy came out into the open when Jesus told John to suffer it to be so to go ahead and baptize Him so that Jesus could fulfill all the righteousness of God that God had called Him to do.

And now when the Spirit descended upon Him like a dove, John saw that. "And I saw, and bare record that this is the Son of God." Now, that's what we call *truth out in the open*. John knew then, and when Jesus left the water and started walking away, John said, "Behold, the Lamb of God, which taketh away the sin of the world." How did he know it? Because the prophet had said it, and the Lord revealed it to John. *Truth in the open* in verse 32 says, "I saw the Spirit descending from heaven like a dove, and it abode upon Him."

"For John truly baptized with water; but ye shall be baptized with the Holy Ghost not many days hence" (Acts 1:5). Truth unfolds. "Wherefore be ye not unwise but understanding what the will of the Lord is. And be not drunk with wine...but be filled with the Spirit;" (Ephesians 5:17-18).

"But the anointing which ye have received of Him abideth in you, and ye need not that any man teach you: but as the same anointing teacheth you of all things, and is truth, and is no lie, and even as it hath taught you, ye shall abide in Him. And now, little children, abide in Him; that, when He shall appear, we may have confidence, and not be ashamed before Him at His coming" (1 John 2:27-28).

Acts 20:19-20 says, "Serving the Lord with all humility of mind, and with many tears, and temptations, which befell me by the lying in wait of the Jews: And how I kept back nothing that was profitable unto you, but have *shewed* you, and have taught you publickly, and from house to house,"

This is a great teaching that came out into the open or came to the understanding of the apostle Paul, formerly called Saul. Saul was not a follower. He was a leader. He believed in what he was doing though it was contrary to God's will. And when the Lord spoke to him, he said this, "Who are you, Lord?" There's nothing more beautiful now to see that a man like Saul was converted and in whom the Lord had become real. He said, "Who are you?" And the Lord said, "I'm Jesus Whom thou persecuteth." The next great thing that unfolded to Paul was, "What would you have me do?" And the Lord told him what to do.

Friends, the will of God is out there. And the Bible gives us three steps to make. He says ask. *If you don't get it in the asking, he says knock. If you don't get it in the knocking, he says seek. And I tell you, ye shall find, and it'll be worth your trip to find truth out in the open.*

We have great manifestations of the wisdom of men today

that are coming out through many inventions. And listen, Friends, the revelation of truth is there for us to make us complete in God. Let's see ourselves complete in Him by understanding truth in God's Word. He wants to reveal it to us. Many of us that are reading this have already tasted of truth. Keep following on. There's much yet that we have need of, and there's much yet in God's Word to bless us.

– 6 –

DIFFERENT WAYS YOU CAN MISS IT

While in The Secret Place this morning, the Lord seemed to bring the whole picture before me of what it's going to mean to miss the way...the door is shut, and there are no more chances. And I began to read in Matthew 25 and began to count the different ways that the Lord went with us to emphasize those that are left outside.

One of them was about the foolish virgins where it says they were with the wise. But then there was a mighty stir come among them to "go out...the bridegroom is going to come." They rose and trimmed their lamps, but the foolish virgins' lamps had gone out.

It seemed like the Holy Spirit just led me right on up to see what a terrible thing it is for the door to be shut, and they were on the outside. I call it, *"Lost believers."* You know, faith without works is dead. The Word tells us that even satan believes and trembles...but he has no place for God in his life.

So, we went on to find that the Lord mentioned those He gave talents to...gave some five, some three, and gave one just *one* talent. When the Lord reckoned with those servants and their talents, He came to the one who had just one talent—he knew the Lord's will, but he buried his talent. What was so touching this morning here in prayer was that the Lord turned him over to the outside where there was weeping and wailing and gnashing of teeth.

Then I went on down counting the many different times the Lord tells us how we can miss it. You know, *we hear so much about how we can make it, but we pay little attention to how we can miss it.* How easy it is to miss it...to overlook some information and direction that God's Word gives. We just skip on over to find something more positive. I know of no truth in the Word more positive than if we disobey God, we're going to suffer.

It started in the Garden of Eden and it's going to end up at the judgment day...where the Word goes on to tell us in Matthew 25 about the nations being gathered together, and the Lord will separate the sheep from the goats. Isn't that plain? How it touched my heart this morning about what it will be like to really be left on the outside. I believe that's the way Jesus felt when He had wept over Jerusalem at the close of His ministry. He said, "All day long I stretched out My hand. And I would have gathered you together as a mother hen gathers her brood." Any of us that have lived on a farm knows about a mother hen. When she has something good, she calls her little ones to her. I've seen that happen...how they run up to her and she chops up a little something she found on the ground with her mouth and drops it down for her little ones.

But then I've also seen her go across the yard and all at once, detect a hawk flying overhead and pick up her little chickens. That mother has an instinct. She's never lost any...never been caught. But she has an instinct there that that's an enemy, and she calls her little ones under her wings. And I've seen the little ones just hide away under her wings and feel so safe while the mother sits down on the ground and the hawk flies and circles around. She knew...instinct was put in her...that there was danger. And she called.

The Lord used that as an example. He called Israel all day long. He stretched out His hand, but He said, "But ye would not." And He wasn't bitter about it, but He wept over Jerusalem and said, "Now then, your house is left unto you desolate." I have never felt more like weeping over those who are just rejecting...who are good people...who are believers but have not received the grace of God, the wisdom of God and the life of Christ in their hearts to change them and *make them ready* for His coming.

Here in The Secret Place, I never felt like weeping more in my life to think, *What if I had a loved one that was left on the outside?* And the Lord began to call my attention to many scriptures and many chapters in which He points out the possibilities of missing Heaven. We, of course, are studying how to get there, but ah, my Friends, the deceiver is at work. And the deceiver isn't only out yonder, but the deceiver can be in you and me to just be willing to be ignorant of what God is really saying.

The Bible says often through the Apostle Paul, "I would not have you ignorant, brethren, concerning these things." And Paul went all out as he ministered unfolding and revealing that the day will come you'll meet God, and then you'll find out for sure whether you're right or wrong. He certainly met the Lord one day and found out he was doing wrong. Being ignorant of it, he repented and turned to God.

So, today let's don't wait too late. I believe even these words will fall on the ears of a lot of people who believe but have not received. Receive God. Receive the Lord. Turn away from unrighteousness and turn to God. How often Paul cried out, "Though you stand by faith, don't be haughty or high minded, but fear." For if God spared not the angels...yes, even the angels that once were in Heaven with God, He spared not those who sinned. And He said the natural branches, which was Israel, to whom God had made many promises, had rejected the promise. They closed their hearts and were cut off!

Fear if we sin today. The Bible says they suffered when they rejected Moses who was on earth...who had received the Word of the Lord for Israel. They paid no attention, but only murmured and complained. And did they pay the price! The Bible says if they suffered when they rejected him who was on earth as a leader, how much more will we suffer if we reject Christ Who has come from Heaven and has walked this earth and shed His blood? And He's given us a Comforter to lead us into truth to set us free. If we reject that, the big question is how do we expect to escape? I want to make it. And I want you to make it, too.

Let's pray again that God will help us to not sleep as others, but be aware of the fact we will stand before the Lord. *So let us weep while weeping will count.* For the day will come, they will weep, but it'll be too late. God help us.

While thinking upon what I have just related, coming to the close of my studying the Word here in The Secret Place, this scripture comes to mind. Jesus spoke to His twelve disciples at the last supper and He said, "One of you will betray Me." The Word says they all began to be very sorrowful and began to ask, "Lord, is it I?" When I read the different ways that people are going to miss it and will miss it, I ended up with that scripture again, "Lord, is it I?" So we actually, with trembling and tears say, "Save our loved ones. Bring us into the fold. Don't let us sleep the sleep of death." We will have to stand before the Lord. So when we see others failing, think of it, *It could be me.* It could be you. Let's take heed lest we ourselves deny the Lord.

The Lord has so emphasized His goodness and His severity. His severity is upon disobedience. His goodness is towards those who will repent of their disobedience, who will turn to God and have a godly sorrow for the things they found they were doing wrong. And God gives us time. In fact, He tells us He has long patience waiting for the precious fruit of the earth. He's not waiting, my Friends, to condone sin.

Let's you and I prepare to meet the Lord. For everywhere we turn, the fulfilling of God's Word we see manifested on every hand. God is faithful to forgive us of our sins if we'll repent, for *the day will come when we'll have no more opportunity.* Today is the day of salvation. None of us can boast of tomorrow. We don't know what tomorrow will bring.

I can hardly grasp that the Lord called upon Noah to build an ark. This ark took quite a long time to build and, no doubt, the Lord was anxious for the people to turn an ear toward Him and hear that His judgment was coming and they needed to repent and prepare. The Bible says that Noah preached around 120 years and built the ark, and the people *still* didn't know and recognize the day of the flood to come until Noah went inside the ark and God closed the door. They might have walked around and laughed and mocked that he was on the inside but there was no rain in sight. All of a sudden, the Bible says, clouds came up and the rain began to fall and fulfilled what God said would happen if the people didn't repent.

And He said it would be that way in the days of the coming of the Son of man. They did not believe, but the flood came and destroyed every living thing...only eight souls were saved. My, the way must have been narrow, Friends.

The Bible says in the last days, it will be as in the days of Noah. Hear the Word of the Lord and repent. God's given you a chance. As the Word says, save yourself from this untoward generation.

Don't try to save others and not save yourself.

Don't try to keep other vineyards and not keep your own.

The War Zone Of Gethsemane Is That Place Where You Have To Give Up Your Will In Order To Carry Out The Will Of The Father...(Now That's A War!)

-J. E. Murdock

STONES

FROM THE

SECRET PLACE

VOLUME 7

DR. J. E. MURDOCK

TABLE OF CONTENTS

—————➤⟊-❍-⟊◄—————

– 1 –

His Cross Was To Give...Our Cross...To Receive

"For ye know the grace of our Lord Jesus Christ, that, though He was rich, yet for your sakes He became poor, that ye through His poverty might be rich" (2 Corinthians 8:9).

The more we meditate upon the scripture concerning the cross of Jesus Christ, the clearer it becomes what Calvary is all about. Some are aware that because of the sins of Adam and Eve in the very beginning, God immediately sought provision for bringing the human race back into a relationship with God rather than to destroy them. We find that His steps were far different than those of Adam and Eve...their direction to meet the need they had now in their lives because of their sin.

They had sewn fig leaves together, the Bible says, to cover their sins. They realized there was a nakedness there they had never known before. Then when the Lord spoke to them in the garden, as He had spoken before, they were afraid and hid themselves. At the very beginning of disobedience... something came into their hearts they had never experienced before. Now they were afraid.

It's a beautiful study in God's Word to see the steps that He has made to bring about the change. We hope that this lesson concerning the cross of Christ will lead you on to a deeper appreciation and acceptance of the cross of Jesus Christ because He sought other ways to save us and to change our lives. He even called out ministers, priests of God, who were to go into a place of worship called the Holiest of Holies, where God would hear their prayers and listen to them and consider the needs they presented to Him. The Word tells us that the priest made steps to obey the Word of God and offered a sacrifice for his sin because he was a man, just like Adam and Eve. He was a man as we are, so he had to first offer a sacrifice for his sin and then offer a sacrifice for the sins of the people. These sacrifices were prolonging a need that could only be met by the cross of Jesus Christ and that's why we want you to stay with us as we go down the road a little ways considering the cross of Christ.

After they had offered sacrifices for the sins of the people, then this had to take place once a year. Then every year they were reminded of their sins. But God didn't get what He desired out of the sacrifices that were made for the people. He wanted to bring them into a relationship where they would have Christ real in their own hearts...to come into their lives...to inhabit their lives. The Bible says He would not have sought this place called Calvary if the sacrifices that were offered would have met the needs in the hearts of the people. But since they did not meet the needs, the Bible says another way was sought.

The scripture goes on to say the prophets declared that the time would come and they prophesied a revelation where God would offer up His own Son on the cross for the sins of the people. The Bible, addressing this Lamb of God, says He was as a lamb, that He opened not His mouth and He went to the slaughter at Calvary for the sins of you and me. So, when you recognize the blessing, the refreshing, the cost of bringing us back to Jesus...how could you ignore the teaching...stop pursuing what God has in store for those who will trust in the Lamb of God, Jesus, Who went to Calvary's cross?

This is just God's way of doing things. We're experiencing the perfection in the hearts of those who believe in the Lamb of God, for they found out His purpose was to take care of our sin problem...our fears...our disappointments...our death that would reign over us forever. To think that Jesus could shed His blood to atone for our sins so we could actually have a relationship with the Lord.

We're not quick to understand the steps that God has

made to save us...the place called Calvary, or the cross, which Jesus went to. We don't understand but we do know this: Our efforts to save ourselves have failed in every respect, for the Bible says that *it's not in man to save himself.*

Jesus went all out fulfilling the will of the Father...giving His life on the cross. I like to put it this way (so you don't have to read a library to understand it), that by faith God has chosen for His Son, Jesus, to die on the cross. We didn't do that...He did that. The Word says that before these days without the shedding of blood there was no remission...no forgiveness of sins. He said the blood of animals that was offered up for the sins of the people at least once a year did not take away the remembrance of their sin, the condemnation. But now Calvary, the Lamb of God at the Cross, took away the sins of the world.

The way it happens, Friends, is that we first have to come to the place that our efforts have failed...we have to see there is still leanness in our own heart and mind and soul after we have done our very best to please God. The Bible says that our righteousness is as filthy rags. So, in spite of the fig leaves that Adam and Eve used to cover their sin, it did not take away the fear and the condemnation.

The Bible tells us that if we will come to the Lamb of God that was on Calvary and accept it by faith and believe it, *then* grace will come to us. Grace will be imparted unto us by faith. Just like water is channeled from a well into your house and made available to you, the grace, God's love and His ability and forgiveness, come through the channel that we call *faith.* *He that cometh to God must believe that He is God and that He will do what He has promised to do.*

The Bible says though Jesus was the Son of God, it was not robbery to be equal with God, yet to *fulfill* the Father's will, He became a servant and a sacrifice for our sins. It was the cross that He placed His life upon for the sins of the world. That takes us completely away from paying for our own sins.

Now, we suffer because we do things wrong, but at the same time we don't pay for our sins...Jesus paid for our sins. The Bible tells us that Jesus, in order to save you and me, to impart the blessing...the hope...the courage...the light that we need, had to die upon the Cross and give His very life that we could be saved. The Bible does make this great expression to us and we find how true it is day by day: *He became poor that we could become rich.* In other words, He had to give up everything and take the ridicule that comes to people who seemingly have lost their life in vain. They certainly whispered those things out loud, "He saved others; Himself He cannot save" (Matthew 27:42).

Every step of Calvary was fulfilling what God called upon Jesus to do. And what a great promise...a great revelation that came to many souls along the way who read about the cross of Christ...what His death was about and what His death, through faith, would impart to those of us who are undergoing a life-changing experience.

Christ's Cross was God's way of redeeming us from our sins and God **is** the only one that can do it. *The only way we can receive it is to accept what God says, "that whosoever believeth in Him should not perish, but have everlasting life. For God sent not His Son into the world to condemn the world; but that the world through Him might be saved"* (John 3:16-17). In other words, we must see the picture of ourselves and find that Christ moved us away, we might say, and has taken our place upon the cross to die for our sins. If we will accept that, He has another cross that we are called upon to pick up and to follow Him so that we will have great riches.

So we find that **His Cross Was To Give...Our Cross...To Receive.** His Cross was to give up everything so that you and I could have everything...could receive of Him by faith the promises that He made to us by the Cross. Just think how He is able and has proven in the lives of many already that what He said is true.

Coming to Calvary was just God's way of saving us. If we come that way for Christ's sake, He will forgive us of our sins if we repent and accept the Lamb of God, the Cross of Christ. Oh, yes, the Cross of Christ in one way is a great mystery, but at the same time, speaking of the death at Calvary, the Bible goes on to say that a grain of wheat would abide alone if it wasn't put into the earth, but if it's put into the earth and dies, it will come forth and bring much fruit. Now that's accepted by anyone who is experienced in sowing Seed into the field to Harvest. Jesus explained it this way, "If I don't die, I'll be like that Seed that was not buried and I will remain alone. But if I give My life that through My life many will come to know God, many will be redeemed, many will become the children of God."

Through faith, there are many who are coming from lives of sin and gaining freedom from condemnation because they read of the Cross of Christ. I will sum it up just like the scripture says that Christ became poor that we could become rich. He became everything in the eyes of our world, a nobody in order that we could be somebody. So we, then, that are somebody, as we claim to be sometime, have to become a nobody to receive somebody. Our cross looks to the outside world like we are losers. But we're really winners if we pick up our cross to follow the Lord.

Don't give up studying, meditating, learning more of why Jesus died. Many of them thought He had lost the battle...that His death upon the Cross meant that He was a loser...He saved others, but He couldn't save Himself. In other words, *know your cross*. We can know our cross better by having a greater knowledge of His Cross.

He explains, my Friends, what He has provided for us, through faith, by His Cross. He explains that through faith, if we'll pick up our cross and deny ourselves and follow Him, we'll have great riches. The Lord is going to emerge at the front of the line before this is over with...He's a winner. And it will prove to you and I, if we follow the Lord by picking up our cross, that we have become rich in Him and will have life eternal.

I think one of the great apostles, the Apostle Paul, found out the riches there were in the Lamb of God that died on the Cross. He finally expressed it and proved his faith in his statement that he would give up everything to know Christ and Him crucified. We surely need to know Christ, but the only way we can truly say we know Him is to find out *why* He was crucified. If we can find out why He was crucified, then we can spell out clearly the reason we have hope in God...through the crucifixion of Jesus at His Cross, He's made a way for us to be saved...to live victorious...to have eternal life in the end. Don't be ashamed of the cross of Christ because many are finding themselves rich in Him because they have found out that Christ died that we might live.

Honor Him by searching more to know the cost of salvation and the gift it has for the lost and for our own souls...*reach for it through faith.*

–2–

WAR ZONE IN GETHSEMANE

Gethsemane was where Jesus often went to pray. As I meditated upon that, I noticed that Jesus carried three of His disciples with Him to the Garden to spend some time in prayer because the hour of crucifixion was upon Him. Of course, that was an experience that His best friends, honestly, didn't understand and you can believe that Jesus, no doubt, felt all alone during this last step of His life upon the earth...the crucifixion. But whenever those words came to me, the "War Zone of Gethsemane," something birthed that was a little bit different than any part of our prayer ministry.

The Lord told these men of God to *sit* and *wait* and mentions carrying them a little bit *closer* in, and He said, "Will you sit here and watch and pray while I go hence?" He was going on into a place to be all alone with the Father. Jesus suffered in all points as we do and was touched in all areas of life just like we are. But what was birthed there that caused us to call this the War Zone of Gethsemane was that's where the real battle was going to wage against Jesus...*where He was face to face with something that He preferred not to do.*

To explain this revelation, we compare it to the many young men who have worn army clothes but who never got into the war zone. They stayed right here in their own country and never knew what it was to really get into where the battle was being fought. But some of them did. Some of them, as soon as they got into the service with almost no training at all were placed in the middle of the war zone. That's what I'd like to build on because, honestly, if we can see this, we will understand more about The Secret Place because a lot of things go on there, in the place of prayer, that very few people come face to face with. Many people have never gone into the War

Zone of Gethsemane.

Now let's take a look briefly at the area of the Garden of Gethsemane. When I was in Jerusalem around the Garden of Gethsemane and Bethlehem, I had to look over a little area I wasn't familiar with.

We went down where we understood Jesus had gone inside the Garden and fell on the ground and prayed unto the Father. All at once I was awakened to the prayer that He prayed. He didn't pray a lot of things there but what came out in the open to us was this, "Father, if Thou be willing, remove this cup from Me: nevertheless not My will, but Thine, be done" (Luke 22:42). That's where the thought that came to me was born into my spirit, that Jesus said it really was not His will to go to the Cross, but since it was the Father's He would surrender His will. Now that's the part that we want to touch on because we're going to experience more and more of what the Bible relates about surrendering our lives unto God...truly denying ourselves and doing things that God has called us to do...that we really don't want to do. That's going to happen more often than we realize.

Many precious people today are not enjoying their experiences because they are meeting up with things that they don't want to go through. First of all, we don't really know for sure that it's the will of God. But now Jesus knew that that was the purpose of Him coming into this world, the plan of God. But if prayer could change it, He said, "I'm going to pray because I have the feeling of being forsaken of the Father. That's a place that I don't want to be. I don't want to suffer, true enough, but the worst thing is to know that the Father could turn His face and not look upon Me in that crucial moment." Think of that, folks, by giving up our will we will experience such a relationship because it seems that just when everybody is against us we're called upon to surrender our will.

I deeply appreciate the revelation of that truth because it's helped me to understand that Jesus was touched in all points just as we are, yet He did not sin, He surrendered to it.

He is touched by us having to give up our will, but He knows it is best...knows how we feel...to suffer feelings that we are forsaken by others. That has helped me a lot.

The War Zone of Gethsemane is that place where we have to give up our will in order to carry out the will of the Father...now that's a war!

You'll find little children who are no more than four or five years old who will almost fight their mother before they'll give up their will. So He knows how attached we feel to doing our will, especially if we see no reason to do anything else...don't see the value of following anybody else...don't see the value or satisfaction in doing anything but our own will.

Reading in the book of Acts, Paul was called upon of the Lord to suffer for the cause of Christ, to preach the gospel, and he was going to experience some severe persecution which could actually come to the point of death. And the news got out quickly among Paul's friends, and they said, "You know, we understand that you are going to Jerusalem." And he said, "Yes, the Lord has called me to go to Jerusalem. It's really not my choice, but I want to do His will at any cost." And they said, "Listen, if you go to Jerusalem, they're waiting for you there. Something is going to happen so you had better not go. Persecution is waiting for you." Would you believe that Paul's revelation of giving up his will had such a value to it that he wept and said, "Why break ye my heart? I'm not just willing to suffer for Christ in Jerusalem, I'm willing to die for Christ." And you know Paul persuaded that group who were trying to change the picture for Paul. They didn't want him to face it but the Bible says they ceased trying to convince Paul otherwise and began to say, "The will of the Lord be done."

Friends, that's where, many times, *if we'll pray long enough about things that we're gravely concerned about, we'll find out that it's really the will of the Lord* and that we should just surrender it to Him. It's wonderful to realize that. Now remember, Jesus had prayed about the will of the Father and about Gethsemane and the Cross. We should pray about these things...cry out to God. Changes could be made...things could be made different. But above all, getting the real understanding and concept of the War Zone of Gethsemane, that's what we want to concentrate on...where you have to give up your will to do the will of the Father. Now we can walk over many areas and enjoy doing what God has called us to do, but *there are places we will come to in which we will be called to do things that we don't want to do.*

The Lord called me back in 1954 to go out into Highway and Hedge Ministry and to place my family and our home in Orange, Texas. I would go out into areas where they needed the gospel. And all at once it dawned on me that I was going to have to give up my family if I did it that way and they needed me then more than ever. So my dear wife and I discussed it and I was praying earnestly and somehow the Lord spoke to me, "Well, you will lose your family anyway, but if you lose them for Me, you'll save them." And you know, I saw something there that helped me to honestly say, "Well, Lord, not my will, but Thine be done." I was just to give up to the will of God in spite of all of my feelings. Would you believe that it was only a short time that I was away from my family?

It worked out in a very few days. In just a few short weeks we were all living together in Franklin, Louisiana, and I was able to go right ahead building the church there. But the point is to grasp the feeling of having to do something that you really don't want to do. I really did not want to do that, but when the Lord spoke to me that way, I could see a picture that was worth saying, *Not my will, but Thine be done.*

So Jesus, no doubt, was touched in all of those points, just like you and I. And when you come to places where it looks like you'll have to give up the only thing that's worth anything to you, *your will*, stay in The Secret Place...stay before the Lord until it works out and you can say, "Not my will, but Thine be done." Not my will, but Your will...not the will of others...not the will of yourself...but the will of the Father.

All of this can be birthed in The Secret Place. Stay there until you can find strength and God's grace to say, "Not my will, but Thine be done." Stay there until you don't have to argue the case at all...until you can move on with peace. That's the fruit of God's ability...to give us a peace of heart...a peace of mind. As Paul said, "If I do this willingly, then there's a great reward for me." And the Bible says that He works in our hearts to will and to do of His good pleasure and that's the way He's chosen for us to pick up our cross, to deny ourselves and follow Him. He doesn't wait long to say the rest of it, but He says you'll have great riches in Heaven.

You know there's no boss out there who wants you to work a week or a month without telling you what you're going to get out of it. So when you're following the Lord and there comes a time to make steps that are contrary to your thinking, God will soon, if we'll stay before Him long enough, let us see the value of following Him all the way, even to the point of self-denial. Find that place and remember to call it the War Zone in Gethsemane...to give up your will.

Don't Let
Anything Steal
Your Prayer Time
With The Lord...
And Your Battles
Will Be Won
Ahead Of You.

-J. E. Murdock

— 3 —

What Cross-Bearers Have To Say

It's very important to say the right thing on the road we're on because somebody is listening and will pick up on what we have to say.

On the subject of cross-bearers...I got saved when I was fifteen years old and one of the first statements that I got from the Bible as I followed on was if any man come after Him, let him deny himself and pick up his cross and follow Him. We were interested in following the Lord because it had been inspired to our hearts that Jesus was coming back again. And we were already old enough to know that we weren't going to be here forever. It seemed like people ahead of us were leaving out...passing on from this life. But it was a marvelous thing to find out that God had a way for us to walk that is pleasing in His sight and we can hear Him say, "Well done."

Before we made these statements about cross-bearers, I noticed that some people were glad to pick up the cross while others complained bitterly about the cross and tried to believe that Jesus' cross was all-sufficient. But I was really attracted to some people in the Bible who actually did have a hard road to travel.

As I began to walk down that road, the first one that seemed to stand out was Jesus who picked up His cross and started up the hill of Calvary. The people were touched, of course, especially those who were followers of the Lord. They were weeping and the Lord made the statement, "Don't weep for Me, weep for yourself." I read different opinions and interpretations of that statement, but I had to settle on the belief that if we will follow the Lord properly, we will be glad that we suffered for the cause of Christ.

Now Jesus was nearing home...most everyone could only see Him stopping at the cross, but He went on beyond that. We have a true revelation and manifestation of the resurrection of Christ *after* the crucifixion. But our thoughts are about what cross-bearers have to say. The Word speaks of it like this in Acts 5:41, "And they departed from the presence of the council, rejoicing that they were counted worthy to suffer shame for His name." What a beautiful picture! Few people have really grasped that...the real value of following the Lord. But the Bible says that this group had been brought before the council. They were going to question them because they were really en route to do something about Jesus who seemed to be stirring up the hearts of people and appeared to be causing confusion. But the Lord had already informed them that they would be brought before rulers and that there would be a persecution to come.

The people were brought before the council, were threatened and had a promise of real chastening to their lives if they continued on in their belief in the Lord. But when they turned away from the council, the Bible says that they turned away rejoicing because they were counted worthy to suffer for the shame and for the name of Christ. How beautiful. That should sound a bell to each of us to look at this again and see that not everybody who follows the Lord turns back. There were some who went right on and came to their end and left an expression of their hope, faith, determination, blessing and strength to become real cross-bearers for Christ.

Real cross-bearers won't be murmuring or complaining. I believe the apostle Paul said that if we do this and we suffer willfully, there's a great reward. Those are the ones we're looking at...the cross-bearers who actually delighted themselves in following after the Lord.

In another scripture, Paul put it this way, "What mean ye to weep and to break mine heart? for I am ready not to be bound only, but also to die at Jerusalem for the name of the Lord Jesus" (Acts 21:13). So this is another beautiful picture...the Apostle Paul had a revelation when he got saved that there was going to be some cross-bearing, some persecution. So he was not ignorant that if he followed the Lord there would be some testings...some trials. In fact, before he was saved, he was one of the main people who put the pressure upon the believers. But now his eyes had been opened and he saw where he had failed in sin. He was ignorant of the things of God, but when the Lord spoke to him the picture changed altogether. Paul actually became a martyr for Christ. So we know that his statement, his confession, held good...he meant it.

We should be encouraged today to pick up the cross that Jesus has for us and begin to enjoy the fact that we can suffer for the cause of Christ. We don't suffer for our sins...*Jesus suffered for our sins*. He's the one that paid the price, but if we serve Him we're going to be *persecuted for righteousness' sake*.

By serving Him, we deny ourselves, put ourselves behind, and our hearts are open to receive what the Lord has for us...the way He wants us to walk.

We have another scripture about a man called Stephen. He was one of the deacons of the church and was called upon to help and encourage the widows and those who were going through hard times. He was a man who really knew God. The scripture says that Stephen met with persecution and people began to stone him. "And they stoned Stephen, calling upon God, and saying, Lord Jesus, receive my spirit. And he kneeled down, and cried with a loud voice, Lord, lay not this sin to their charge. And when he had said this, he fell asleep" (Acts 7:59-60). Now then those were the closing words of Stephen who had picked up his cross to follow the Lord and suffered for believing in the Lord...but he gladly did it.

We are encouraged to follow the Lord to the extent that we'll actually suffer for His cause. We should be close enough to Him that it can bring a persecution...like darkness and light. When light walks in, darkness has to move out. So it brings a great stir when a person turns to the Lord. And these that we have mentioned today are men who are just like you and me...didn't know the Lord, but God made Himself real and they accepted it and they picked up the cross and met persecution just as well as Jesus.

The Word tells us that we're not only to believe on Him, but we are to suffer with Him. Here's another scripture, "For even hereunto were ye called: because Christ also suffered for us, leaving us an example, that ye should follow his steps:" (1 Peter 2:21). In other words, all that live godly in Christ Jesus will suffer persecution. "Forasmuch then as Christ hath suffered for us in the flesh, arm yourselves likewise with the same mind: for he that hath suffered in the flesh hath ceased from sin;" (1 Peter 4:1).

The Bible says, "Wherefore seeing we also are compassed about with so great a cloud of witnesses, let us lay aside every weight, and the sin which doth so easily beset us, and let us run with patience the race that is set before us, looking unto Jesus the Author and Finisher of our faith; Who for the joy that was set before Him endured the cross, despising the shame, and is set down at the right hand of the throne of God. For consider Him that endured such contradiction of sinners against Himself, lest ye be wearied and faint in your minds." No greater scripture than that we've just read from Hebrews chapter 12, verses 1-3, goes on and tells so many important things about suffering for the cause of Christ.

I've often thought that much of my sufferings came from my mistakes. So I began to think *if I'm going to suffer, I want to suffer for right-doing.* For the Bible says that there will be a lot of your friends who will pull aside. Now you don't go to the same places they go to and your entertainment doesn't come from the same things that it used to come from. You have made a difference in your life by accepting the Lord and following Him. The Bible says they think it's strange...you don't look to them anymore. I think we need a little more of that...that is to come out from among them and be ye separate, saith the Lord. You don't have to read a library to find out the reward of following Jesus. You won't read the words "Pick up your cross" but just a moment and you'll read the reward right ahead. So let's take new courage today and get close enough to God that we are actually persecuted for right-doing...right-living.

The Apostle Paul gave us these words, "I am crucified with Christ: nevertheless I live; yet not I, but Christ liveth in me: And they that are Christ's have crucified the flesh with the affections and lusts. If we live in the Spirit, let us also walk in the Spirit" (Galatians 2:20;5:24-25). That's where the difference comes in. Our lives are truly changed as we start following after the Lord.

You don't have to travel far sight-unseen...God's promise of blessing is just a step past the cost. If we suffer for His cause, we will also reign with Him. The battle will be over and what a joy it will be to find the reward. *He learned obedience through the things that He suffered.* We are surprised to find out that most of our knowledge comes through suffering.

The Lord wants us to know the value of obedience...the payday that's coming for those who will obey Him. So He is willing to allow the road that's displeasing to Him to become a rough road in order to get us on the road that leads on to righteousness.

Hebrews 13:14 says, "For here have we no continuing city, but we seek one to come." That's the thing that caught my eye many years ago, that we actually won't stay here whether we want to go or not. So let's prepare for it because there is a truth in God's Word that puts a light upon the future of our lives. *Everyone will stand before God.* We want to be ready.

The Lord turned my feet around towards Him when I truly realized and accepted the fact that here we have no continuing city, so now we're seeking one to come. It's like a building or your home or your automobile being on fire. We don't have to be begged to get out of there. We will immediately turn to flee because we know that the fire is not going to fool around...it's going to burn down everything in there so we want to be ready to vacate.

Realize this vessel of clay that we're living in is going to stand before the Lord and have to give an account. Many people have accepted that and have found out there is a new life.

There are still people who are willing to bear the cross...willing to serve the Lord. Let's join this group of cross-bearers and have the same joy, peace and confidence in our hearts knowing that if we'll pick up our cross, there will be a crown for us.

Paul said we labor for things that are corruptible, things that perish; we spend a lifetime on something that could actually be gone tomorrow. He was concerned why don't we labor for a crown that's *incorruptible*. If we're going to suffer, we want to suffer and go the route that has a payday. Let's deny ourselves...pick up the cross and follow Him. We'll be glad.

– 4 –

DON'T OVERLOAD THE DOLLAR

The statement "Don't overload the dollar" is a very attractive statement. You know, everyone of us who gets hold of a dollar are glad because we have found out that the dollar really means something. You can't go anywhere that you don't have to have a dollar. So it isn't long until the dollar stands out in a real big way.

It's hard to believe, but it's true, that before we went out in the Lord's work I was working in a dairy and getting $35.00 a month and had a house to live in. It was hard work. But then the call to go into the ministry came and the church said they would come with a truck and move me there if I would come and work with their young people and help them in the church. They said they would give me $8.00 a week. Well, I'll tell you what, we weren't going for the $8.00. We truly were going because we wanted to answer the call of God.

I've heard some say, "Oh, there's nothing that looks better than a hundred-dollar bill!" It's very easy to get distracted, to put too much dependence upon the wrong thing. That's where the trap really comes...we actually overload the dollar. There are many of us, truly, who are like the prodigal son. We don't know how to use the dollar and the first thing you know, why, it's all gone and we don't even have what we wanted. So, to say those words, "Do not overload the dollar" is not stretching the statement because it's hard today, and anytime, to get enough of those dollars to cover all of our needs.

Many times in these days of pressure when there's a lack somewhere else, we try to meet that need in another area. There are people who have found that the dollar didn't do everything, didn't bring true happiness. They heard the gospel and heard that there was hope. When the dollar bill had done it's best and still hadn't brought satisfaction, they have truly turned to the Lord and begun to hope in God. Some have actually given everything they had in order to answer the call of the Lord.

There are some, the Bible says, who put great emphasis upon the dollar supposing that gain is godliness. From such, the Scripture says to withdraw thyself. But godliness with contentment is great gain. Can you see the route to gain here? *God never directs us down a path seeking anything that detours from Him.* We do find that a lot of times when there is a sufficiency of material things laying before us that it's *hard* to find the path that leads us to *true* commitment to God. True happiness comes through knowing the Lord. The Bible says, "Let him rejoice in this that he knoweth the Lord."

It's a blessing to see God supplying our needs, bringing in the material blessings. We certainly have a testimony of that. I don't mean to tell you that we've got silver and gold stacked up, but the very fact that He gives us food, daily bread, clothing and protection and helps us to learn how to use what He gives us is a great reward and a great blessing. And the Lord does promise to do that. But our main thought today is, *Don't depend on the dollar doing it all...it can't!* It is impossible.

When we take hold of anything that leaves God out, we are missing the real lifeline...for happiness...for peace...for joy. So, let's look again and see there are many precious people who have a lot of material things who are unhappy. They are trying to be happy and they feel like they should be happy. They are blessed and they have enough to pay the bills, that's true. But listen, the goal is this: getting Christ into our lives by faith...reading His Word...having hope that the dollar bill cannot give. Much of our unhappiness overtakes us because we've left God out. I'm so glad I found out early that real satisfaction comes through true commitment to the Lord.

I'm going to read a little bit more from the Word to see what Jesus has to say about money and material things. "But thou, O man of God, flee these things; and follow after righteousness, godliness, faith, love, patience, meekness. Fight the good fight of faith, lay hold on eternal life, whereunto thou art also called, and hast professed a good profession before many witnesses" (1 Timothy 6:11-12).

Paul wanted to give Timothy a charge. Timothy was a young man who was saved under the ministry of the apostle Paul, and Paul was as a father over him. Look at 1 Timothy 6:13 and 14, "I give thee charge in the sight of God, who quickeneth all things, and before Christ Jesus, Who before Pontius Pilate witnessed a good confession; That thou keep this commandment without spot, unrebukeable, until the appearing of our Lord Jesus Christ."

Further on in 1 Timothy 6:19, he says, "Laying up in store for themselves a good foundation against the time to come, that they may lay hold on eternal life." Above everything, see that your heart is right with God... "For we brought nothing into this world, and it is certain we can carry nothing out. And having food and raiment let us be therewith content. But they that will be rich fall into temptation and a snare, and into many foolish and hurtful lusts, which drown men in destruction and perdition. For the love of money is the root of all evil: which while some coveted after, they have erred from the faith, and pierced themselves through with many sorrows" (1 Timothy 6:7-10).

How the Lord wants to caution us of all of these things. I have found out that we can know the perfect will of God for our life, but how easy it is to *neglect* what it takes to stay in that perfect will of God. That is to take time to pray...take time, as the Word says, to be holy...to be what God wants us to be.

Now the enemy will seek to bring satisfaction to us and cause us to settle down with just the dollar bill. But don't overload the dollar...it will never bring satisfaction for the soul. There are many "Perverse disputings of men of corrupt minds," that is the trap that's laid for every one of us, "destitute of the truth, supposing that gain is godliness: from such withdraw thyself. But godliness with contentment is great gain" (1 Timothy 6:5,6). So, regardless of how much we have in the way of the dollar, there is a trap and that's what we are cautioned to warn against. *If these things increase,* the Bible says *not to set your heart upon them.*

Godliness doesn't shut the door...it is the route to great gain.

God wants to give you and me a relationship with Him where we can actually handle blessings. You know, you can have God but if you allow discontentment to get a hold of you and begin to think that your satisfaction is going to come through the material things of this world...that's the trap. We often think, "If I could just get this, if I could just have that, if I could just achieve this, oh, I'd be a better church member, I could serve God better." No, the only way we can serve God better is to get more of God, to get the revelation of God, to come to know God. As Paul says, "I count all things but loss for the excellency of the knowledge of Christ Jesus my Lord: for whom I have suffered the loss of all things, and do count them but dung, that I may win Christ," (Philippians 3:8). So we are not headed towards happiness until we're headed towards increasing our knowledge of God.

We have a teaching in God's Word where Jesus taught of a young man who had two sons. One day the younger son said, "Father, give me all that belongs to me." And so the father gave him all that belonged to him and then he left home. And the Word says he began to spend his living in a wrong way and with wrong relationships. The time came that everything that the father had given him was gone and he was about to go hungry. Instead of turning to go back home, he just joined himself with the citizens of that country, but they didn't give him anything to eat. In fact, the Word says they didn't give him as much as the husk from the hog pen. Then he came to himself and realized what he had done, and he said, "I will arise and go to my father, and will say unto him, Father, I have sinned against heaven, and before thee, And am no more worthy to be called thy son:" (Luke 15:18-19).

What we are trying to get into now is this: The importance of our relationship with God...getting to the point that we can handle prosperity. I'll tell you, Friends, there are only a few who can handle it. I wouldn't boast that myself. I don't know enough about prosperity, really, to set my affections on it to the extent that I lean upon it and stop my prayer meeting, stop reading, stop praying through and touching God. But, oh, it's deceiving on every corner. Satisfaction, my Friends, does not come by the things of this world. So let's not overload the dollar by thinking if we can just get a little bit more, we can serve God better. It's a marvelous thing to have God to the extent that you are content with what He has for you.

God wants to prepare us for the blessing as well as give us the blessing. We're not trying to say to you that we're against finances. *We need finances*...that's not the point. But the Bible does say *if riches do increase, if the time of prosperity does strike in an unexpected way, do not set your heart upon them.*

Don't let anything distract you from serving the Lord.

"Charge them," the Word says in 1 Timothy 6:17, "that are rich in this world, that they be not high-minded, nor trust in uncertain riches, but in the living God, Who giveth us richly all things to enjoy;"

As I have taught these lines to you today about not overloading the dollar, I take caution of what we are saying as well as I want you to take the caution. Don't think that your happiness will come through that channel because it can cut you off quicker than anything else...it can change your relationship. It doesn't mean that God doesn't want us to have it, but it does mean that He wants to *prepare* us for the blessing.

Getting God into our lives is great gain. You can't buy contentment with a dollar.

You Don't Have
To Travel Far
Sight-Unseen...
God's Promise Of
Blessing Is Just
A Step Past
The Cost.

-J. E. Murdock

STONES

FROM THE

SECRET PLACE

VOLUME 8

DR. J. E. MURDOCK

Table Of Contents

WHY STONES FROM THE SECRET PLACE?

Before we begin our walk together in my book that I've called "Stones From The Secret Place," I want to take you to the book in the Bible named Joshua. I've just been re-reading some of it. The many times I've read it, I've always been blessed because we seem to get two sides of the picture of God's work with His people. It is most beautiful and clear to us today what we want to bring to you. Before we go into *Stones From The Secret Place,* it would be well to get this picture in mind.

God had brought Israel out from the land of Egypt, and His plan was to take them into the Promised Land, a land that was flowing with milk and honey. As we followed Moses' leadership and his period with the children of Israel, why they had some beautiful experiences crossing the Red Sea. "Then sang Moses and the children of Israel this song unto the Lord, and spake, saying, I will sing unto the Lord, for He hath triumphed gloriously: the horse and his rider hath He thrown into the sea. The Lord is my strength and song, and He is become my salvation: He is my God, and I will prepare Him an habitation; my father's God, and I will exalt Him. The Lord is a man of war: the Lord is His name. Pharaoh's chariots and his host hath He cast into the sea: His chosen captains also are drowned in the Red Sea. The depths have covered them: they sank into the bottom as a stone. The enemy said, I will pursue, I will overtake, I will divide the spoil; my lust shall be satisfied upon them; I will draw my sword, my hand shall destroy them. Thou didst blow with thy wind, the sea covered them: they sank as lead in the mighty waters. Who is like unto Thee, O Lord, among the gods? who is like Thee, glorious in holiness, fearful in praises, doing wonders? Thou stretchedst out Thy right hand, the earth swallowed them. Thou in Thy mercy hast led forth the people which Thou hast redeemed: Thou hast guided them in Thy strength unto Thy holy habitation. Thou shalt bring them in, and plant them in the mountain of Thine inheritance, in the place, O Lord, which Thou hast made for thee to dwell in, in the Sanctuary, O Lord, which Thy hands have established. The Lord shall reign for ever and ever" (Exodus 15:1-5,9-13,17-18).

Now today, we want to bring out the picture a little further of what God has brought to Israel. The Bible really makes it clear that somehow God couldn't go very far with the Israelites because of their lack of faith...actually trusting in the Lord. During their trials and testing in their walk, they would continually murmur and complain, so God couldn't get very far with them.

Even Moses himself actually became weary in leading the children of Israel. Moses told the people. "The Lord was wroth with me for your sakes, and would not hear me: and the Lord said unto me, Let it suffice thee; speak no more unto Me of this matter...behold it with thine eyes: for thou shalt not go over this Jordan. But charge Joshua, and encourage him, and strengthen him: for he shall go over before this people, and he shall cause them to inherit the land which thou shalt see" (Deuteronomy 3:26-28).

Moses spoke to all Israel in the desert east of the Jordan— and told them everything they were to do. He said, "And the Lord said unto Me...I will raise them up a Prophet from among their brethren, like unto thee, and will put My words in his mouth; and he shall speak unto them all that I shall command him. And it shall come to pass, that whosoever will not hearken unto My words which he shall speak in My name, I will require it of him" (Deuteronomy 18:17-19).

So, the call came to another man of God. His name was Joshua. It's beautiful when we look into that and see how God has not given up on His people. He actually wants to lead us right on and show His arm strong in behalf of His people. But, at the same time, He wants to get inside our lives and our hearts.

Joshua steps into the leadership, and they have come now to the river of Jordan. Then, the river of Jordan flowed with water from one end of the year to the other. The water was flowing from the top of the banks to actually overflow, at times, the river of Jordan, so it is going to take another miracle. I don't know whether they repeated what had happened in the past when God brought them over the Red Sea. We do quickly get a viewpoint of them standing there at the river of Jordan.

The Lord told Joshua, and the priests of God that bear the ark of the Lord, to take steps toward the river. As they did, the river parted. "And the priests that bare the ark of the covenant of the Lord stood firm on dry ground in the midst of Jordan, and all the Israelites passed over on dry ground, until all the people were passed clean over Jordan" (Joshua 3:17).

After this wonderful experience and they'd crossed over Jordan and were standing on the bank on the other side, God wanted that testimony of what He had done for Israel to live on for a future time and a future generation. They had placed some stones in the river where the priests stood as the Israelites were crossing over the river. The waters had been backed up and a clear, clean path was before the Israelites as they crossed over.

God wanted this testimony to live on so that others could see the hand of God, so He said, *"Take those twelve stones out of the river and place them on the bank."* Read Joshua 4:20: "Those twelve stones, which they took out of Jordan, did Joshua pitch in Gilgal." "And he spake unto the children of Israel, saying, When your children shall ask their fathers in time to come, saying, What mean these stones? Then ye shall let your children know, saying, Israel came over this Jordan on dry land" (Joshua 4:21-22).

Now really that's what we want you to see as you step into our book, *Stones From The Secret Place.* See what God continues doing and leading and saying to those who are willing to follow on and come into The Secret Place. I trust that you will get much out of this and you will be blessed.

Really, the purpose of those stones on the bank were to help the generation to come know the testimony of God's grace, God's ability, God's mindfulness of Israel to cross them over where they could go on into the good land that the Lord had prepared for them. "The land you are entering to take over is not like the land of Egypt, from which you have come, where you planted your seed and irrigated it by foot as in a vegetable garden. But the land you are crossing the Jordan to take possession of is a land of mountains and valleys that drinks rain from heaven. It is a land the Lord your God cares for; the eyes of the Lord your God are continually on it from the beginning of the year to its end. So if you faithfully obey the commands I am giving you today—to love the Lord your God and to serve Him with all your heart and with all your soul—then I will send rain on your land in its season, both autumn and spring rains, so that you may gather in your grain, new wine and oil" (read Deuteronomy 11:10-14).

Israel said, "Had it not been the Lord, the waters would have overflowed us" (read Psalm 124). The Lord loves for us to see the miraculous because He does things in such a way that really the natural man wouldn't even think of such. There's no one who would actually think of crossing a million people over on dry land across a river. God wants us to look back and recognize "If it had not been the Lord, these waters would have overflowed us."

That's the purpose, Friends, of relating to you these actual personal experiences and relationships with the Lord, and how He has led our lives from the time I got saved at the age of 15. Now we want you to step right on with us into *Stones From The Secret Place.* May the Lord bless it to your hearts as you read carefully from page to page.

– 1 –

THE BEGINNING

The first Stone that we actually want to look at is the very first thing that began to happen in our Christian relationship and change of heart in the Lord.

I was standing in the yard on a mid-summer day when a car drove up in front of the house. It was an aunt of mine who had been to the house and picked up my mother and two of my sisters to go to a prayer meeting. I knew nothing about it. We'd never had a prayer meeting like that at all.

But, when they returned and stopped in front of the house, my aunt reached back in the back seat and picked up a sister of mine who was only ten years old. I thought when she carried her into the house that something must be seriously wrong. I soon found out that they had just come in from a prayer meeting, and my sister had been saved and filled with the Spirit and was speaking in a heavenly language. You may know how that attracted me. I had never heard of such an experience as that.

As they went on into the house where we lived, my aunt says, "We're going to have a prayer meeting here tomorrow evening." I didn't say it out loud, but I said to myself, "I'm going to be in that prayer meeting." I looked forward to it because my little sister had just come from a prayer meeting and I saw something in her face. From that moment until the next evening, I heard her, along with two of my other sisters, in prayer. They were talking to the Lord just as if the Lord was right there in the room. I had never heard anyone talk to the Lord in such a way. That really got my attention, so I could hardly wait until the next evening.

Sure enough about 3:00 in the afternoon I got this thought and this first stone that we want to look at from The Secret Place. I stepped into that prayer meeting at 3:00 and three or four others knelt down and began to talk quietly before the Lord. I heard some of them begin to cry. Then I heard this little sister of mine began to speak in a heavenly language.

I looked around real quietly. Remember, this was my first time to get into a prayer meeting. I believed in prayer like many times you'll find people who believe in prayer, but they don't ever pray. It's quite obvious everywhere you turn these days that there are a lot of people who believe in God, but they don't serve God. They don't seek after God. But that's the purpose of this book, *Stones From The Secret Place,* to relate to you the definite personal relationship that we've had with the Lord. Not only us, but there are many others who have stepped into the presence of God and have never been the same.

I just kind of knelt around on the floor. Then I'd crawl on my knees over to one of the others real quietly and listen. After a while, I found something happening in my own heart, and I began to cry a little bit. I told the Lord, "Oh help me. Help me." That's about all I could say. "Help me, Lord. Help me and save me, Lord." Every now and then I would hear them in prayer speaking very softly. It wasn't boisterous, but with a broken spirit they would say, "Lord, You're coming back again. You're coming back again. You're soon to return back again." Now I knew and had related that message that Jesus would return again, but that really got a hold of me that *He's coming soon.*

So, I began that very evening my first prayer meeting. I noticed that eight hours had passed when this little teenage boy of 15 began his first prayer meeting. My mother had told me, "Son, if you don't change, you are going to go to the pen before you get grown." I certainly believed in God, but I didn't know how to reach for God. I didn't know how to lay hold upon God. And that's really a concern that has stayed with me...to try to know how to lay hold upon the Lord. That's why we began, in these later times, to look and to consider writing this book that you've started to read, *Stones From The Secret Place.*

That evening something happened that has lived on and on and on. How beautiful it has been and how helpful it has been, because we've come to some rivers to cross, too. We've come to valleys to walk through. We've come to mountains to climb. We've met opposition, just like we related to you how Israel came to the Red Sea and then she came to the Jordan. Then, we ourselves often face different things and obstacles. I trust that these *Stones From The Secret Place* will reveal something to you, and you'll find something that will be very helpful to you. That was the purpose of the Israelites putting the stones on the bank of the river that we related in the beginning of this book.

So the eight hours began to go on by, we might say. I didn't pay any attention to it until it was over, and I found that we had been there right about eight hours. I had a twin sister who had been filled with the Spirit that evening. The Lord gave her such a vision of Heaven and a call into the ministry that it wasn't long until she was preaching the gospel and young people were hearing and turning unto the Lord.

There is power in the presence of the Lord. But, to recognize His presence is the real purpose of writing and relating these wonderful days and experiences, and we might say, years that have gone by. How the Lord has been faithful of His promise and has been teaching us a little more each day on how to come before the Lord.

That evening as I observed these things, something was planted into my heart that I certainly was not able to get away from. In fact, I really did not want to get away from it. I really felt and tasted and witnessed something very real, very precious. I like to relate it this way. There was a little lady, the book of John relates, who was at one of Jacob's wells. She went to get water. She met a Man there Who was named Jesus, but she didn't know who He was. Jesus asked her to give Him some water. She couldn't understand how He would even talk to her because she was a Gentile and He was a Jew, and they had nothing to do with each other. So a mystery now came forth as the Lord began to talk to her.

Finally, He said something to her that really got her attention. He asked her about the condition of her life. She saw immediately that He must be a prophet for He began to get into her private life she thought was covered and no one knew about. After He talked about her fathers, the woman said, "I know that Messiah (called Christ) is coming. When He comes, He will explain everything to us." Then Jesus declared, "I Who speak to you am He" (read John 4:25-26).

And really, Friends, back to the prayer meeting, that eight hours in The Secret Place, I thought of a lot of things. I thought of everything I had done wrong, every thought and every action, that I found out was not good. It was the presence of the Lord, no doubt, that had brought it to my attention. So when Jesus comes to you, you may sometimes hear things about yourself that is necessary for you to be reminded of. There's One Who knows all about you. One Who is interested in you and is offering you living water now, also, as there at the well.

So when Jesus was through talking to the little lady "she left her waterpot, and went her way into the city, and saith to the men, Come, see a man, which told me all things that ever I did: is not this the Christ?" (John 4:28-29). Well you can say a whole lot of things along that line...to think about hearing somebody tell you everything you've ever done. Who wants to hear that? But that's what the Lord wants us to recognize. He knows all about us. He knows all about us whether we tell Him or not.

And with this experience she had at the well, which we'd now like to say from The Secret Place, she told people in the city of Samaria. "And many of the Samaritans of that city believed on Him for the saying of the woman, which testified, He told me all that ever I did. So when the Samaritans were come unto Him, they besought Him that He would tarry with them: and He abode there two days. And many more believed because of His own word; And said unto the woman, Now we believe, not because of thy saying: for we have heard Him ourselves, and know that this is indeed the Christ, the Saviour of the world" (John 4:39-42).

I'll tell you Friends, that's exactly what we desire to relate to you. It's not altogether what others have said, but we have heard from the Lord, too. That's the purpose of Jesus coming. That's the purpose of His patience and long suffering today.

He wants us all to hear the voice of the Lord. May you hear something and receive something as you read the pages of *Stones From The Secret Place.*

I will relate more and more, but at the same time, I do want to say that at that first time and that one visit in the presence of the Lord, my heart was changed. I was amazed to end that day with a hunger for God that I tell you still reaches out today...that thirst for God.

I shall never forget it, and it might be worthwhile to relate. I had joined a certain church when I was 13. I do not blame the church, but I do say this, I didn't know how to take hold of the Lord by faith and no one told me. All they asked was if I wanted to accept the Lord. I said, "Yes, and I want to join the church." They asked, "Do you want to be baptized?" I said, "Yes." All of that is very clear teaching. We need that. We need those questions asked to us, but we need a follow up on how to receive the Lord...how to accept Him by faith.

So, with this great desire to please God, I really felt it was all up to me to do the rest. I got me a little New Testament, and I began to seek to be different. But I did not know how to lay hold of truth, so in a very short few weeks, I had misplaced my little New Testament. A little opposition rose up between other brothers and sisters. They questioned why I still acted like I did if I had joined the church. They said, "Oh, you joined the church. Look at you now." I had lost my temper, you see. I had reacted in a way that they themselves wondered if the church meant anything to me.

I traveled that road for about two years until the testimony of one who had actually come from The Secret Place, and my little sister from a prayer meeting the evening before, actually put a thirst in my heart that lasted. I began to seek the Lord, and their words of exhortation to me were like this, "I saw you in prayer at home." We didn't have a church to go to then to reach out for God like we wanted to, so we took it to the Lord in prayer. That's why The Secret Place means and spells out so much to me today because that's where really I got born again. I got my sins forgiven. And I got a relationship with the Lord that gave me a peace and a hunger and a thirst for more of God in such a way that I began to pursue the Lord almost day and night when I'd come in from school.

The three that had been saved and filled in the Spirit in our home were continuing their relationship. That certainly helped me to pray and to seek the Lord because I knew I was saved, but I knew I didn't have that relationship of being filled with the Spirit. I read later in the Bible how the world cannot receive that. He says we that receive it are not of the world. We've been saved. We have, through faith in God, had our sins taken away and blotted out. We have a peace, and it's left us with a hunger that we had never had before…and that's to know more about Jesus. So, my Friends, we will be saying a lot about those eight hours…the very roots of The Secret Place and what it means.

I began to seek the Lord and ask that He would fill me with the Spirit. My sister would say, "John, just surrender all." Whatever that means. Remember that's the first time I'd ever heard anybody say, "Surrender all, John. Just seek Him with all your heart." Well that's the first time I'd heard that. I'd heard them say, "You want to accept the Lord." But I never had heard, "Seek Him with all your heart. Surrender to the Lord. He loves you. He wants to help you. He'll save you. Keep your mind on the Lord." I called those words of exhortation.

It was back there that I heard in my first time in The Secret Place what I call my ABC's. I explained that relationship as when I went to school I really had learned to say my ABC's before I went to school. I really felt proud of my education, but I knew there was more yet to learn. Whenever the spelling teacher asked us to spell words, then to reach into that alphabet and take out the right letter to spell that word, that's when I saw the need of more study. So after we got saved and turned our hearts to the Lord, we were aware very quickly that there was more yet for us from the Lord and to seek after God. Oh how beautiful it has been!

Friends, do keep following on in The Secret Place and this book, *Stones From The Secret Place*. I believe it will help you and me because, to this very day, if we're sitting here unhappy or dissatisfied, if we're sitting here with a knowing that God has yet more in store for us...we shall have that satisfaction as we follow on. So, follow on and let's enjoy together wonderful experiences, changes that have taken place, strength that came, encouragement that came, even along with tears and hardships and trials.

I found His peace in The Secret Place and then to read and to find scriptures later to say to me, "When you seek the Lord, enter into your closet and shut the door and seek Him in secret" (read Matthew 6:6).

I'll tell you, there's more to that than just words. God bless us as we move on down the road and on into The Secret Place. *There's more yet to come!*

To Get What God Has For Us, The Pathway Will Be Strange To The Natural Man.

-J. E. Murdock

– 2 –

THE BREAD THAT I GIVE YOU WILL EAT AND NOT DIE

I know of no other scriptures that offer so much as these in John 6 where Jesus tells us, "Verily, verily, I say unto you, he that believeth on Me hath everlasting life. I am that bread of life" (John 6:47-48). Then He goes on a little further in verse 58 and says, "This is that bread which came down from heaven: not as your fathers did eat manna, and are dead: he that eateth of this bread shall live for ever." He says, "I am the living bread which came down from heaven: if any man eat of this bread, he shall live for ever: and the bread that I will give is My flesh, which I will give for the life of the world" (John 6:51).

I never shall forget one of the greatest experiences that I had shortly after I had given my life over to the Lord. I actually was just a young fellow. I hadn't even gotten married. But I loved the presence of the Lord in our home. We didn't have a church to go to.

One Saturday afternoon after I had done the work my dad had assigned me to do as a little farm boy, I wanted to go to town. I was living a Christian life. I was serving the Lord and the Lord was very real to me, but I knew a lot of friends there in town. I loved to play ball, and I loved to talk about the Lord when I found someone who enjoyed the Lord. So, I decided every Saturday evening after I'd done my work at home, it was no problem to go to town.

About the first or second week, after I had been saved and turned to the Lord, I was getting ready to go to town. I was not going to do anything wrong, and there was nothing wrong about going to town. I was just going to go stand around and visit with my friends.

Then, the still small voice in my heart, the Holy Spirit,

just spoke very gently. I didn't have to have anybody else to tell me this, and I'm not quoting what somebody else said. The Spirit of the Lord actually seemed to speak to me and say, "Had you rather go to town and stand around on the streets and talk to the people, or had you rather take My Word and go down into the woods and pray and seek Me?" I had prayed there in the woods often. It was not a voice saying, "You'd better go down into the woods" or "You'd better not go to town." It was just like a little soft voice. I didn't hear it audibly, but it came into my spirit, "Had you rather?"

Well really, as a young man then, there was something in me that wanted to go to town. But there was something else in me that wanted to go into the woods and wait on the Lord. I knew what that was, too. I'd already experienced that. So I said to myself, "I believe I'll go down in the woods on the creek. I'll sit there and wait on the Lord and read His Word instead of going to town." No one else was against me going to town, and nothing was wrong, as far as I know, about going to town. But this other seemed to be the best choice to make. Go and sit down on the bank of the creek and read His Word.

I shall never forget it. I went across the field and knelt down on the creek among the shady trees, laid my Bible down, and said, "Lord, let Your Word be real." I started reading His Word. I'd read one line in the Bible, and I would break weeping before the Lord. It was such a beautiful touch of God. Then I'd open my eyes and read another line, and the same thing would happen. I don't recall just how much of that chapter I read line upon line. When I'd read it, I would break before the Lord. I found out in those days crying...breaking before the Lord is good for you. I found out then, once and for all, how powerful and how real God's Word is.

Then I began to study His Word more than ever, get the touch and get inside God's message. We read in the Scripture where people were very concerned about the bread for the natural body. It seems that the top need of our time is to have plenty of bread on the table. If we have plenty of food in the pantry shelves and in the refrigerator, we feel like we are doing well. But really, friends, if we haven't gotten hold of the Word of the Lord, we haven't really gotten hold of the bread of life. And that's where the difference comes in. "For the bread of God is He which cometh down from heaven, and giveth life unto the world. Then said they unto Him, Lord, evermore give us this bread. And Jesus said unto them, I am the bread of life: he that cometh to Me shall never hunger; and he that believeth on Me shall never thirst" (John 6:33-35).

That's what I began to reflect on at an early age...what the Word of the Lord would mean.

In one place, it says the Word of the Lord is *like a hammer.* It can just break things away and break up the hard surface of our hearts and begin to bless us so God can get hold of our life. "Is not My Word like as a fire? saith the Lord; and like a hammer that breaketh the rock in pieces?" (Jeremiah 23:29). There's nothing like letting the Holy Spirit or the voice of God in your own heart talk to you, and that's what began to take place. From that moment on, I saw the importance of God's Word.

You cannot tell how powerful God's Word is until you taste of it. Until you get the feel of God's Word, it's hard to estimate the power of the Word of the Lord. It's like Job in his trial. He came out saying, "Oh, before this trial came, I just heard about the Lord, but since the trial has come, God has worked in such a way that I have truly seen the hand of the Lord." "I have heard of Thee by the hearing of the ear: but now mine eye seeth thee" (Job 42:5). And truly, my friends, whenever you and I can hear, it's a good thing, but I like to say that to see is to understand. Hear the Word and understand it! Actually, when we hear God's Word, that's good, but when we come to understand it, there's nothing better.

As the Word says, "No man spake like this man." And the Lord says, "The bread I give you is not like the bread that Moses called down whenever he was hungry in the wilderness. It's different than that." He said they ate that bread and they died. Though they had manna in the wilderness, they died because it couldn't give eternal life. He says, "This is the bread which cometh down from heaven, that a man may eat thereof, and not die" (John 6:50). That means His bread will give eternal life. Regardless of what happens in this world, His Word will prepare us for eternal life, and give us hope even in this frail body of ours. The Word of the Lord gives hope.

Peter must have recognized something about the Word of the Lord. At one point in Jesus' ministry, some people had heard so many things that they could hardly grasp that Jesus was really all that He confessed to be. Many of them turned away because He said a few things that offended them. When they began to turn away it was to the extent that Peter recognized, "Lord, there are many that are turning way from You." And Jesus said, "Well, will you turn away also?" And Peter said something that's good to think of and that's been proven. Peter says, "Lord, to whom shall we go? Thou hast the words of eternal life" (John 6:68).

Now He could multiply the loaves and the fishes. He could bless the garden of the man who was planting his garden. He could bless the field. He could bless every part of life.

To hear God's Word brings eternal life. So He says to us, "The bread that I give you, you will eat and not die." That means even while you are dead, yet ye live. He said, "Though they died, yet they speak" for there's a life in them that's given by the promises of God. It works in our life as we release His Word by faith in the Lord. How important it is for us to see that.

The Word says there are many voices in the land, and many will say, "I am the way." In fact Jesus says, "For many shall come in My name, saying, I am Christ; and shall deceive many" (Matthew 24:5). And some of them will say, "Come over here. Christ is over here." But remember this, only the Lord Himself has the words of eternal life. It doesn't mean that God has to speak in person, but God can cause His ministers to speak the word of the Lord, and, as the Word says, He'll confirm it to us. If they had believed what the prophets had to say, their peace would have been like a river. Why? It's the Word of the Lord. So, it's important for the believer today to catch on to how thirsty our world must be for this bread that we can eat and that gives us hope in the face of every trial...in the face of death itself. Only God's Word can give hope.

Everything that God created, He created by speaking The Word. "And God said, Let there be light: and there was light. And God saw the light, that it was good: and God divided the light from the darkness. And God called the light Day, and the darkness He called Night" (Genesis 1:3-5). And everything that was accomplished, everything today in the way of creation, He spoke it into existence. And when the Lord says today, for instance, "Thy sins be forgiven thee," that means He has power to speak the Word and take away condemnation and sin out of our life.

I can remember when I began to take hold of God's Word. By faith, I began to *hear* it. It began to *work* in my own heart and in my own life mightily. And so how the Lord wants to show you and I the difference that by laboring and seeking, reading, meditating in the law of God day and night...the Word can give life eternal. And He has given a Word that has promised to meet our needs while we are in this world, and at the same time, a Word that can prepare us for the world to come.

There were many of them that began to detect, "Lord, You speak like no other man speaks." When Jesus spoke, there was something about His message that was different than any other. And oh, it makes a difference even today. How blessed we are to be able to tell the difference between even the written Word of God and the word that's written that's really not the Word of God. For we are told there will be many who will wrest the Scriptures and twist them in such a way that it takes from them the affect that God wants it to have. We are told that. But if we can hear the voice of the Spirit of God, He'll speak the word that we need to hear. He'll speak in order that we can begin to understand it, and it will do things for us.

He says, "And Jesus said unto them, I am the bread of life: he that cometh to Me shall never hunger; and he that believeth on Me shall never thirst" (John 6:35). And when you think about what God has done for the human heart of those who have believed His Word, it should put you and I in pursuit after the things of God. We have really too few that have tasted of the Word of the Lord that gives hope of eternal life...His

306 – Dr. J. E. Murdock

Word that gives faith in His forgiveness. His Word that gives faith in His Second Coming... His returning back again. His Word says, "Call unto Me, and I will answer thee, and shew thee great and mighty things, which thou knowest not" (Jeremiah 33:3). Everything you have need of you will find written in the promises in the Word. How we need to study the Word!

In fact, the Bible speaks of the blessedness of the man who loves the Word. "But His delight is in the law of the Lord; and in His law doth he meditate day and night. And he shall be like a tree planted by the rivers of water, that bringeth forth his fruit in his season; his leaf also shall not wither; and whatsoever he doeth shall prosper" (Psalm 1:2-3).

Have you ever noticed, somewhere around your home or on the old farm place, the difference of a plant that was near the water where it could give life? And you're not shocked to find how it grows. What a difference in plants that are nourished by the water or the rain that falls from Heaven.

It's the same way with the Word. We can hear many voices, and the Word says there are many voices, but there's no voice like the Word of the Lord. He has the words of eternal life. And I'll tell you the day will come when every knee will bow when the Lord speaks. Every tongue will confess when the Lord speaks. "Wherefore God also hath highly exalted Him, and given Him a name which is above every name: That at the name of Jesus every knee should bow, of things in heaven, and things in earth, and things under the earth; And that every tongue should confess that Jesus Christ is Lord, to the glory of God the Father" (Philippians 2:9-11).

How important it is today while we can hear a word from God to take time to hear the Word. Often the Lord called to the seven churches in Revelation. He said, "He that hath an ear, let him hear what the Spirit saith unto the churches." And many of us have tasted and have witnessed already many times and many occasions what the word of the Lord has done.

Think of God taking men like Paul and Silas, men in the Scripture that were lost and undone, that didn't know God. The Word of the Lord was so real and so life giving to them that they could sing when they were put in prison for the cause of Christ. And some of them, like Stephen when he was stoned because of his faith in God, said, "Father, lay not this sin to their charge." Think of how powerful the Word worked in his life. Think of grace coming from the word of God and hope that builds such courage that Paul and Silas could even sing in prison and have life. "And at midnight Paul and Silas prayed, and sang praises unto God: and the prisoners heard them" (Acts 16:25).

And oh, we wouldn't argue the fact that there are people that can have plenty of this world's food and goods and then still pass away from this life. But the Word says that if we have the true bread, though we are dead, yet we are speaking, yet our hope is much alive because His Word is life and it gives life.

We beg of you today as never before to find out through reading the Word it's power. Begin to taste and witness how powerful the Word is. In fact, the Bible tells us beautiful things voiced by others after the death of Jesus, because it looked like truth had fallen in the streets. It looked like hope was gone. They said, "He promised life, and now He's in the tomb. What are we going to do?" But Jesus had said, "I'm going to be raised the third day. The tomb is not going to hold Me there. I am the resurrection. I proved it to you when I raised Lazarus from the dead." "I am the resurrection, and the life: he that believeth in Me, though he were dead, yet shall he live: And whosoever liveth and believeth in Me shall never die" (John 11:25-26). And just to think that actually while He was speaking, they were sorrowful.

As two of the disciples walked along on the Emmaus road and Jesus, The Resurrection, was raised from the dead, He walked along in their midst. He hid Himself in such a way they didn't know it was Jesus Whom that they had put in the tomb. And He asked them the question, "Why are you sorrowful?" They said, "Well, are you a stranger here that you do not know what happened? Jesus of Nazareth, the man that we thought was the Christ, they have taken Him and crucified Him. Our hearts are heavy." Jesus was there talking to them about it, but He hid Himself and they didn't know it was Him.

Oh, don't you hate to think that God would hide Himself? Don't you hate to think that we wouldn't discover truth, that we wouldn't recognize His Word? Oh, how blessed it is Jesus taught us to have ears to hear. But now He's talking to them. As they went on they entered into a village, and Jesus still hadn't revealed Himself. "And it came to pass, as He sat at meat with them, He took bread, and blessed it, and brake, and gave to them. And their eyes were opened, and they knew Him; and He vanished out of their sight. And they said one to another, Did not our heart burn within us, while He talked with us by the way, and while He opened to us the scriptures?" (Luke 24:30-32).

So, His Word still opens the eyes of our understanding. His Word is still real. If we'll follow on, the Holy Spirit can break the Word so that we'll know He's alive and we'll know He's coming back again.

Now the food and the prosperity and the things of this world do not promise that, do not give that. You'll meet no one who has hope of eternal life if they don't have Christ. Christ's Word gives hope and such hope that masters our life even in the midst of sorrow and disappointment and even death. We can say with Jesus, "Father, forgive them; for they know not what they do" (Luke 23:34). We can say with Job, "Though He slay me, yet will I trust in Him:" (Job 13:15), and as Stephen who, in the very midst of his persecution, said, "Lord, lay not this sin to their charge."

So if you want to find out if God's Word is still working, just walk down the street a little way. You'll find somebody that has heard the voice of the Lord. He still speaks. And then pray that we'll hear His voice, and we'll understand His voice. Really that's what The Secret Place is about, and that's to get alone with God and seek Him in secret, and He will reward us openly. I've had great touches of God and His Word that have made me a strong believer from my boyhood that God still works. So in all of our getting, understand this, we can eat of this Word, the Bible says, and not die.

He made it clear to us that all the things that God had

done for Israel under the leadership of Moses, getting them bread that wasn't from Heaven...they ate that manna that fell from Heaven and they died. But He says if you eat this Bread that I give you, My Word that I give you...

▶ It will *build courage,*

▶ It will help you *not* to be faint-hearted,

▶ It will *strengthen* you,

▶ It will give you *life,*

▶ It will bring the *resurrection life to you,* and even when we pass from this life, we'll awaken in His likeness.

With that hope, it works in the believer mightily. The Bible says he that hath the hope that God gives in His Word will perfect himself...he will draw nigh to God. "For the law made nothing perfect, but the bringing in of a better hope did; by the which we draw nigh unto God" (Hebrews 7:19).

He that does the will of God will purify himself knowing this that the Word of the Lord is true. All will stand before the judgment and all that's right will make Heaven their home. All that's wrong and refuse to make things right will spend eternity away from God. "For we shall all stand before the judgment seat of Christ. For it is written, As I live, saith the Lord, every knee shall bow to Me, and every tongue shall confess to God. So then every one of us shall give account of himself to God...For the kingdom of God is not meat and drink; but righteousness, and peace, and joy in the Holy Ghost" (Romans 14:10-12,17).

So let's take the Word. Let's have faith in God's Word. As the Bible says, "O taste and see that the Lord is good: blessed is the man that trusteth in Him. O fear the Lord, ye His saints: for there is no want to them that fear" (Psalm 34:8-9).

"The fear of the Lord is the beginning of wisdom: and the knowledge of the Holy is understanding" (Proverbs 9:10). There are hearts that have been changed, lives that have changed, and lives have been surrendered all because of the influence and the power of this Bread that we can eat from the Word of God. It gives life. I can testify to that truth. He'll give you life, too. Read on and move on and get alone with the Lord in The Secret Place!

Only
God's Word
Can Give Hope.

-J. E. Murdock

⫸ 3 ⫷

HOW CAN YOU LOVE HIM WHOM YOU HAVEN'T SEEN?

I find out a lot of times in The Secret Place God, through the Spirit, will reason with us on things. That's what we find in this heading and message of The Secret Place. "How Do We Expect To Love Someone Whom We Haven't Seen If We Can't Love Someone Whom We Have Seen?"

There's nothing more powerful, more rewarding and stricter in a person's life than the love of God. That's why all things actually are set forth to us because of love. "We love Him, because He first loved us. "If a man say, I love God, and hateth his brother, he is a liar: for he that loveth not his brother whom he hath seen, how can he love God Whom he hath not seen? And this commandment have we from Him, That he who loveth God love his brother also" (1 John 4:19-21).

I shall never forget a few times how the Lord spoke to me about the importance of a relationship with God that spreads our love towards our fellow man. After I found this out, I try to daily live in that place where God's love, not what I try to love, would be free to flow in my life. For we have been in The Secret Place long enough to know that God knows all about us. He cares, and He wants us to be able to receive from Him the greatest reward that He has for us. So the question is, "How Can We Expect To Love Someone That We Haven't Seen If We Don't Love Him Whom We Have Seen?"

Actually, that Scripture in 1 John 4 seems to bring out to us this question. How can we expect to stretch ourselves to love some we know who are very unloveable if we haven't had the love of Christ shed abroad in our hearts by the Holy Spirit? "And hope maketh not ashamed; because the love of God is shed abroad in our hearts by the Holy Ghost which is given unto us" (Romans 5:5). That's the life of the Lord. Really, we don't put on His life. It's His life that is manifested through us.

The Word reveals how Jesus dealt with those that were disrespectful to Him and how He answered so gracefully those who had rejected Him. We find out that it's truly a manifestation of God's life in Jesus. How did Jesus know how to flee from those who rejected Him and hated Him and those who would kill or destroy Him? I fully believe that the way Jesus was able to shoulder the great responsibility of walking against the currents and the winds that blew against Him in life was because He spent His nights in prayer.

I really don't think that He was praying all the time, "Father, prove that I'm Yours by healing the lame and the halt and the blind." I believe that He actually focused on the will of the Father. He was sold on the fact that if He would do the will of the Father, He had the Father's approval. He knew He then would have everything He needed to fulfill the Father's will. "I must work the works of Him that sent Me, while it is day: the night cometh, when no man can work" (John 9:4).

Doing the will of the Father still gets us out of trouble, and, more than that, doing the will of the Father can keep us out of trouble. What I mean by trouble is when we are displeasing the Father. We've used the statement much along the way of how the Lord takes giant steps with us. In other words, we are called upon to measure up to a measurement and to a place of maturity in Him. "Not every one that saith unto Me, Lord, shall enter into the kingdom of heaven; but he that doeth the will of My Father which is in heaven" (Matthew 7:21).

How can you love God Whom you haven't seen...you've just heard about Him...if you don't love him whom you have seen? I really think that the Lord is not trying to say something to us to shame us. I think that He's trying to reveal to us the need of loving our brother if we expect to have God's approval. He's saying, "Don't be shocked if you don't obey or pay attention or pursue Me, One Whom you haven't seen, if you don't pay attention to others."

We're actually told in the Scripture of the importance of the child of God who has a message, a visitation from God. It says if you don't hear them, how can you hear One that you have never seen, you have never met? "Ye are of God, little children, and have overcome them: because greater is He that is in you, than he that is in the world. They are of the world: therefore speak they of the world, and the world heareth them. We are of God: he that knoweth God heareth us; he that is not of God heareth not us. Hereby know we the spirit of truth, and the spirit of error" (1 John 4:4-6).

You know there was a man the Bible says who ended up in eternity without God in the place called hell. He was in torment. He said, "I'm locked in." Then he said, "I pray thee therefore, father, that thou wouldest send him to my father's house: For I have five brethren; that he may testify unto them, lest they also come into this place of torment" (Luke 16:27,28).

He sees Lazarus and he says, "Send Lazarus, one that's already raised from the dead, to my five brothers and they will believe him." Abraham said to him, "They have Moses and the prophets; let them hear them. And he said, Nay, father Abraham: but if one went unto them from the dead, they will repent. And he said unto him, If they hear not Moses and the prophets, neither will they be persuaded, though one rose from the dead" (Luke 16:29-31). Abraham was saying, "No, they have the prophets...someone they can look at in the face, someone they can sit in the pew and hear, someone whose writings they can read, someone they can know personally."

So really, God is trying to emphasize through 1 John the importance of knowing the Lord. We can know Him to the extent that we can trust His grace to do what is impossible for us to do. And that's to love others who don't love us. So we have actually felt blessed to see and understand the possibilities of loving those who don't love us.

I never will forget. I was in prayer many years ago concerning an in-law of our family who was mistreating one of my loved ones. I was a Christian, but I just didn't like the person at all. So in The Secret Place seeking the Lord, He was mindful of my need of grace to care for this person. They were wrong, but His grace enabled me to care for them in the face of their wrong and pray that God could help them.

While I was thinking over the seriousness of abusing and hurting my own testimony by not going God's way towards the person, I seemed to have a revelation. In my spirit I saw this person in great tribulation. The expression he had on his face caused a sorrow and pity to come over me in my heart for him. I never felt the same again. It wasn't that I accepted his way, but it was looking at him in a way of saying, "Be merciful to him, Lord. Help him to turn to You. Help him to be saved." It was altogether a different feeling, just like another world I was drifting into.

So in our day, God knows we can't love the love He has without His love. And the Bible said that His love can be shed abroad in our heart by the Holy Spirit. There's nothing more wonderful to get the feeling of love for those that don't love you. It doesn't mean at all that you are endorsing the wrong, but there's something about love that makes you comfortable.

I think what makes us comfortable in our relationship with God is to have a right relationship with others. If we have a wrong relationship with others and a wrong attitude, it isn't long until we question our love for God. "Beloved, let us love one another: for love is of God; and every one that loveth is born of God, and knoweth God. He that loveth not knoweth not God; for God is love. In this was manifested the love of God toward us, because that God sent His only begotten Son into the world, that we might live through Him. Herein is love, not that we loved God, but that He loved us, and sent His Son to be the propitiation for our sins. Beloved, if God so loved us, we ought also to love one another. No man hath seen God at any time. If we love one another, God dwelleth in us, and His love is perfected in us" (1 John 4:7-12).

The question was, "How can you love Him Whom you have not seen, if you don't love him whom you have seen?" Now He is not trying to introduce you and I to a life of love apart from Him. He wants you and I to recognize His love. While we were yet sinners, He died for us. He forgave us and He seeks to save us. In this world, that kind of touch of the Lord's love in our heart toward others solves and gives us the answer to "How can we love Him Whom we haven't seen if we don't love him whom we have seen?"

If we don't love our brother, we are short of the relationship with God that we have need of. We need to understand the reproofs of God without being offended and accept the question and study it over seriously. He doesn't expect us to love Him, Whom we haven't seen, if we don't love those whom we have seen. Neither does He expect us to love our brothers, whom we have seen, if our relationship with Him hasn't imparted His love in our hearts so that we can forgive others even as the Father has forgiven us. We can go on in this life as a true example of Christ who shed His love abroad in our hearts through the Holy Spirit. We can, through this love, forgive others their trespasses as the Father has forgiven us.

I find the seriousness of the statement so much that I realize the importance of His love and the importance of knowing Him in order to have His love. That relationship with Him is so important that I've used this statement, "How to keep the forgiveness God has given us...how to keep it in force...how to continue to enjoy the forgiveness God has given us." We find the answer in this parable the Lord spoke.

"Therefore is the kingdom of heaven likened unto a certain king, which would take account of his servants. And when he had begun to reckon, one was brought unto him, which owed him ten thousand talents. But forasmuch as he had not to pay, his lord commanded him to be sold, and his wife, and children, and all that he had, and payment to be made. The servant therefore fell down, and worshipped him, saying, Lord, have patience with me, and I will pay thee all. Then the lord of that servant was moved with compassion, and loosed him, and forgave him the debt" (Matthew 18:23-27).

The Lord of that servant felt such sincere compassion for this old sinner that he says, "I'll tell you what I'm going to do. I'm going to forgive you that debt. I'm going to do it, and you won't have to pay it." He didn't wait on him to pay. He just said, "Just forget it. You don't owe it." What a beautiful place to rejoice. What a beautiful answer. What beautiful results we get sometimes when we cry out to God.

But, when we do that and we receive mercy, then we are responsible to show mercy to others. "But the same servant went out, and found one of his fellowservants, which owed him an hundred pence: and he laid hands on him, and took him by the throat, saying, Pay me that thou owest" (Matthew 18:28).

Now the Lord is trying to make us understand that He's not trying to get us to do things and minister to others what we haven't had ministered to us. But when we've had the Lord's forgiveness, then we're responsible to forgive others. "Then his lord, after that he had called him, said unto him, O thou wicked servant, I forgave thee all that debt, because thou desiredst me: Shouldest not thou also have had compassion on thy fellowservant, even as I had pity on thee? And his lord was wroth, and delivered him to the tormentors, till he should pay all that was due unto him. So likewise shall my heavenly Father do also unto you, if ye from your hearts forgive not every one his brother their trespasses" (Matthew 18:32-35).

I asked the question, "How can you love someone that you haven't seen?" You say you love God, but you hate your neighbor. How does that work? How can you do that? He certainly does explain the importance of having a relationship with God so that the Holy Spirit can enable us to forgive others the same as God has forgiven us.

So study that question again. Hold it in The Secret Place if it's not clear. Hold it before you as you get before the Lord. Think it over clearly. God's not trying to put us down. God's trying to show us the necessity of having a relationship with Him, or we can never, never help others even though we've been helped. We must come to have the love of God shed abroad in our heart.

We must know more than what to do for it to count. We must have the grace of God to do what He requires. And we get that grace by getting away in The Secret Place, and telling God, "I'm having trouble, Lord, forgiving someone who is continually doing me wrong. They ask me once in a while to forgive them, but I think I've gone far enough. Help me here,

Lord." And the Lord will help you to forgive to a measure you'll be so proud of. You'll be so thankful for you and I never cease to be helped by a measure. Any measure of relationship we've had from the Lord, if we've still got it, will work for us if that relationship was once strong enough to love those you didn't know. Somehow you find God in doubt of your love for Him because of the way you treat others.

Now is the best time in the world to steal away before the Lord and say, "Lord, I know I'm supposed to love them. In the natural that's impossible, but according to your word, You loved others that hated You. Now let that life come forth in me so that I can, not only be blessed here, but I can so let my light shine when I leave The Secret Place so that others will know I've been with You."

It's all for us, and it's not far off. Those who enter the closet and shut the door and seek Him in secret, He'll reward openly. The shock of your life...the joy and peace of your life will come when you find you love your enemies. You will then have more faith that the love you said you had for God is real. Love can all be found in The Secret Place!

Don't Labor
In Vain...
Labor In Love.

-J. E. Murdock

— 4 —

IF YOU SEE ME WHEN I'M TAKEN

These are Scriptures that, while waiting on the Lord in prayer, have really come alive to me. In fact, our early experience in the Lord took place when we waited on God in prayer. We began to find it was very scriptural that men should always pray and never to faint. We came to places we would have fainted if we had not prayed. But, we saw the importance of believing that truth, and we began to keep our eyes on the Lord through staying and tarrying in The Secret Place waiting upon the Lord.

Now this scripture today that has been so inspired as we waited upon Him is another Stone From The Secret Place. A stone that carries a message, a stone that represents a message, a stone that reminds us of the importance of obeying God every step of the way. You know it's so easy to start out. And it comes to mind that when Peter was standing on his boat, along with the other apostles, they looked out and saw Jesus walking on the water.   At first they were much afraid and the Lord spoke to them and said, "Be not afraid. It is I." Peter got a glimpse of Him and said, "That is the Lord." And he put an if with it, he says, "If that be You, bid me come." And the Lord says, "Come on." So now then he is seeing the Lord on the water to the extent he's ready to step out on the waves.

But, we're going to find later the importance of keeping Jesus before you, of seeing the Lord all the way. The rest of the way. It's good to see the Lord when the impossible is taking place, but when the tests come, that is the time our faith must begin to operate. Faith in what? Faith in the Lord Who walked on the water. Faith in the Lord Who could sleep in the midst of the storm.

This scripture is a statement that Elijah in the book of 2 Kings related to Elisha. These two prophets of God and ministers of the Lord were walking along together. A latter day had come upon Elijah. Elijah had experienced a lot of things and his very life reflected the human side as a person like you and I. He was a person that could get afraid. He was a person that could get discouraged. But, he was also a person who could stay before the Lord and get prayers through. He was a man, as the word says in James, of like passion as we are, but he prayed and things were done.

So we can't say, "Oh well, if I had the chance that Elijah had, I could find myself in his shoes now at the end of the way." But, Friends, you and I can have that ending if we will walk daily, and, even in the midst of our trial, we'll cry out to God. See Elijah had a feeling that he was the only one left who was actually following God. But the Lord broke the news to him in the midst of his terrible shake up when he thought he was alone and everybody else against the Lord. But the Lord spoke to him. "Yet I have left Me seven thousand in Israel, all the knees which have not bowed unto Baal, and every mouth which hath not kissed him" (1 Kings 19:18).

The Lord said, "You're not really alone. They're not around you, they're not cheering you, but they're there. And now arise and eat." The only way I can rejoice and enjoy what he ate is to see the result of it. It must have been good because the Bible says he ate and he went 40 days in the strength of what the Lord gave him when he was discouraged. "And he arose, and did eat and drink, and went in the strength of that meat forty days and forty nights unto Horeb the mount of God" (1 Kings 19:8).

But going on with the thought, "If You See Me When I Am Taken." While they were in route from the Gilgal to Bethel to Jericho and to Jordan, these different places, they stopped before Elijah was to cross over the Jordan and be taken up to Heaven. There were some sons of the prophets in each place who said to him, "Didn't you know that Elijah, your master, is going to be taken from you?" Elisha would only answer, "Yea, I know it. Hold your peace." He didn't enter into a conversation with others I noticed because he had one goal in mind and that was to follow this man, Elijah.

I believe he had enough revelation and a witness to know that there was something in store for him if he'd just follow on. God wanted him to follow on, no doubt, and not be discouraged when Elijah said three times as they were traveling from Bethel, to Jericho to Jordan, "Tarry here, Elisha." Each time Elisha would say, "As the Lord liveth, and as thy soul liveth, I will not leave thee."

Then, he comes to the place we all like to have brought to our attention every day. We like to quote this scripture because it's so true, it's so real, so helpful, so encouraging to us. "Ask what you will and it shall be done." We like to quote that every day of the week, but this opportunity didn't come to Elisha until he had shown a determination that he was going to go on. He didn't say, "Elijah, I'm not going to go any further if you don't promise that you're going to do this for me." He didn't do that. He knew that there would be a rewarding moment...if he'd just follow on.

That's the reason we encourage people not to faint when their third prayer isn't heard. Don't faint, my friends, until you get an answer...whether it's the answer you want or whether it's the answer you didn't intend to get. The answer the Lord gives you will help you keep your faith in God whether He answers it like you want or He doesn't. But, He'll have a plan.

So, here they go. Elisha had no opportunity to ask or tell Elijah what he wanted out of the walk. He was to just stay with the walk. We don't wait like that, do we, folks? We hardly hit The Secret Place until we are telling God what we want. But the Lord knows how frail we are. That's the reason He's long suffering and patient with us.

I never will forget how I wanted to drive the old Model T truck my dad bought when I was growing up. I'd get out there and just work my feet fast on the clutches, and I'd make sounds like that old car. I looked forward to the day when I could drive it. And a lot of times we get to the place where we say, "Oh, dear Lord, give me this, give me that." We are pretty much like the younger son that Jesus mentioned. "And the younger of them said to his father, Father, give me the portion of goods that falleth to me. And he divided unto them his living. And not many days after the younger son gathered all together, and took his journey into a far country, and there wasted his substance with riotous living" (Luke 15:12-13).

We're really not in position to take care of what God has given us. If He blesses us with important things down through life too soon, we will actually lose them before we need them. God knows how to grow us, doesn't He? That's why we've used the statement, "Lift the pressure off your faith with patience."

No doubt Elisha was aiming at something that God had impressed him to receive, or to pick up and continue the work and ministry of Elijah. Since Elijah was going to be called away, he was to carry on. So, he had something in mind, but he never was asked the question until they crossed over the Jordan. What do I see in that? They crossed over the Jordan. God has a real place He wants to reward us. He wants to bring us to a certain place. Now the Bible speaks of Jordan as a type of the world He wants us to cross. He says, "Come out from among them, and be ye separate, saith the Lord, and touch not the unclean thing; and I will receive you, And will be a Father unto you, and ye shall be my sons and daughters, saith the Lord Almighty" (2 Corinthians 6:17-18).

It appears that Elijah never had received Elisha until he got over Jordan. Now, instead of telling him stay here, he is saying, "What do you want me to do for you before I am taken?" That's another thing, friends, that if we'll tarry in The Secret Place long enough, we'll be praying and focusing in the right direction and for the right thing. Best of all, He'll prepare us to receive, and we won't spend it and throw it away in riotous living. Don't we need to grow so we can come to the point where we know the time has come we can handle things? We know the time has come that receiving is important.

God is patient to take away things that are not right for us. Why don't we be patient enough to wait and receive what is right? "They that wait on the Lord"…He will offer something good to us. So many follow on and never get anywhere. They even get to the door, and know what it takes and still don't have it all because they didn't prepare for it.

But Elisha is making preparation. Brother he's not letting the encouragement of Elijah to "stay here while I go to Bethel...stay here while I go to Jericho...stay here while I go to Jordan," stop him. He didn't tell him to "stay here" now at Jordan. He didn't say, "Come on, let's go." He raised up his mantle, and knew, "There's no use to say more. If he's going to go across with me, he's ready." "Fifty men of the sons of the prophets went, and stood to view afar off: and they two stood by Jordan. And Elijah took his mantle, and wrapped it together, and smote the waters, and they were divided hither and thither, so that they two went over on dry ground. And it came to pass, when they were gone over, that Elijah said unto Elisha, Ask what I shall do for thee, before I be taken away from thee" (2 Kings 2:7-9).

So he goes on across and Elisha is right behind him. They talked along after they got out of Jordan, and began to talk together. How beautiful. Wouldn't you love to talk to someone that's about to go in the air to meet the Lord in a few minutes? "And it came to pass, when they were gone over, that Elijah said unto Elisha, Ask what I shall do for thee, before I be taken away from thee? And Elisha said, I pray thee, let a double portion of thy spirit be upon me." He said, "I want a double portion of the Spirit that's resting upon you."

You know, the Word does say "ask ye largely." He wants to do abundantly, but too often we leave before we get enough. We need to stay there until we are able to make the trip. We need to stay before God until strength is renewed. We will learn that if we stay in The Secret Place long enough. And we'll be able to apply that knowledge if we stay there long enough. God's presence will build us to qualify, not only to follow on, but to receive. And not only to receive, but to be able to handle that which we receive.

More and more I've said to myself, "Maybe if I'd have been a minister who was able to have thousands of people in my services, I might have begun to bend and compromise in a way to keep those thousands with me. I might have found myself compromising the truth that's able to keep me when I'm having to walk alone." So, I believe it was the wisdom of God to show Himself strong in my behalf to surrender to Him. At whatever path He led me through, to be contented in Him and in letting His presence satisfy.

Jesus, when He was told that many people were leaving Him, said, "I haven't lost any that the Father gave Me, and I'm satisfied with what the Father does." "I came down from heaven, not to do Mine Own will, but the will of Him that sent Me. And this is the Father's will which hath sent Me, that of all which He hath given me I should lose nothing, but should raise it up again at the last day. And this is the will of Him that sent Me, that every one which seeth the Son, and believeth on Him, may have everlasting life: and I will raise him up at the last day."

That's the place we need to be. "What and if ye shall see the Son of man ascend up where He was before? It is the Spirit that quickeneth; the flesh profiteth nothing: the words that I speak unto you, they are spirit, and they are life...And He said, Therefore said I unto you, that no man can come unto Me, except it were given unto him of My Father. From that time many of His disciples went back, and walked no more with Him. Then said Jesus unto the twelve, Will ye also go away? Then Simon Peter answered Him, Lord, to whom shall we go? Thou hast the words of eternal life" (John 6:38-40,62-63,65-68).

So, friends, to get what God has for us, the pathway will be strange to the natural. That's why we should say daily in The Secret Place, "Lord, don't be silent to me. Keep working with me. Be patient with me." "Then Jesus said unto them, Verily, verily, I say unto you, Except ye eat the flesh of the Son of man, and drink His blood, ye have no life in you. Whoso eateth My flesh, and drinketh My blood, hath eternal life; and I will raise him up at the last day. For My flesh is meat indeed, and My blood is drink indeed. He that eateth My flesh, and drinketh My blood, dwelleth in Me, and I in him. As the living Father hath sent Me, and I live by the Father so he that eateth

Me, even he shall live by Me" (John 6:53-57).

Pray, "Work in me to will and to do of Your good pleasure." "Being found in fashion as a man, He humbled Himself, and became obedient unto death, even the death of the cross. Wherefore God also hath highly exalted Him, and given Him a name which is above every name: That at the name of Jesus every knee should bow, of things in heaven, and things in earth, and things under the earth; And that every tongue should confess that Jesus Christ is Lord, to the glory of God the Father. Wherefore, My beloved, as ye have always obeyed, not as in My presence only, but now much more in My absence, work out your own salvation with fear and trembling. For it is God which worketh in you both to will and to do of His good pleasure" (Philippians 2:8-13).

Can you see two of those fellows walking along now? They'd already passed by the prophets of Jericho. They've already gone on across Jordan. Now they're walking along together. Elijah said, "Thou hast asked a hard thing: nevertheless, if thou see me when I am taken from thee, it shall be so unto thee; but if not, it shall not be so. And it came to pass, as they still went on, and talked, that, behold, there appeared a chariot of fire, and horses of fire, and parted them both asunder; and Elijah went up by a whirlwind into heaven" (2 Kings 2:10-11).

Suddenly the angel of the Lord comes down in a chariot and just sweeps Elijah away, and he's out of sight. I think that's one reason it was necessary for Elijah to tell him, "If you see me, oh boy, you're going to have to be watching. You asked a hard thing." And Elisha saw it, and he cried, "My father, my father, the chariot of Israel, and the horsemen thereof. And he saw him no more."

You know people used to look for the coming of the Lord, but they're not looking any more. And the Bible warns us of that. He's coming for those that love His appearing...not who loved Him last year, not who loved Him 20 years ago, but who love Him to the end. "Henceforth there is laid up for me a crown of righteousness, which the Lord, the righteous judge, shall give me at that day: and not to me only, but unto all them also that love His appearing" (2 Timothy 4:8).

Eagerly watch. Expect His return. Be ready to meet Him. Follow Him all the way. "For Christ did not enter a holy place made with hands, a mere copy of the true one, but into heaven itself, now to appear in the presence of God for us...now once at the comsumation of the ages He has been manifested to put away sin by the sacrifice of Himself. And inasmuch as it is appointed for men to die once and after this comes judgment, so Christ also having been offered once to bear the sins of many, will appear a second time for salvation without reference to sin, to those who eagerly await Him" (read Hebrews 9:24-28).

The Lord called a little early in Matthew 25. He gave all the virgins a little time to look around and see how things were. And the Bible said the foolish virgins found out their oil lamps had gone out. And in their pursuit quickly to get their oil, the Lord came. "And while they went to buy, the bridegroom came; and they that were ready went in with Him to the marriage: and the door was shut. Afterward came also the other virgins, saying, Lord, Lord, open to us. But He answered and said, Verily I say unto you, I know you not. Watch therefore, for ye know neither the day nor the hour wherein the Son of man cometh" (Matthew 25:10-13).

Ah, he believed, but he didn't see. He wasn't ready when He came. "But If You See Me When I Am Taken." I wish we could just grasp really the importance of keeping our eyes on the Lord. Keeping our minds on Him. Not turning aside or looking back. Just a little distance more and Mrs. Lot would have been just as safe as Lot, but she just decided to look back. I don't think she says, "I'm going to go back." She just looked back. She didn't see the importance of going on...and she turned to a pillar of salt.

Elisha is still going on, and just as soon as it happened, he got busy. Elijah is already gone, but he saw him when he left. And he saw the mantle of Elijah. He pulled off the mantle that was on him and put on the mantle of Elijah. "He took hold of his own clothes, and rent them in two pieces. He took up also the mantle of Elijah that fell from him, and went back, and stood by the bank of Jordan; And he took the mantle of

Elijah that fell from him, and smote the waters, and said, Where is the Lord God of Elijah? and when he also had smitten the waters, they parted hither and thither: and Elisha went over" (2 Kings 2:12-14).

We must let The Secret Place and the revelation of truth and the impartation of The Secret Place work in our lives. Now, we see that Elisha picked up the responsibility and the ministry of Elijah, but he's got a double portion of the Spirit. He's going to meet some children as he crosses over who laugh at him. "And he went up from thence unto Bethel: and as he was going up by the way, there came forth little children out of the city, and mocked him, and said unto him, Go up, thou bald head; go up, thou bald head" (2 Kings 2:23). But, Elijah has what it takes to handle them.

So Friends, let's you and I stay in The Secret Place until we get what it takes...because I'll tell you, there's going to be some contrary winds to blow. They may blow from directions that will be hard to take, but let's live in that place where God can impart to you and me what it takes. "Raise the war cry, you nations, and be shattered! Listen, all you distant lands. Prepare for battle, and be shattered! Prepare for battle, and be shattered! Devise your strategy, but it will be thwarted; propose your plan, but it will not stand, for God is with us. The Lord spoke to me with His strong hand upon me, warning me not to follow the way of this people. He said: Do not call conspiracy everything that these people call conspiracy; do not fear what they fear, and do not dread it. The Lord Almighty is the One you are to regard as holy, He is the One you are to fear, He is the One you are to dread, and He will be a sanctuary...

Bind up the testimony and seal up the law among My disciples. I will wait for the Lord, Who is hiding His face from the house of Jacob. I will put my trust in Him. Here am I, and the children the Lord has given me. We are signs and symbols in Israel from the Lord Almighty, Who dwells on Mount Zion. When men tell you to consult mediums and spiritists, who whisper and mutter, should not a people inquire of their God? Why consult the dead on behalf of the living? To the law and to the testimony! If they do not speak according to this word, they have no light of dawn" (read Isaiah 8:9-20).

And the Bible says it takes waiting on the Lord until we are endued with power from on high. "He giveth power to the faint; and to them that have no might He increaseth strength. Even the youths shall faint and be weary, and the young men shall utterly fall: But they that wait upon the Lord shall renew their strength; they shall mount up with wings as eagles; they shall run, and not be weary; and they shall walk, and not faint" (Isaiah 40:29-31).

So immediately now it is happening. He has raised up his mantle that he's picked up, and Elijah was gone, but he saw him when he was taken. He knew what to do. So he goes back to the Jordan and he raises the mantle and he cries out and says, "Where is the Lord God of Elijah?" And the Word says the river was parted back and he crossed over on dry ground.

So in order to see the work of God, and do the works of God, we're going to have to see Him in resurrection power and life in eternal things, and go from there. Because if we don't have the hope and we're not sure that He's coming again, we can't very well be like Him when we go back to the Jordan.

Much to learn in The Secret Place, but it's available if we'll stay there until…

"If You See Me When I'm Taken…"

— 5 —

It Was More Than I Could Bear...Until I Came Into The Sanctuary

———◦———

There are certain times in our pursuit of the things of God when we feel so established that we just believe nothing can move us. But, there's nothing like reconsidering. We need to follow on and begin to walk softly before the Lord.

The Apostle Paul mentions that we must know from whom we have received the blessings or the revelations we embrace...to be sure that we build properly. "According to the grace of God which is given unto me, as a wise masterbuilder, I have laid the foundation, and another buildeth thereon. But let every man take heed how he buildeth thereupon. For other foundation can no man lay than that is laid, which is Jesus Christ. Every man's work shall be made manifest: for the day shall declare it, because it shall be revealed by fire" (1 Corinthians 3:10-11,13).

As we see the real characteristics of someone we were supposed to know and love, and have been deceived, we become moved and shaken, discouraged and confused. We cannot put our confidence in them any more. That's why the important thing for us to do is to come to know the Lord daily...*to know Him.* He'll always guide us through those places. We will be exposed to many things that will cause us to wonder and will put the real test into us.

A lot of people have turned away from the Lord's place of worship because of things that are happening. But what we love to point out in *Stones From The Secret Place* is the privilege God has made for everyone of us. We do not have to build our relationship on others without knowing what they are giving to us. God can make that sure. You take even a child and give it something that doesn't taste right, why it shows up on his little face. And if there's something that comes our way that's not right, God has fixed it to where, if we'll listen closely, we won't be swayed by it. We've experienced what we read in Psalm 73:1-3: "Truly God is good to Israel, even to such as are of a clean heart. But as for me, my feet were almost gone; my steps had well nigh slipped. For I was envious at the foolish, when I saw the prosperity of the wicked."

How much of that scripture is read? You find where the Lord spoke of it. "Your words have been stout against Me, saith the Lord. Yet ye say, What have we spoken so much against Thee? Ye have said, It is vain to serve God: and what profit is it that we have kept His ordinance, and that we have walked mournfully before the Lord of hosts? And now we call the proud happy; yea, they that work wickedness are set up; yea, they that tempt God are even delivered" (Malachi 3:13-15).

Whenever things are taught from the lips of Jesus, He says, "Blessed are they that mourn: for they shall be comforted" (Matthew 5:4). He encourages us in every way that we can know His voice as little sheep. Honestly, we can know His voice. "My sheep hear My voice, and I know them, and they follow Me: And I give unto them eternal life; and they shall never perish, neither shall any man pluck them out of My hand. My Father, which gave them Me, is greater than all; and no man is able to pluck them out of My Father's hand" (John 10:27-29).

We've often said this concerning being envious of wrong things or wrong people or being envious of anyone. He tells us the importance of coming to know the Lord individually for yourself by the Spirit that He gives you. He wants us to know Him. Then, we should seek to build our relationship strong enough that we find everything that we have need of. That scripture says he was envious at the prosperity of the wicked. And the Word says that's a powerful force if it catches you and in a wrong position of envy. "Behold, these are the ungodly, who prosper in the world; they increase in riches. Verily I have cleansed my heart in vain, and washed my hands in innocency. For all the day long have I been plagued, and chastened every morning" (Psalm 73:12-14).

I went through that very serious thought a lot of times. The suggestion would come, "If you were what you ought to be, it wouldn't be this way or it wouldn't be that way." Now, if He's challenging us with a truth, that things will be better if you seek Him more earnestly, that's good. But what the enemy does is bring the picture of some personality up before you, and it isn't long until it appears they are in much better shape than you are. And it isn't long until you wonder, "Why are things working out for me like this? I'm serving the Lord, too." Honestly, I wish I could wash away all those kind of things that come through the minds of people.

Being a pastor for many years, I was seeking to lead people to the place they could truly say as Paul, "Not that I speak in respect of want: for I have learned, in whatsoever state I am, therewith to be content. I know both how to be abased, and I know how to abound: every where and in all things I am instructed both to be full and to be hungry, both to abound and to suffer need. I can do all things through Christ which strengtheneth me" (Philippians 4:11-13).

A lot of times you will find precious souls who have gotten their eyes upon the prosperity of the wicked and they wonder why the wicked live like they live and yet they are blessed. But those things do not always spell approval. "When I thought to know this, it was too painful for me; Until I went into the sanctuary of God; then understood I their end. Surely thou didst set them in slippery places: thou castedst them down into destruction. How are they brought into desolation, as in a moment! they are utterly consumed with terrors" (Psalm 73:16-19).

It was told many years ago about a minister who had ministered about how God would bless us if we would give our tithe or gifts to the work of the Lord. He spoke about how important it was to serve the Lord and remember the Sabbath which is clearly taught to us in the law of Moses. And the minister went on to say that a man came to him one day and said, "Listen, I want you to explain something to me. You talk about how the Lord will bless you if you keep the Sabbath day. I want to tell you something, preacher, I've got a piece of land that I break and prepare on Sunday." He says, "This particular ground, why I sow it on Sunday. I work it on Sunday. I even harvest it on Sunday. And this statement about how you should keep the Sabbath day doesn't ring a bell." He goes on to tell the minister, "I even gather it on Sunday and I sell it on Sunday. And listen, preacher, that piece of ground does better than any other plot of ground that I have worked. Now what do you say?"

The preacher must have had a word from the Lord for it truly bears truth. He said, "I can tell you this, God doesn't always collect in October. In other words, God doesn't always destroy our ways the same day we do them, but the day will come when He will reward us for wrong doings. He will collect it. It may be on a Monday. It may be on a Tuesday. It may be on a Friday. But remember, just because you seem to think it's all prospering, things are going good, and you're doing something contrary to God's Word, He doesn't always collect in October." I believe this person got a thought there.

A lot of times we have seen God's judgment fall and the same thing happened a week from then. Somebody who is caught in the same thing may even get saved and forgiven and the sin blotted out where judgment or death has taken over. For instance, we read in the New Testament where Ananias and Sapphira came into the house of the Lord. The minister was the Apostle Peter. Ananias wanted to make it appear that he and his wife, Sapphira, were doing the same thing that the other Christians were doing, that they sold their possessions. For many Christians had sold their possessions and their property and even shared it with many others. They collected the money and helped others. These two wanted to make Peter think they were people of that nature, but they weren't really. "But a certain man named Ananias, with Sapphira his wife, sold a possession, And kept back part of the price, his wife also being privy to it, and brought a certain part, and laid it at the apostles' feet" (Acts 5:1-2).

Peter discerned by the Holy Spirit it was not so. He said "Ananias, why hath satan filled thine heart to lie to the Holy Ghost, and to keep back part of the price of the land? Whiles it remained, was it not thine own? and after it was sold, was it not in thine own power? why hast thou conceived this thing in thine heart? thou hast not lied unto men, but unto God" (Acts 5:3-4).

And the Word says clearly that he immediately fell dead. "And Ananias hearing these words fell down, and gave up the ghost: and great fear came on all them that heard these things" (Acts 5:5).

Scripture reveals that his wife came and related seemingly the same story to the Apostle Peter. "And Peter answered unto her, Tell me whether ye sold the land for so much? And she said, Yea, for so much. Then Peter said unto her, How is it that ye have agreed together to tempt the Spirit of the Lord? behold, the feet of them which have buried thy husband are at the door, and shall carry thee out. Then fell she down straightway at his feet, and yielded up the ghost: and the young men came in, and found her dead, and, carrying her forth, buried her by her husband" (Acts 5:8-10).

A lot of times we think punishment for liars is over, but really it's never over. Now, there's forgiveness for people who lie or deceive others when they repent. God wants us to repent, but many times we will not repent until we have a picture of judgment set before us. "But the fearful, and unbelieving, and the abominable, and murderers, and whoremongers, and sorcerers, and idolaters, and *all liars,* shall have their part in the lake which burneth with fire and brimstone: which is the second death" (Revelation 21:8).

That is why we are exhorted in the Word to behold the goodness and severity of God. Look at both sides of the picture because they both play a part. "Behold therefore the goodness and severity of God: on them which fell, severity; but toward thee, goodness, if thou continue in His goodness: otherwise thou also shalt be cut off. And they also, if they abide not still in unbelief, shall be graffed in: for God is able to graff them in again" (Romans 11:22-23).

The goodness of God is upon those who will turn to the Lord, and His severity teaches us that wrong will end up bad if a change doesn't come. God delights in mercy. He delights to show goodness and mercy. He rejoices any time that He can show forth His mercy. But we have to walk in a certain path of godly sorrow in order to receive the mercies of the Lord. He loves for us to have a godly sorrow. "For godly sorrow worketh repentance to salvation not to be repented of: but the sorrow of the world worketh death" (2 Corinthians 7:10). Not just sorrow because we got caught, but sorrow because we have grieved the Lord.

We find out that after the Lord has gone all out to bless us and help us, save us and give us a future, if we overlook godly sorrow and repentance for our sins, we are in a bad shape. How important it is to see both pictures the Lord has laid before us. How long would it last do you think if the Lord had never given us any danger signs or cautions? What if He never told about the punishment that comes with wrong doing, the danger of missing it? I just wonder where we would go from there.

Well first, the Bible says, "My people are destroyed for lack of knowledge: because thou hast rejected knowledge, I will also reject thee," (Hosea 4:6). God wants us to know these things...not wait until it's too late. That's why preparation for what's coming upon the earth is one of the greatest cries of our time. We need to get our hearts right with the Lord, and let God be the real chief Shepherd of our lives. "And take heed to yourselves, lest at any time your hearts be overcharged with surfeiting, and drunkenness, and cares of this life, and so that day come upon you unawares. For as a snare shall it come on all them that dwell on the face of the whole earth. Watch ye therefore, and pray always, that ye may be accounted worthy to escape all these things that shall come to pass, and to stand before the Son of man" (Luke 21:34-36).

So many things will come for the simple reason of teaching us to cast our care upon the Lord. "Casting all your care upon Him; for He careth for you. Be sober, be vigilant; because your adversary the devil, as a roaring lion, walketh about, seeking whom he may devour: Whom resist stedfast in the faith, knowing that the same afflictions are accomplished in your brethren that are in the world" (1 Peter 5:7-9).

The sad part about it is when we allow our trials and our testings to cause us to become bitter and resentful to the things of God or to the directions He gives. We should truly be glad, and sometimes I think it would be good to pray the prayer that David prayed. He said, "Unto Thee will I cry, O Lord my rock; be not silent to me: lest, if Thou be silent to me, I become like them that go down into the pit" (Psalm 28:1).

I believe he learned the importance of being cautioned. He also prayed a prayer which would be good for you and me to get in on the answer every now and then, and that is, "Lord, make me to know mine end, and the measure of my days, what it is; that I may know how frail I am" (Psalm 39:4). So it's the frailness of life that moves us for a remedy or for help.

Surely it should be known to the generation on the earth today that there is a lack. There is a lack of turning to the Lord with all of our heart. Having faith in God. The day will come when the storm will increase until only the things that will stand will be those who have hearkened unto God's directions to build. "Except the Lord build the house, they labour in vain that build it: except the Lord keep the city, the watchman waketh but in vain" (Psalm 127:1).

He spoke it in the simplest way. Actually, you can read in just seconds what it means to build according to the Lord. He speaks of the trials, the tests, the things that are going to come. And, saddest of all, David said, "For it was not an enemy that reproached me; then I could have borne it: neither was it he that hated me that did magnify himself against me; then I would have hid myself from him: But it was thou, a man mine equal, my guide, and mine acquaintance. We took sweet counsel together, and walked unto the house of God in company" (Psalm 55:12-14).

That's where many bruises come from among the children of God. That's why Jesus placed emphasis on the importance of believers loving one another. Jesus said to His disciples, "A new commandment I give unto you, That ye love one another; as I have loved you, that ye also love one another. By this shall all men know that ye are My disciples, if ye have love one to another" (John 13:34-35).

Now, we are actually thinking about it. Keep in mind, as we mention these few things here from the *Stones From The Secret Place,* we're talking about the revelation God gave us while we waited on the Lord in The Secret Place. It's amazing how much preaching can be done, and yet, much of the time, we get very little out of it. I think one of the greatest needs of our day is to get still before God, and even get to the place where the Lord can talk to us through the ministry that's before us today...to be in the place where we can hear the voice of the Lord. It's God's business to get a message over to us, and He uses a lot of patience to bring it about.

It was important for us to get hold of these things and know that we could not have made it had it not been the Lord. Israel certainly had that phrase made real to them. They said, "If it had not been the Lord Who was on our side...Then the waters had overwhelmed us, the stream had gone over our soul:" (Psalm 124:1,4).

The beautiful part about it is that we can't erase the fact that God cares because He makes a way. But to find His instructions, the Word says, is in His sanctuary. Come into His presence in the sanctuary. David continues, "Until I went into the sanctuary of God; then understood I their end. So foolish was I, and ignorant:...Nevertheless I am continually with Thee: Thou hast holden me by my right hand. Thou shalt guide me with Thy counsel, and afterward receive me to glory. Whom have I in heaven but Thee? and there is none upon earth that I desire beside Thee. My flesh and my heart faileth: but God is the strength of my heart, and my portion for ever. For, lo, they that are far from Thee shall perish: Thou hast destroyed all them that go a whoring from Thee. But it is good for me to draw near to God: I have put my trust in the Lord God, that I may declare all Thy works" (Psalm 73:17, 22-28).

I have noticed in reading the travail of David in the Psalms, the desire of his soul, the frailness, the failures and the mistakes. He cried out, "O God, Thou art my God; early will I seek Thee: my soul thirsteth for Thee, my flesh longeth for Thee in a dry and thirsty land, where no water is; To see Thy power and Thy glory, so as I have seen Thee in the sanctuary" (Psalm 63:1-2). So, David found out God's ways in the sanctuary. And in the sanctuary, we find out how to rid ourselves of unnecessary things and how to be able to bear whatever comes against us. We find out how to do all things in the sanctuary of the Lord.

Let's you and I begin as never before to meditate in the law of God. Be still in His presence. We might say *Stones From The Secret Place* is actually true revelation, the true voice of God in the understanding we get as we sit in His presence. In the sanctuary, God has a word for us today. Let's be still, as the Scripture says, and know that He is God. "Be still, and know that I am God: I will be exalted among the heathen, I will be exalted in the earth" (Psalm 46:10).

I remember reading and ministering about how Israel was doing pretty good in her route to the Canaan land, the promised land, but they came down to the Red Sea and Pharaoh and his army had followed them. They were about to panic. They didn't know what to do. "The Egyptians pursued after them, all the horses and chariots of Pharaoh, and his horsemen, and his army, and overtook them encamping by the sea…And when Pharaoh drew nigh, the children of Israel lifted up their eyes, and, behold, the Egyptians marched after them; and they were sore afraid: and the children of Israel cried out unto the Lord. And they said unto Moses, Because there were no graves in Egypt, hast thou taken us away to die in the wilderness?

wherefore hast thou dealt thus with us, to carry us forth out of Egypt?" (Exodus 14:9-11).

It's hard to believe how Israel received as much attention as God gave them, not just bringing them out of the land, but blessing them and keeping them even in their bondages there in Egypt...but nevertheless, Pharaoh's army overtook them. The Lord spoke to Moses. "And Moses said unto the people, Fear ye not, stand still, and see the salvation of the Lord, which He will shew to you to day: for the Egyptians whom ye have seen to day, ye shall see them again no more for ever. The Lord shall fight for you, and ye shall hold your peace" (Exodus 14:13-14).

A few times we have waited on the Lord until that quietness, that stillness, that calmness came to us from the Lord. I could name quite a few times we just waited quietly before the Lord. As the Word says, "Be still and know." Then, the Lord also tells us, "In returning and rest shall ye be saved; in quietness and in confidence shall be your strength;" (Isaiah 30:15).

So God has a way, Friends. When you and I have actually used up all of our energy and we feel like there's nothing left, God still has a way to win the battle...if we can just hear His voice and obey Him. Let's press on to the point where we learn to truly wait on the Lord. Let's shut out things that hinder us from hearing God's voice and allow enough of God to come into our hearts so He can take charge of our lives and take hold to the reins of our life.

Yes, I wish we could say that when one victory is won, there will be no more battles, but we are only told there will be no more tears, no more sorrow, no more pain and no more death *in Heaven.* Until then, it seems to be necessary to have things that woo us to the realization that we must follow the Lord with all of our heart, soul, mind and strength. God wants us to do that.

Just think of it. You're not by yourself with your troubles and trials. The whole earth today is groaning. But listen, there's some who actually are able to declare to us that our trials are just God's opportunity to make Himself real to us.

I think of how Goliath was out in the valley walking up and down talking to Israel at a distance there on the hill and daring them to come and fight against him. Believe it or not, they were all afraid to go. Then the Lord chose one little boy who was watching over the sheep. I doubt if anyone knew about it up to this point, but a bear had come out to destroy little David's group of sheep. I don't guess the bear would have paid any attention to David, but David knew he was to watch over the sheep. No doubt, he prayed a prayer, and went for the bear. Also, at one time, he went for the lion that came out against the sheep. And the Word says the Lord gave him victory over the lion and the bear.

I've often said this, "Don't forget the bear fight. Don't forget the victory that God gave you yesterday." You'll need another surge tomorrow against discouragement or however the enemy may approach you. God doesn't mean for it to destroy you. He just wants to get your attention and get you to learn to lean on Him, to trust in Him and believe in Him. So, we will see at the end, why actually, all these testings and trials were working for our good...if we recognized them. "And we know that all things work together for good to them that love God, to them who are the called according to His purpose" (Romans 8:28).

If we'll follow on, we can even thank the Lord for the storms that come our way for had it not been for them who knows how far away we would have wondered? "My brethren, count it all joy when ye fall into divers temptations; Knowing this, that the trying of your faith worketh patience. But let patience have her perfect work, that ye may be perfect and entire, wanting nothing" (James 1:2-4).

We do know that Israel made a bad mistake when they murmured in their trial. They couldn't murmur and say God never had done anything for them. "The Lord spake unto Moses and unto Aaron, saying, How long shall I bear with this evil congregation, which murmur against me? I have heard the murmurings of the children of Israel, which they murmur against me. Say unto them, As truly as I live, saith the Lord, as ye have spoken in Mine ears, so will I do to you" (Numbers 14:26-28).

God had done a lot for them. He made a difference between them and the Egyptians when they were in the land of Egypt. He blessed them in many ways. "But against any of the children of Israel shall not a dog move his tongue, against man or beast: that ye may know how that the Lord doth put a difference between the Egyptians and Israel" (Exodus 11:7).

Whenever God tested them to find out what was in their hearts, He found them murmuring and complaining at every little test. They would go to Moses and Moses would intercede. It was unbelievable almost when you read of the concern that Moses had for Israel. It was even to the point where God was ready to destroy them because they had murmured so much. "And when the people complained, it displeased the Lord: and the Lord heard it; and His anger was kindled; and the fire of the Lord burnt among them, and consumed them that were in the uttermost parts of the camp. And the people cried unto Moses; and when Moses prayed unto the Lord, the fire was quenched" (Numbers 11:1-2).

If they'd have paid attention properly, they would have known the Lord did bless them. He answered their prayers. They had plenty. They never actually grew feeble in the wilderness. "He brought them forth also with silver and gold: and there was not one feeble person among their tribes. Egypt was glad when they departed: for the fear of them fell upon them. He spread a cloud for a covering; and fire to give light in the night" (Psalm 105:37-39).

But, the Bible says, they did always err in their hearts in unbelief. "For some, when they had heard, did provoke: howbeit not all that came out of Egypt by Moses. But with whom was he grieved forty years? Was it not with them that had sinned, whose carcases fell in the wilderness? And to whom sware he that they should not enter into his rest, but to them that believed not? So we see that they could not enter in because of unbelief. Let us labour therefore to enter into that rest, lest any man fall after the same example of unbelief" (Hebrews 3:16-19;4:11).

The next time you enter into The Secret Place I think it would be wise for you to ask as the apostles did, "Lord, Increase our faith" (Luke 17:5). It would be very good for without faith it is impossible to please Him. "But without faith it is impossible to please Him: for he that cometh to God must believe that He is, and that He is a rewarder of them that diligently seek Him" (Hebrews 11:6).

This message from The Secret Place hasn't promised you and me that we'll never have another trial or storm. God has brought you through trials until now, and He can keep you in the future. Release your faith. Let the sanctuary of God, let His presence, build your faith like little David did. He was ready. He was prepared not only to go against Goliath, but he knew *how* to go against him. As we fight our battles, God has a way for us to win.

Now Saul decided to put his armor on David. "And Saul armed David with his armour, and he put an helmet of brass upon his head; also he armed him with a coat of mail. And David girded his sword upon his armour, and he assayed to go; for he had not proved it." He had not done that before. "And David said unto Saul, I cannot go with these; for I have not proved them. And David put them off him. And he took his staff in his hand, and chose him five smooth stones out of the brook, and put them in a shepherd's bag which he had, even in a scrip; and his sling was in his hand: and he drew near to the Philistine" (1 Samuel 17:38-40).

That's not easy is it, folks? To pull off the armor of another soldier. But say, God has a way for you to fight your battles. Find out how He wants you to win. He likes to talk to you personally. Let The Secret Place say it to you so you can enjoy hearing from God, then it won't be so hard for you to get back into The Secret Place.

The Lord bless you good now!

Live Daily In That
Place Where
God's Love Will
Be Free To Flow
In Your Life
Towards Your
Fellow Man.

-J. E. Murdock

– 6 –

JESUS IS THE WAY TO PERFECTION

―――⟫•◦•⟪―――

It is a marvelous thing to find out that Jesus doesn't expect you and me to walk in a state of pureness and holiness before Him in ourselves. He came Himself and fulfilled the demands the Law gave. The demands of the Law were so strict that the Word says no one was able to keep the Law.

God was pleased with the nature and the discipline and the kind of a life that obedience to His Law would bring. So, He didn't stop because we were unable to obey the law which would set us free from our old way of life and free us from condemnation. The Word says that Jesus came and He fulfilled the Law. He fulfilled the Law in every respect and in every way. They could actually find no fault in Him.

So, if Jesus fulfilled the Law, then we find scriptures that point out that Jesus is the way to perfection. "If perfection could have been attained through the Levitical priesthood (for on the basis of it the law was given to the people), why was there still need for another priest to come—one in the order of Melchizedek, not in the order of Aaron? For when there is a change of the priesthood, there must also be a change of the law...The former regulation is set aside because it was weak and useless (for the law made nothing perfect), and a better hope is introduced, by which we draw near to God...For the law appoints as high priests men who are weak; but the oath, which came after the law, appointed the Son, Who has been made perfect forever" (read Hebrews 7:11-12,18-19,23-28).

The seventh and eighth chapters of Romans contain a volume of information, wisdom and instructions. We find our condition in the seventh chapter. "For I delight in the law of

God after the inward man: But I see another law in my members, warring against the law of my mind, and bringing me into captivity to the law of sin which is in my members. O wretched man that I am! who shall deliver me from the body of this death? I thank God through Jesus Christ our Lord. So then with the mind I myself serve the law of God; but with the flesh the law of sin" (Romans 7:22-25).

We find the remedy for our condition in the eighth chapter. I'd like to read something right from Romans 8. I think three or four verses would help you and me to begin to hunger and thirst after the truth and for it to be made plain. "There is therefore now no condemnation to them which are in Christ Jesus, who walk not after the flesh, but after the Spirit. For the law of the Spirit of life in Christ Jesus hath made me free from the law of sin and death. For what the law could not do, in that it was weak through the flesh, God sending His own Son in the likeness of sinful flesh, and for sin, condemned sin in the flesh: That the righteousness of the law might be fulfilled in us, who walk not after the flesh, but after the Spirit" (Romans 8:1-4).

Wouldn't it be nice if when you had problems and you needed help and some attention in your body, there would be somebody who could help you in whatever need you had? All you'd have to do is just go down the road a little way and find someone there who could meet that need. Well, in the Scriptures, we are told that the Lord Himself is the example. He is the way to perfection. And anyone who comes to Him, He doesn't only heal them in their body, but He heals them in their heart and soul and mind. "And if Christ be in you, the body is dead because of sin; but the Spirit is life because of righteousness. But if the Spirit of Him that raised up Jesus from the dead dwell in you, He that raised up Christ from the dead shall also quicken your mortal bodies by His Spirit that dwelleth in you" (Romans 8:10-11).

I doubt if I'm actually speaking to anybody that wouldn't like to be better and have greater love, greater peace and greater perfection in their life in one area or another...

financially, mentally, spiritually, physically. How wonderful it would be to have such a relationship with God to the extent that when we call He will answer, "Here Am I."

How beautiful it is to find a place that you can get your call through to God immediately. "And this is the confidence that we have in Him, that, if we ask any thing according to His will, He heareth us: And if we know that He hear us, whatsoever we ask, we know that we have the petitions that we desired of Him" (1 John 5:14-15).

The Bible calls Him a Present Help in time of need. "God is our refuge and strength, a very present help in trouble. Therefore will not we fear, though the earth be removed, and though the mountains be carried into the midst of the sea;" (Psalm 46:1-2). I'll tell you what, if we have to go days without finding help from the Lord from something that's needful, then there may be a loose connection and relationship in our walk with the Lord. But through it all, try to remember this: find the key that gets Gods attention...a *present* help in the time of need.

So our thought and our one liner now is that "Jesus Is The Way To Perfection." But listen, if we live after the flesh, we shall die. That's the carnal nature that's in everyone. It's through the Spirit that we live. "But ye are not in the flesh, but in the Spirit, if so be that the Spirit of God dwell in you. Now if any man have not the Spirit of Christ, he is none of His. For if ye live after the flesh, ye shall die: but if ye through the Spirit do mortify the deeds of the body, ye shall live" (Romans 8:9,13).

Now many precious souls are already beginning to experience a deliverance of some measure or other from things of the old carnal nature. I'm talking to people, no doubt, who are listening or reading *The Road To Perfection* or *Stones From The Secret Place* who are already tasting a measure of what God has promised to those who will mortify the deeds of their body by the Spirit. It says we shall live if we do that.

"For as many as are led by the Spirit of God, they are the sons of God" (Romans 8:14). Can it be said stronger? And can it be emphasized more of what and how to be called the sons of God. Just to be led by the Spirit of the Lord. Now I can say I'm led by the Spirit of God. But really, am I? Is the Lord saying that I'm being led by the Spirit? I may be doing some right things, but I may still not be doing the most important thing to meet the need that I have at that moment. So, it's important to find out where the need is in your life.

The Scripture says there was a man who was praying and offering up a gift to the Lord. While he was in prayer the Lord spoke to him and said, "Arise and leave there your gift at the altar and go to your brother and correct some things." You may not have anything against him but you know he's got something against you, either way you want to look at it. It says to just leave your gift there. "I can't do any more for you. I can't respect your gift now until there's a little correction made." "Therefore if thou bring thy gift to the altar, and there rememberest that thy brother hath ought against thee; Leave there thy gift before the altar, and go thy way; first be reconciled to thy brother, and then come and offer thy gift" (Matthew 5:23-24).

I'm sincere when I talk to you like this, because I'll tell you what, The Secret Place certainly combs our lives with a very fine comb and we are going to see and find things out in our day that we used to overlook. God doesn't overlook it because we can have something better. He has what it takes.

He's longing to make us what He would have us to be. "Not that we are sufficient of ourselves to think any thing as of ourselves; but our sufficiency is of God; Who also hath made us able ministers of the new testament; not of the letter, but of the Spirit: for the letter killeth, but the Spirit giveth life...But even unto this day, when Moses is read, the vail is upon their heart. Nevertheless when it shall turn to the Lord, the vail shall be taken away. Now the Lord is that Spirit: and where the Spirit of the Lord is, there is liberty. But we all, with open face beholding as in a glass the glory of the Lord, are changed into the same image from glory to glory, even as by the Spirit of the Lord" (2 Corinthians 3:5-6,15-18).

How the Lord wants to speak to us today about how we may be led by the Spirit and the importance of it. We don't cry "Abba, Father" just from our lips, but we have received the *Spirit* of adoption. We have truly gotten into the family of God through the precious Spirit of the Lord so that we can call Him, "Abba, Father." "For ye have not received the spirit of bondage again to fear; but ye have received the Spirit of adoption, whereby we cry, Abba, Father. The Spirit itself beareth witness with our spirit, that we are the children of God:" (Romans 8:15-16).

Can we truly say beyond a doubt that our hearts are right with God, that we are His children? There were plenty of people, even in the day when Jesus was on the earth, who claimed to be the children of God and at the same time they were persecuting Jesus and what He had to say. So it is not what we say that's really speaking the loudest today. It is actually what we are doing. I've got a little poem that I wrote. It goes like this:

> Your walk is your talk, my child
> No matter what you say
> Your walk is your talk all along the way.
> So watch your walk which is your talk
> That others may see you clear
> For the walk you walk is the talk you talk
> No matter what you say.

And what it is, Friends, is not putting a caution sign to what we say, but what we say doesn't really spell out the true picture of our lives. It's how we walk. In fact, the Lord says, "And why call ye Me, Lord, Lord, and do not the things which I say?" (Luke 6:46).

Don't depend upon what others say about you. Ask God, and don't be offended if God says you lack one thing. There's something just not right. Listen to Him closely for you will not only reap comfort and consolation here now, but when we stand before God, we can hear Him say, "Well done, thou good and faithful servant." Friends, Jesus is our example. If we'll follow Him, we'll not be ashamed whenever He comes.

How beautiful the eighth chapter of Romans is and what it will add to our faith is actually indescribable. Many people never refer to this wonderful chapter. They are looking over to find other things they are wanting from God. They are wanting to find peace and comfort without any perfection in their life and in their walk. "The Spirit itself beareth witness with our spirit, that we are the children of God: And if children, then heirs; heirs of God, and joint-heirs with Christ; if so be that we suffer with Him, that we may be also glorified together" (Romans 8:16-17).

We are back again to the day when God is going to test us. I really do believe our choices are very few. We'll either go the way of the world or we'll go the way of God. Let's reach on out higher. Let's not try to describe our idea about perfection. "But God forbid that I should glory, save in the cross of our Lord Jesus Christ, by Whom the world is crucified unto Me, and I unto the world. For in Christ Jesus neither circumcision availeth any thing, nor uncircumcision, but a new creature. And as many as walk according to this rule, peace be on them, and mercy, and upon the Israel of God" (Galatians 6:14-16).

No one spoke it plainer than Jesus. He made it plain to us what He, not only expects us to do, but He tells us the way we will walk and the way we will live if we'll follow Him. Let's follow Him into The Secret Place. Stay before Him long enough so that the reward meets us in the face when we leave The Secret Place. He said if we would seek Him in secret, He would reward us openly. "The Spirit itself beareth witness with our spirit, that we are the children of God: And if children, then heirs; heirs of God, and joint-heirs with Christ; if so be that we suffer with Him, that we may be also glorified together. For I reckon that the sufferings of this present time are not worthy to be compared with the glory which shall be revealed in us. For the earnest expectation of the creature waiteth for the manifestation of the sons of God" (Romans 8:16-19).

I know of nothing more wonderful than to have a good

clean, consecrated heart towards the Lord. I pray for that daily. I trust, my friends, that these thoughts we discover in The Secret Place, will enable us to "walk in the Spirit and not fulfill the lusts of the flesh." I love to say this: What God gives you will be something that will talk to you tomorrow. It will help you next week. It will help you in days to come.

Jesus made it very clear that Moses gave the Israelites manna from Heaven in the wilderness. He said they ate that bread and they died. "Verily, verily, I say unto you, He that believeth on Me hath everlasting life. I am that bread of life. Your fathers did eat manna in the wilderness, and are dead. This is the bread which cometh down from heaven, that a man may eat thereof, and not die" (John 6:47-50).

In The Secret Place, you learn how to live in the face of your adversaries and how to shoulder the responsibility God gives you and everyone who follows Him. "Likewise the Spirit also helpeth our infirmities: for we know not what we should pray for as we ought: but the Spirit itself maketh intercession for us with groanings which cannot be uttered. And He that searcheth the hearts knoweth what is the mind of the Spirit, because He maketh intercession for the saints according to the will of God. And we know that all things work together for good to them that love God, to them who are the called according to His purpose. What shall we then say to these things? If God be for us, who can be against us? Who shall lay any thing to the charge of God's elect? It is God that justifieth" (Romans 8:26-28,31,33).

Christ enables us to pick up our cross daily and follow Him. "Who is He that condemneth? It is Christ that died, yea rather, that is risen again, Who is even at the right hand of God, Who also maketh intercession for us. Who shall separate us from the love of Christ? shall tribulation, or distress, or persecution, or famine, or nakedness, or peril, or sword? As it is written, For Thy sake we are killed all the day long; we are accounted as sheep for the slaughter. Nay, in all these things we are more than conquerors through Him that loved us" (Romans 8:34-37).

So don't let perfection warp our thinking. Everyone of us

are seeking a better way some how, some way. Let's find God's way and begin to reap a Harvest even now in this present life. "And we know that all things work together for good to them that love God, to them who are the called according to His purpose. For whom He did foreknow, He also did predestinate to be conformed to the image of His Son, that he might be the firstborn among many brethren. Moreover whom He did predestinate, them He also called: and whom He called, them He also justified: and whom He justified, them He also glorified. He that spared not His own Son, but delivered Him up for us all, how shall He not with Him also freely give us all things?" (Romans 8:28-30,32).

He says we'll have great riches in Heaven. "Every good gift and every perfect gift is from above, and cometh down from the Father of lights, with Whom is no variableness, neither shadow of turning. Of His own will begat He us with the word of truth, that we should be a kind of firstfruits of His creatures" (James 1:17-18).

God bless you!

— 7 —

MARY GAVE THE PATTERN

I can't forget how the Lord quickened that thought, Mary gave the Pattern, to my heart. Mary's statement was far reaching for us in our progress in the Lord, in our place of revelation or in our need being met. It is for us to find out what our part is in the plan of God and getting things done.

Jesus was invited to a wedding there in Cana. This is what is revealed in John 2:1-5. "And the third day there was a marriage in Cana of Galilee; and the mother of Jesus was there: And both Jesus was called, and His disciples, to the marriage. And when they wanted wine, the mother of Jesus saith unto Him, They have no wine. Jesus saith unto her, Woman, what have I to do with thee? Mine hour is not yet come. His mother saith unto the servants, *Whatsoever He saith unto you, do it.*"

That actually sets the stage for you and me and our approach in whatever need we have. God knows the way, and Mary has actually, I would say, spoken one of the greatest messages that could be spoken to the believer or to the person who is in need. I have used that to answer a lot of hard questions that have been asked me. I've had people ask me who they should marry. I've had people ask me what I think they should do about answering their call into the ministry. Those are just a few of the many questions that we've been asked. I'm glad to be asked the questions. Most of all, I rejoice in the fact that I feel that the Lord, many times, has given me just exactly the message they need. And there never has been anything more important than to find what God's will is.

It actually seemed to satisfy many who have asked who were smart enough to play their role to bring a need or an answer to pass. They knew they had to be involved. I've had it repeated from the pulpit. Someone would say, "I was asking about a certain thing. Brother Murdock told me to just stay before the Lord, hear what He has to say and do what He says." Well what more could you say? They couldn't say, "God doesn't know the answer." So they had to say, "Well, after all, I'm going to have to position myself to do what the Lord says."

Now the need arose there at the marriage in Cana. I want us to picture that. Jesus and His disciples accepted the invitation, and they were at the marriage. I've heard some wonderful encouraging remarks on that very thought. How Jesus had set His approval upon marriage by going to the wedding and by performing and working in the wedding to meet a need. I have said it this way and thought, "Oh how many weddings have fallen short of what they expected." Now when Jesus is there, it seems to me like there is always a lack. Whenever Jesus appeared to the seven churches in Revelation, He didn't overlook what they had, but He also mentioned what they lacked.

The message that got to Jesus at this wedding was, "Well, we weren't expecting so many here at the wedding." No doubt, some of them were there because they heard that Jesus and His disciples were going to be there. Because of that, the crowd that day at this wedding was larger than expected. They had prepared, but they didn't have enough wine. How true it seems to be that when Jesus shows up there is a lack. The good part about it is He wasn't going around condemning them or complaining about it, but He was available if anybody wanted to talk to Him.

So, somebody told Mary. They knew that if anybody could influence Jesus, Mary could. And it was embarrassing to have to report to their guests that, "Hey, we have run out of wine." They wanted to get this thing fixed so the guests would never need to know they were short of wine, so they told Mary. Mary, of course, goes and tells Jesus. She must have said it in such a way that she expected Jesus to step in now and get something going, but Jesus said, "Woman, why do you involve Me? My time has not yet come."

Now listen, folks, you and I can be blessed if we'll stay

before the Lord long enough to find out the importance of hearing what He really is saying in this very first miracle that He performed. He said, "My time has not yet come." We've used the phrase like this. If it's not His time, then whose time is it? We're out of wine. We need some wine. Well, if you're in need, you're going to have to get involved with it, as well as Jesus getting involved.

So, they've got it before the Lord and He says, "My time hasn't come." And something happened that caused Mary to speak the words we're talking about today. "His mother saith unto the servants, Whatsoever He saith unto you, do it." Did she know He was going to say something? I don't know. But she had already gotten the message when Jesus said to her, "Woman, what have I to do with thee? Mine hour is not yet come."

So, if anything needs to be done, why we've got to get somebody involved, and who should step into this? We should. We're the ones who are in need. We should find out. Jesus loves for us to approach Him regardless. Though it's not His time, He has made a way for somebody, even like Mary, to speak up and tell us, "Hey, do what He says."

As I've stated already, I've told others, "Just stay before the Lord, and do what He says." Do what He says. Think of having to tell someone in our day the person they should marry. Oh, what a responsibility. Who? Where? When? There's one thing about it that's been impressed upon our hearts. If we follow God, it doesn't mean that everything is going to work out perfectly. After all Jesus was at the wedding, and now they're out of wine. So you will find out that any time Jesus has made Himself available, we're going to need His help. He's going to make Himself useful somewhere.

The wine was needed. Now, it's not His time. If it's not His time, then it must be ours. Mary got that word of wisdom. Somehow it just broke through, and we're using it today. She said to the servants, "Do what He tells you." She believed that Jesus was interested in that need being met. She believed that Jesus had a way of doing it, and He would tell them. "And there were set there six waterpots of stone, after the manner of the purifying of the Jews, containing two or three firkins apiece." If He didn't do it Himself, He'd tell them what they could do. He told them. "Fill the water pots with water. And they filled them up to the brim."

Just think how direct God is. It's like when you pray, pray earnestly. When you pray, pray believing. Don't forget you can pray all day if you don't believe and nothing will happen. In other words, the miracle won't start until you come up to par. We like to say God is too strict. But no, He's not too strict. He is just direct, and it works. "And He saith unto them, Draw out now, and bear unto the governor of the feast. And they bare it. When the ruler of the feast had tasted the water that was made wine, and knew not whence it was: (but the servants which drew the water knew;) the governor of the feast called the bridegroom," (John 2:7-9).

If He ever broke down and did it like us, we'd change His plan again tomorrow. But it's always, "Do it, and do what He said to do." What a beautiful picture we see! We shouldn't be discouraged if we've got to make another move before the miracle happens. Just do it. Just do it. If He says to stand still, well, don't run then. Stand still. Whatever He says, do it.

The Bible gives Jesus Himself as a real example even in the prayer life. The Word says that Jesus prayed in the garden. "And they came to a place which was named Gethsemane: and He saith to His disciples, Sit ye here, while I shall pray. And He taketh with Him Peter and James and John, and began to be sore amazed, and to be very heavy; And saith unto them, My soul is exceeding sorrowful unto death: tarry ye here, and watch. And He went forward a little, and fell on the ground, and prayed that, if it were possible, the hour might pass from Him. And He said, Abba, Father, all things are possible unto Thee; take away this cup from Me: nevertheless not what I will, but what Thou wilt. He came back and found the disciples asleep. And He cometh, and findeth them sleeping, and saith unto Peter, Simon, sleepest thou? couldest not thou watch one hour? Watch ye and pray, lest ye enter into temptation. The spirit truly is ready, but the flesh is weak" (Mark 14:32-38).

He went back again and the Word said He prayed *more earnestly*. I've used this phrase. The Lord forbid that I change God's Word, but I did use this thought. When He went back and prayed more earnestly, I wonder if He didn't pray for His disciples that time who had gone to sleep. He prayed more earnestly for them. Who knows? Well, that's food for thought, so think about it. At the same time, if it was necessary for Jesus to pray more earnestly, we certainly will find ourselves where there's a place to pray more earnestly. "And being in an agony He prayed more earnestly: and His sweat was as it were great drops of blood falling down to the ground" (Luke 22:44).

Now Friends, concerning the shortage there at the wedding, it was an embarrassing situation for those who had prepared for this marriage. They had prepared the supper but ran short of wine, so a miracle had come. Really, a lot of times that's the only way God gets a chance at us, folks, to give us a miracle...for us to find out we've run short. A lot of times I've left the prayer room with short change, you know, and it will never work. We never can get by properly until we do what God said. Now it doesn't mean He's that hard to please. There was no one going to faint because they ran out of wine, but they did get the message to Jesus. Now then, do what He says.

I have used this subject for myself often...I would say almost daily. It isn't that I just want God to do things for me, but I want to do what He wants me to do. I want to say what He wants me to say. How beautiful it is to study this first miracle that Jesus did. Study it thoroughly. Re-read this article from *Stones From The Secret Place*. Re-read it again. Think it over seriously. Think over the steps that were made. Why did we run short and Jesus and His disciples are here? My, how embarrassing it is. Don't be embarrassed, but just be ready to report it to Jesus. Be ready to do and go the route that He may suggest.

Now, if they had had a cupful left, He could have done it like the loaves and fishes. That's the way we usually like it. We like for Him to stretch this thing and get it over with and let us be on our way. He says, "Well, find something here that's got a cupful or spoonful left." And then He begins to stretch it out. Why He could have done the same as He did with the loaves and fishes. But no, He's going at it a different way. He said, "It's not My time." And Mary said, "Do what He tells you." So you're not left alone, folks. You and I are left with a word from God on what to do, or we listen until He tells us what to do.

After Mary said that, I imagine they began to watch Him and say, "Well, I wonder what's next." And the Lord looked around and He saw water pots. Very common, isn't it? They had brought water in there. To go get water isn't that easy to do. But I think one of the most important things we should really look at to get the spiritual application that God wants us to get. He tells us how full to make it. How much water to put in the pail. He says, "Fill it up to the brim and bring it on in." Now folks, God doesn't want you to be short handed. He tells you exactly. If He'd have just said, "Go and bring in a half a pail"...okay, just do what He said.

The Scripture says there was a leper who went to the prophet to get healed of leprosy. And he expected the prophet to come out and to say a word, "Be healed." But, the prophet gave him a message that he turned away pouting over. "And Elisha sent a messenger unto him, saying, Go and wash in Jordan seven times, and thy flesh shall come again to thee, and thou shalt be clean. But Naaman was wroth, and went away, and said, Behold, I thought, He will surely come out to me, and stand, and call on the name of the Lord his God, and strike his hand over the place, and recover the leper" (2 Kings 5:10-11).

You say, "Oh my, I'll do anything." But you'd be surprised to know how some people rebel against God's way of doing things. We want it to work another way. But, he's in a bind now. The thing has come before the Lord's servant. God has told him what to do. He turned and went away in a rage. "And his servants came near, and spake unto him, and said, My father, if the prophet had bid thee do some great thing, wouldest thou not have done it? how much rather then, when He saith to thee, Wash, and be clean?" (2 Kings 5:13).

But what the enemy had flashed before Naaman's mind was, "The river of Jordan is a muddy river. There are better rivers to wash in and be clean." God will always do things a little bit different, but the thing about it is you can be assured that the job will be done if you do it like he says. I've often pictured going with Naaman down to the river and watching him as he dipped. I've often gone through the motions with him. He would be about to stop because he lost count, but I would say, "Hey, Naman, that's just six times. You need to dip one more time." And when he dipped that seventh time, he was made clean. "Then went he down, and dipped himself seven times in Jordan, according to the saying of the man of God: and his flesh came again like unto the flesh of a little child, and he was clean" (2 Kings 5:14).

So, don't forget now that at the wedding they are short, and don't be surprised about feeling a shortage when Jesus is around. But say, what of it? I'd rather feel it now when I can do something about it than to feel it too late and I can't do anything about it. You see, just to say to the foolish virgins, "Hey, you are out of oil. Go get some"... is not enough. They do go, but sadly in their case, they went too late and the door was shut when they came back. "And while they went to buy, the bridegroom came; and they that were ready went in with him to the marriage: and the door was shut. Afterward came also the other virgins, saying, Lord, Lord, open to us. But He answered and said, Verily I say unto you, I know you not. Watch therefore, for ye know neither the day nor the hour wherein the Son of man cometh" (Matthew 25:10-13).

Are you in shortage of something in a most embarrassing stage now? Re-read the verses that we have read about Mary. She said, "Do what He tells you." Think it over. You may already have the answer, but you haven't responded to it. You may already know what to do, but you haven't done it right. But know this, staying before the Lord in The Secret Place is the way to get the answer. There is no better way to get the pattern and the strength to do what God tells you to do than to stay in The Secret Place. *Then, it will happen.*

– 8 –

NONE OF THESE THINGS MOVE ME

I don't know of any statements that have been more real to me than these two scriptures. And I don't know of two more important scriptures to learn what all is involved in the Christian life in following the Lord. "Save that the Holy Ghost witnesseth in every city, saying that bonds and afflictions abide me. But none of these things move me, neither count I my life dear unto myself, so that I might finish my course with joy, and the ministry, which I have received of the Lord Jesus, to testify the gospel of the grace of God" (Acts 20:23-24).

Jesus made it very clear that we should count the cost. "And whosoever doth not bear his cross, and come after Me, cannot be My disciple. For which of you, intending to build a tower, sitteth not down first, and counteth the cost, whether he have sufficient to finish it? Lest haply, after he hath laid the foundation, and is not able to finish it, all that behold it begin to mock him, Saying, This man began to build, and was not able to finish" (Luke 14:27-30).

It's all in His Word actually about the path of a person who is going to follow the Lord Jesus. "For I am now ready to be offered, and the time of my departure is at hand. I have fought a good fight, I have finished my course, I have kept the faith: Henceforth there is laid up for me a crown of righteousness, which the Lord, the righteous judge, shall give me at that day: and not to me only, but unto all them also that love His appearing" (2 Timothy 4:6-8). I am going to take a little time here to relate what the Lord inspired to us while we were in prayer studying about the trials and the tests.

The Apostle Paul was formerly a persecutor of the church.

He was persecuting the church because he thought he was doing God's service. You wouldn't think there would be people that far from the plan of God and from what God says about loving people, but that's what deception and ignorance can do. That's why you'll read in Paul's writings many times where he said he would not have us ignorant. Being ignorant is very expensive. We are to know about the path we are stepping into. "For as the sufferings of Christ abound in us, so our consolation also aboundeth by Christ. And our hope of you is stedfast, knowing, that as ye are partakers of the sufferings, so shall ye be also of the consolation. For we would not, brethren, have you ignorant of our trouble which came to us in Asia, that we were pressed out of measure, above strength, insomuch that we despaired even of life: But we had the sentence of death in ourselves, that we should not trust in ourselves, but in God which raiseth the dead:" (2 Corinthians 1:5,7-9).

Jesus makes it very clear. He spoke of one man who was a ruler among the Jewish people, a religious person named Nicodemus, who came to Him by night and said to Him, "Rabbi, we know that Thou art a teacher come from God: for no man can do these miracles that Thou doest, except God be with Him." Nicodemus wanted to know "What can we do to be saved...or to make heaven our home...or to please God?" Jesus answered and said unto him, "Verily, verily, I say unto thee, Except a man be born again, he cannot see the kingdom of God."

That was Greek to Nicodemus. He asked, "How can a man be born when he is old? Can he enter the second time into his mother's womb, and be born?" Jesus went on to explain "I say unto thee, Except a man be born of water and of the Spirit, he cannot enter into the kingdom of God. That which is born of the flesh is flesh; and that which is born of the Spirit is spirit" (John 3:1-6).

The point we are making is that God doesn't want us to be ignorant. Jesus doesn't want to leave you and me anywhere in our journey with Him in an embarrassing situation. That's why He wants us to know who we're following and to know what to do to follow Him. Saul was one of those persons the Lord spoke to on the road when he was en route to Damascus to persecute the believers in Christ.

When the Lord got through with him, he says "...the Holy Ghost witnesseth in every city, saying that bonds and afflictions abide me" (Acts 20:23). How would you like to start out and find out that there's nothing ahead of you but bonds of afflictions? Well many jobs actually face such opposition. That's why Paul says to us later, "And every man that striveth for the mastery is temperate in all things. Now they do it to obtain a corruptible crown; but we an incorruptible. I therefore so run, not as uncertainly; so fight I, not as one that beateth the air: But I keep under my body, and bring it into subjection: lest that by any means, when I have preached to others, I myself should be a castaway" (1 Corinthians 9:25-27).

Paul seems to start out with a balance. He's looking back now. He found out that the road he was traveling before certainly had nothing to offer. Now then, if there's anything else to do, it is to turn another direction. So the Lord didn't let him start in this place without letting him know. "Say, it's not a bed of roses." He told him he was going to suffer. "For I will shew him how great things he must suffer for My name's sake" (Acts 9:16).

Later on Paul says, "But none of these things move me, neither count I my life dear unto myself, so that I might finish my course with joy," (Acts 20:24). I have quoted that since I have moved on up in years. You take on different feelings. I'll tell you birthdays have more ways of talking than from just the calendar's standpoint. You can almost feel it from head to toe. But at the same time, following God has a way of bringing you through all those places. And if we embrace them, we can do and have the hope that this apostle has written. We can finish our course with joy.

And he says, "...and the ministry which I have received of the Lord Jesus, to testify of the gospel of the grace of God" (Acts 20:24). Being in the ministry, we have invited some people along the way who wanted to serve the Lord, but they didn't want to start if they weren't going to go through with it. I've actually left a few on the pew not coming to the altar because they had the feeling that they couldn't make it. They didn't want to go to the altar and act as if they were Christians only to find out later that they couldn't hold out. Really there's nothing wrong with that, but you need to discover as you begin in this walk that you've got to trust the Lord for that born-again experience. That's a great step itself, and that's a great understanding of God being able to change our hearts and give us an appetite for the milk of God's Word.

You are not going to have to step into this barehanded, but listen, you do have to step into it with faith in the Word of God. And there's no better way to do that than to get still before the Lord. How the Lord is calling upon us, my friends, to build and not be embarrassed by not being able to go through. He doesn't want to discourage you. He wants to let you know what you can expect. Then He wants to let you know that really you've got nothing else to turn to anyway. There's no hope outside of the road He's got for you.

Many times we have to come to a realization of the dead-end street that's in this world, so we can try to find one that goes on through to the better world. How good it is to find in the Scripture that we do have some who have come to the end of the way and who have said, "None of these things have moved me." There's no one who spoke of the trials with a less complaining attitude or feeling than the Apostle Paul.

He says, "Of the Jews five times received I forty stripes save one. Thrice was I beaten with rods, once was I stoned, thrice I suffered shipwreck, a night and a day I have been in the deep; In journeyings often, in perils of waters, in perils of robbers, in perils by mine own countrymen, in perils by the heathen, in perils in the city, in perils in the wilderness, in perils in the sea, in perils among false brethren; In weariness and painfulness, in watchings often, in hunger and thirst, in fastings often, in cold and nakedness" (2 Corinthians 11:24-27). I'll tell you, he suffered, but he surely started out good.

He started out knowing something about the cost of following and with the realization of what he had left behind. There was nothing he could offer himself through the life that he had been living after now coming to the truth.

You know it's one thing to think you're right, and it's another thing to not be right and to think you're right. It takes a really good shaking, but I've said this, "Oh Lord, do anything to put me on the right path." Paul must have had that feeling, and he proved to be sincere even when he was far from doing the right thing at first.

God will give us a chance, folks. Don't be afraid, but He is going to show us that there is a cross to bear. We're going to bear one anyway, so why not pick up the cross He has for us and go for it? We'll not only have His good promises at the end, but He'll give revelation of truth to encourage us in the walk.

He's left it with us here through these scriptures where Paul says, "None of these things move me." I have followed this scripture reading concerning the servants of God, and I'll tell you they have made a believer out of me. They really have. "And when they had called the apostles, and beaten them, they commanded that they should not speak in the name of Jesus, and let them go. And they departed from the presence of the council, rejoicing that they were counted worthy to suffer shame for His name. And daily in the temple, and in every house, they ceased not to teach and preach Jesus Christ" (Acts 5:40-42).

It's a marvelous thing to see people at the end of the road who are actually forgiving of all their enemies. Forgiving of those who have actually persecuted them unto death. It's a marvelous thing to see truth prevailing and keeping them in God's will and God's pleasure in the midst of their trial. "And they stoned Stephen, calling upon God, and saying, Lord Jesus, receive my spirit. And he kneeled down, and cried with a loud voice, Lord, lay not this sin to their charge. And when he had said this, he fell asleep" (Acts 7:59-60).

I hope that we will stay in the presence of the Lord in

what we call The Secret Place until we can begin to see *the importance of our trials and troubles.* David says "Before I was afflicted I went astray: but now have I kept Thy Word. It is good for me that I have been afflicted; that I might learn Thy statutes" (Psalm 119:67,71). Our troubles and our trials actually may be the very thing that's keeping us moving in the right direction. That's why we're told His grace is sufficient. "And He said unto me, My grace is sufficient for thee: for My strength is made perfect in weakness. Most gladly therefore will I rather glory in my infirmities, that the power of Christ may rest upon me. Therefore I take pleasure in infirmities, in reproaches, in necessities, in persecutions, in distresses for Christ's sake: for when I am weak, then am I strong" (2 Corinthians 12:9-10).

We read in the Scripture where the Lord has a gospel, not only of mercy, but of grace also. The mercy of God is not condoning wrong doing, but it's forgiving us of our wrong doing. The grace of God is given to us so that we can carry out His will and His plan and the pattern He has for us to walk in after He has forgiven us of our sins. "And I thank Christ Jesus our Lord, Who hath enabled me, for that He counted me faithful, putting me into the ministry; Who was before a blasphemer, and a persecutor, and injurious: but I obtained mercy, because I did it ignorantly in unbelief. And the grace of our Lord was exceeding abundant with faith and love which is in Christ Jesus. This is a faithful saying, and worthy of all acceptation, that Christ Jesus came into the world to save sinners; of whom I am chief. Howbeit for this cause I obtained mercy, that in me first Jesus Christ might shew forth all longsuffering, for a pattern to them which should hereafter believe on Him to life everlasting" (1 Timothy 1:12-16).

I do not have time in one little *Stones From The Secret Place,* to tell of the many ways the Lord has helped me through difficult places. I never shall forget some of them. That's the reason I would encourage you, not condemn or put you down, when you are in your trial. I would say with assurance and hope that you will receive it. "Beloved, think it not strange concerning the fiery trial which is to try you, as though some strange thing happened unto you: But rejoice, inasmuch as ye are partakers of Christ's sufferings; that, when His glory shall be revealed, ye may be glad also with exceeding joy. If ye be reproached for the name of Christ, happy are ye; for the spirit of glory and of God resteth upon you: on their part He is evil spoken of, but on your part He is glorified" (1 Peter 4:12-14).

Think about it. How many have had pressures and trials, and finally, they learn a little bit about how to trust God with them. When two or three days pass, those same trials are trying to get back upon our lives. Many times they are very successful in getting back into our lives. The enemy seeks to wear us out by repeating those pressures again and again. "Be sober, be vigilant; because your adversary the devil, as a roaring lion, walketh about, seeking whom he may devour: Whom resist stedfast in the faith, knowing that the same afflictions are accomplished in your brethren that are in the world" (1 Peter 5:8-9).

But listen, stay before the Lord. Seek His face. And God will have grace. "But the God of all grace, Who hath called us unto His eternal glory by Christ Jesus, after that ye have suffered a while, make you perfect, stablish, strengthen, settle you" (1 Peter 5:10).

The Word says to just keep looking toward the Lord and His sufferings. It says if we look to Him and His sufferings, then we won't faint in ours. I've studied that statement because it came to be very real as we were waiting on the Lord. It says to consider the Lord in His sufferings, not the neighbor's sufferings and not yours, but consider Him in His sufferings lest we become weary and faint in our own. "Looking unto Jesus the Author and Finisher of our faith; Who for the joy that was set before Him endured the cross, despising the shame, and is set down at the right hand of the throne of God. For consider Him that endured such contradiction of sinners against Himself, lest ye be wearied and faint in your minds" (Hebrews 12:2-3).

There's a revelation that God means for us to get in His sufferings that will unload us of our own. We'll find His yoke turns out to be easy, His burden to be light. "None of these things move me." When you first hear that, you think of someone who is saying, "I'm strong. You're weak." No, when you follow the footsteps of this that the Scriptures point out, you'll have to admit they had to get in harmony with the Lord to be able to say that and to be able to end their course with joy.

Friends, actually the will and the grace of God and His ability will come to those, as the Word says, that wait upon the Lord. "He giveth power to the faint; and to them that have no might He increaseth strength. Even the youths shall faint and be weary, and the young men shall utterly fall: But they that wait upon the Lord shall renew their strength; they shall mount up with wings as eagles; they shall run, and not be weary; and they shall walk, and not faint" (Isaiah 40:29-31).

He knows of weary moments that are going to come even though we're bearing the very cross we're supposed to bear. A parent who is loaded with the care of a family, especially in our day, can get mighty weary. But somehow God has looked out for all these times that come our way. He's already prepared for it and has proven to us that we can overcome and come forth strong.

Even when Jesus was taking the last steps up the hill of Calvary and others were weeping for Him, Jesus turned to them and said, "Daughters of Jerusalem, weep not for Me, but weep for yourselves, and for your children" (Luke 23:28). I have a feeling He thought, "In just three days, I'll be home with the Father, so don't worry about Me. But you are still here, and don't be surprised if you find yourself weeping while you're here. It won't be long until you'll say with Me, Don't weep for me. Weep for yourselves."

You'll find out that your trials and troubles are what keep you in The Secret Place.

Don't be discouraged.

Go and seek the Lord in secret.

Meditate in His Law and refuse to let meditations of other things rob you of this wonderful truth that will help you say along with Paul, "None of these things move me. I have learned in whatever state that I'm in therewith to be content." Paul said to Timothy, "Godliness with contentment is great gain" (1 Timothy 6:6). If the enemy can make you discontented following God, he's on his way toward you into a wrong area in your thinking and in your position. Don't tolerate it.

Stay on the alert, and you can by staying before the Lord. I look back even today and think of things that could have happened so that I wouldn't be talking about The Secret Place today. I wouldn't know anything about His grace, His blessing, His revelation, His strength. So I thank God for every trial that has kept me focused in the right direction. And listen, He knows what to choose for us. Know this, regardless, the Lord will carry us through if we will wait on Him. Seek His face. *Read on, my Friends.*

Faith Will Not Rid The Child Of God From Suffering.

-J. E. Murdock

– 9 –

NOT JUST TO BELIEVE BUT TO SUFFER WITH HIM

It's amazing that so many of us experience a touch from God and get a heavy load moved away and are able to testify, "My sins are forgiven. They're gone." And oh, to see God as One Who will and Who is able to cushion our lives where all we have to do is to believe God and the road will be smooth. But remember, the Scripture reveals to us that He has not only called upon us to believe, but to suffer with Him. Dear friends, we need to stay before the Lord until we can receive a revelation of that truth. We must understand the value of not only believing, but also the suffering that goes with it. As the Word says, "If we suffer with Him, we shall also reign with Him:" (2 Timothy 2:12).

Jesus certainly didn't hold back from us that there is some suffering if we follow in His steps. There are also sufferings in the path of every other walk, but the sufferings in those paths are not rewarding. To suffer for right doing brings rewards. "But let none of you suffer as a murderer, or as a thief, or as an evildoer, or as a busybody in other men's matters. Yet if any man suffer as a Christian, let him not be ashamed; but let him glorify God on this behalf" (1 Peter 4:15-16).

Most of the time we come to the Lord because we feel like we're suffering for wrongdoing, and we are. Most people who go to the altar for the first time to accept the Lord are suffering for their own wrongdoing. They are doing like the Pharisee that Jesus spoke of. "The Pharisee stood and prayed thus with himself, God, I thank thee, that I am not as other men are, extortioners, unjust, adulterers, or even as this publican. I fast twice in the week, I give tithes of all that I possess." The other man is suffering. "And the publican, standing afar off, would not lift up so much as his eyes unto heaven, but smote upon his breast, saying, God be merciful to me a sinner" (Luke 18:11-13).

It's a beautiful thing. In fact, it's the mercy of the Lord that wrongdoing carries with it some suffering. But at the end of the day there, you'll find God is stretching forth His hand and He's saying, "Come unto Me, all ye that labour and are heavy laden, and I will give you rest" (Matthew 11:28). And we are told in Romans 10:11-13, Anyone who trusts in Him will never be put to shame. For there is no difference between Jew and Gentile—the same Lord is Lord of all and richly blesses all who call on Him, for, "Everyone who calls on the name of the Lord will be saved."

We are to enjoy and to receive and know that the touch He gives us has worked wonderfully in our lives. But to follow on then, that's the importance of reading a little bit more in the truth of God. We, of course, are children. We start out as children, and that's why reproof doesn't go over big. But as we meditate upon it, we'll see the necessity of it. "All scripture is given by inspiration of God, and is profitable for doctrine, for reproof, for correction, for instruction in righteousness" (2 Timothy 3:16). We'll find out it's not only important, but it's really a must for you and me. Somehow it fits in because we hardly make a turn to the right until we suffer from the wrong. But at the same time, to begin to suffer for the right, there is a beautiful place in that.

I can't say it happened many times, but I can say it has happened that after being persecuted and laughed at or mocked, I was able to turn away and weep, we might say, for joy. I turned away from a family member of mine years ago. I was sitting in the house talking to them about the Lord and the coming of the Lord. My sister said to her husband, my brother-in-law, "Oh, get him on out. He's religious." To me, the Lord was very precious. I didn't know it was weighing that heavy upon them. I got up and started walking down the hallway in their home. I stopped at the door and said a little bit more.

I know I was a bit forward in those times. I walk a little

softer now I guess, but I'll never forget that. I wasn't driven out because I was calling them bad names. We were talking about the Lord, and what the Lord could do and wanted to do for us. I guess I stood at the door there a little too long because my sister said to her husband again, "Oh, get him on out. Shut the door." So this time I stepped on outside.

I don't know what it was, but I never felt so good considering I hated to be misunderstood. But I knew they needed what I said, and I had already seen the Scripture that said there was going to be some suffering doing this. I can't say that that is easy to step over into, but I do say this, if we'll stay in the presence of God and wait long enough, we can carry out this part of the gospel, too. We will be persecuted for right doing, but Jesus says to rejoice. "Blessed are ye, when men shall revile you, and persecute you, and shall say all manner of evil against you falsely, for My sake. Rejoice, and be exceeding glad: for great is your reward in heaven: for so persecuted they the prophets which were before you" (Matthew 5:11-12). If we're persecuted for wrong doing, we have nothing to rejoice in but to back up and make it right.

It's important for the believer today to know that faith will not rid the child of God from suffering. But listen, Jesus didn't suffer because of a need of repentance. He suffered for right doing. "For even hereunto were ye called: because Christ also suffered for us, leaving us an example, that ye should follow His steps: Who did no sin, neither was guile found in His mouth: Who, when He was reviled, reviled not again; when He suffered, He threatened not; but committed Himself to Him that judgeth righteously:" (1 Peter 2:21-23).

And when the real showdown came to find fault with Him, they couldn't. They actually had to persecute Him even though they had no true witnesses that He had done anything wrong. He was just doing the Father's will. "Then said Pilate to the chief priests and to the people, I find no fault in this man" (Luke 23:4).

This is important to me, and it's important to you as well. We don't have to live under the shadow of conviction. There is a place to actually feel good in your sufferings and know that it's for a good cause. Now that there's purpose for our sufferings is not easy to discover because it has to be real. A person cannot use, we might say, a lack of real wisdom or a lack of true love or respect for the other person. It has to be real, or we'll feel it.

Oh yes, I said the right thing to my sister and her husband, but I said it in the wrong way. I said it in the wrong spirit. God doesn't overlook those things because He is able to help us in a more perfect way. He's patient to lead us on and let us suffer for our little errors that we make sometime by saying the right thing, but in the wrong spirit. "But and if ye suffer for righteousness' sake, happy are ye: and be not afraid of their terror, neither be troubled; But sanctify the Lord God in your hearts: and be ready always to give an answer to every man that asketh you a reason of the hope that is in you with meekness and fear: Having a good conscience; that, whereas they speak evil of you, as of evildoers, they may be ashamed that falsely accuse your good conversation in Christ. For it is better, if the will of God be so, that ye suffer for well doing, than for evil doing" (1 Peter 3:14-17).

If you are reading this message from The Secret Place, don't slap yourself too hard. Don't put yourself down too quickly now. Take a little time. You're not by yourself. We've all said the right thing but have mixed up our own spirit in it, and it wasn't pleasing to the Lord. We haven't hurt anyone else, but God wants it done right. Then, He can honor it.

Above all, our lesson today from The Secret Place is that we're called upon, not only to believe, but to suffer with Him. Let's go for it. That kind of grace and understanding won't be found everywhere you look. *But, you can find it as you wait on God in The Secret Place.*

– 10 –

Now My Eyes Have Seen The Lord

$\Longleftrightarrow$

I read from the book of Job a lot. It's amazing how important it is to just read it over and over and over again. It's surprising how much more revelation of the truth can come to us as we meditate in the law of God. I've often wondered really about Job. He is addressed by the Lord Himself as being an upright person. "Then the Lord said to satan, And the Lord said unto satan, Hast thou considered My servant Job, that there is none like him in the earth, a perfect and an upright man, one that feareth God, and escheweth evil?" (Job 1:8).

In many ways God was honoring Job and Job was blessed. "Then satan answered the Lord, and said, Doth Job fear God for nought? Hast not Thou made an hedge about him, and about his house, and about all that he hath on every side? Thou hast blessed the work of his hands, and his substance is increased in the land" (Job 1:9-10). Then, to find him in a great trial, and his friends coming and talking to him and trying to get him straight and explain why he's in his trials.

I didn't have to read Job many times to realize, "Hey, I would hate to have to pass through those waters." Job is really faced with something. You can tell it wasn't easy on Job for I'll tell you what, he cursed the day he was born to think of, "I've tried so hard, and now look what's happening to me." "After this opened Job his mouth, and cursed his day. And Job spake, and said, Let the day perish wherein I was born, and the night in which it was said, There is a man child conceived" (Job 3:1-3).

That's why we need to read just a little more in the Word of Truth to find out that there are things that we don't know about, things that we don't understand. We feel that we have put it all before the Lord. Somehow and for some reason perfection doesn't always come so that we can enjoy what we expect to enjoy. But in continuing to read about Job, we find he comes out with something very good. That's why, as the scripture says, we need to follow on to really know the Lord.

Some have followed on enough to know and appreciate the Lord's sufferings, but very few have learned to appreciate their own. Yet, there are some wonderful, strong statements that have come from the lips of those who saw the importance of their suffering. For instance, David said, "Before I was afflicted I went astray: but now have I kept Thy Word" (Psalm 119:67).

Don't be too hard on yourself, but seek to find out, "Why is this happening to me?" Hearing Job's conversation with his friends, why I can tell it wasn't very easy to discover what God was really seeking to do with Job. And not only to do with Job, but through Job's experience, to get a lesson over to you and me. That's why the scripture says in the Song of Solomon, "If you would know, if you want to find out what's going on, follow the footsteps of the flock."

So, God's very best, who have followed on in the Scriptures, have a beautiful lesson for us and something that should encourage us regardless of where we are coming from. We can still find some tracks that have been made along that same path. You and I are not the first ones. "Remember them which have the rule over you, who have spoken unto you the Word of God: whose faith follow, considering the end of their conversation" (Hebrews 13:7).

Our thought today is, "Now My Eyes Have Seen The Lord." I don't think Job had ever really discovered this part, or he would have already talked more about it earlier. There was a little something wrong with Job that you seldom hear about. But if you read it carefully and slowly, you'll find that God didn't send the trial just to get a lesson to you and to me. His trial was so, we might say, bring about a little more perfection.

Think about just being able to hear and not being able to see. That seems to be what happened in Job's experience that the Lord seemed fit to carry him through. The Lord wasn't afraid to carry Job through this. Though he might have thought, "Well, what else, Lord?" He was far enough along that he didn't faint in his trial and test. He found it hard to defend himself, but he made a statement that seemed to uncover what the Lord was really seeking after. It will be worthwhile for you and me to consider all these areas. His friends seemed to want to prove to Job that, "You're bound to have done something badly wrong, or you wouldn't be going through what you are going through."

Now most every believer can take that phrase and say, "Hum, that's passed my way, too. That's been my thought on life a lot of times. What have I done that is wrong?" That's just a part of life. There's no way to erase it because there will be enough to happen to everyone that will cause us to wonder. Oh, I'll be glad when the day comes that we won't have to wonder any more like that, but we can be like the Lord. I had to throw that in for good measure right here.

Job made a statement when they were ready to put him down, and explain to him, "Listen, something is bound to be wrong, or you wouldn't be going through this." Finally, to tamper with Job's feeling of his surrender to God. It looked like everything was surrendered to God. But he made a statement that caught my attention, and I began to look at it to see really what it was all about. He said, "My righteousness I hold fast, and will not let it go: my heart shall not reproach me so long as I live" (Job 27:6). "My righteousness I will not let go." Now you'll find out that his friends got nowhere in pointing these things out. No doubt they didn't understand anything like that. All they understood was, "If you are having trouble, you've done something bad." But it really wasn't that. God wants to thoroughly perfect our lives, and He's able to do it. He's not wondering, "I don't know whether you'll make it or not. You'll just have to go through it and see." No, He's able to bring it about if we'll just stay in the place so that God can go ahead and bring it about.

Finally, the Lord Himself began talking to Job, and Job to the Lord. Something came out of Job's lips there that make us see that the Lord was trying to get rid of something that had somehow gotten into Job's life. You know, it's not easy to climb over the wall of self life though we want to honor God with everything that we say. But, Job said, "My righteousness." You know what the Lord says about our righteousness. "But we are all as an unclean thing, and all our righteousnesses are as filthy rags;" (Isaiah 64:6).

With this viewpoint in mind then, we can see what's going on. And it'll help us because He is not going to let anything escape. It takes a long time to do that. It just takes a little time to recognize it. Sometimes God has to carry us through things before we recognize them. Job had already made the statement, "My righteousness I will not let go." I don't think he really understood what it was. Self righteousness can leak in somewhere if we don't recognize it. That's why we must be on guard. We certainly wouldn't take the credit intentionally, but somehow it had got into Job's life. My righteousness.

If he had not surrendered to God, he wouldn't be so righteous. "Then the Lord answered Job out of the whirlwind, and said, Who is this that darkeneth counsel by words without knowledge? Gird up now thy loins like a man; for I will demand of thee, and answer thou Me. Where wast thou when I laid the foundations of the earth? declare, if thou hast understanding" (Job 38:1-4).

When the Lord got through asking Job some questions, Job had to stop. He couldn't answer. He could answer his friends and argue with them pretty good. But then the Lord came with this idea and asked him, "Where were you when I did these things?" He asked some pretty hard questions for Job found out, "Hum, I don't know it all, do I? I'm not up to par on those kind of questions." Finally, he couldn't answer the Lord. He said, "I know that thou canst do every thing, and that no thought can be withholden from Thee. Who is he that hideth counsel without knowledge? therefore have I uttered that I understood not; things too wonderful for me, which I knew not. Hear, I beseech Thee, and I will speak: I will demand of Thee, and declare Thou unto me" (Job 42:2-4).

Now we come to the point. Job said, "I have heard of Thee by the hearing of the ear: but now mine eye seeth Thee.

Wherefore I abhor myself, and repent in dust and ashes" (Job 42:5-6). In other words, he knew that he wasn't able to answer all those questions.

The Lord knows how to touch us, doesn't He? He knows how to talk to us. It's almost like the parable He gave about the king who made a wedding for his son. When he came in to see the guests who had been invited, he saw a man having no wedding garment, and he said to him, "...Friend, how camest thou in hither not having a wedding garment? And he was speechless" (Matthew 22:12). He couldn't answer, so the king had him cast out.

So Job had a question and if you'll meditate in the many parts of the book of Job and get a clear picture, it'll be helpful and will bless you to find out that God doesn't allow things just for fun. He has a purpose in everything that He does with His children. And He's there to work with you patiently. He's there to honor that which needs to be honored as well as to bring to light that which needs to be revealed.

That's exactly where we went in the trials and tests. We bypassed the friends that couldn't understand or diagnose the case to satisfy Job. Whenever Job got before the Lord and began to talk with Him and God talked with Job, understanding came. He said, "Oh my, I abhor myself, and I repent." Then, he let go of his righteousness, but before he had said, "I will not let go my righteousness." He got a true glimpse of the greatness of God and said, "I've just been hearing of You by the ear, but now my eyes see You."

I'll tell you really, I wanted to find a little fault with God for allowing such a test and trial to come on Job. God had said earlier, "There is none like him on earth, a perfect and upright man, one that feareth God and escheweth evil." But, then I found out the value of going on with God and coming into the place where you can become more of what He wants you to become. That is very worthwhile. Just don't fall out with God.

A man came to Jesus when He was healing the lame and the halt and the blind and said, "You've got a servant over here in jail. He wants to know for sure if you are the Christ." Would you believe it was John the Baptist? Yes sir, it was

John the Baptist. It was the man who at first refused to baptize Jesus for he said, "Oh, I'm not worthy to baptize You." He had such a revelation of Jesus, the Son of God. He said to those who asked him who he was, "I am the voice of one crying in the wilderness, Make straight the way of the Lord," He said, "I'm just a voice." When he saw Jesus coming to him, he said, "Behold the Lamb of God, which taketh away the sin of the world. This is He of Whom I said, After me cometh a man which is preferred before me: for He was before me" (John 1:29-30).

But now, John in his test and trial sent his disciples to Jesus to ask Him if He was the Christ. "When the men were come unto Him, they said, John the Baptist hath sent us unto Thee, saying, Art Thou He that should come? or look we for another?"

So, we know this. John, too, was seeking for a little more information and a little more light upon what seemed earlier to have no need for more light. "Then Jesus answering said unto them, Go your way, and tell John what things ye have seen and heard; how that the blind see, the lame walk, the lepers are cleansed, the deaf hear, the dead are raised, to the poor the gospel is preached" (Luke 7:20,22).

I think John the Baptist could have gone along with that because he knew the ministry of Jesus. But Jesus said something else. "And blessed is he, whosoever shall not be offended in Me." John could say, "Well I know He's healed them. I know that, but why am I in jail? Why am I in prison?" There might have been a point that John could have accepted it gladly and maybe rejoiced. But somewhere or other his trial offended his revelation or vision of Jesus, and he sent two of his disciples to Jesus saying, "Art Thou He that should come? or look we for another?" (Luke 7:19).

So, don't grow weary and faint, but inquire again in The Secret Place. God will make clear what your trial is about. He'll also make clear the importance of your trial. Let's stay in The Secret Place until our soul is cheered up, and so we may not stumble or be confused in the Word. "Jesus answered and said unto them, Go and shew John again those things which ye do hear and see: The blind receive their sight, and the lame walk, the lepers are cleansed, and the deaf hear, the dead are raised up, and the poor have the gospel preached to them. And blessed is he, whosoever shall not be offended in Me" (Matthew 11:4-6).

Thank the Lord that now we see more clearly. That's why the Lord teaches us that while we are in this earthly house, there is going to be a need. "For we know that if our earthly house of this tabernacle were dissolved, we have a building of God, an house not made with hands, eternal in the heavens" (2 Corinthians 5:1). We wouldn't be able to understand the full revelation anyway. But one of these days we'll understand it. We used to sing the song, "We'll Understand It Better By And By."

Another thought that came so real to our heart from The Secret Place was, "Don't Faint Under Your Trials. Just Follow On." Don't talk it just among your friends. God wants to talk it over with you. That's what happened that opened the eyes of Job when he said, "I know that Thou canst do every thing, and that no thought can be withholden from Thee. Who is he that hideth counsel without knowledge? therefore have I uttered that I understood not; things too wonderful for me, which I knew not. Hear, I beseech Thee, and I will speak: I will demand of Thee, and declare Thou unto me. I have heard of Thee by the hearing of the ear: but now mine eye seeth Thee" (Job 42:2-5).

How beautiful to get the answer when you're having so much trial. *It's for us, too, if we'll stay in The Secret Place.*

The Testings In Today's Experiences Are Actually An Arm Reaching Out To Things Eternal... Things Of Tomorrow.

-J. E. Murdock

– 11 –

PRAYER AND PRAISE IN A SONG

I don't suppose that I have talked from any subject that's more alive to my heart than the title we have on these Stones From The Secret Place, "Prayer and Praise In A Song." When I got saved at the age of 15, I immediately bought a little guitar. I dedicated it to the Lord. I wasn't taught that I should do that. I just felt the Holy Spirit wanted me to. I dedicated it to the Lord and asked Him to help me learn to play and sing to worship Him.

Remember, I had no church to go to or group to follow. We had no one to lead us out from our time of prayer at home and being saved and filled with the Spirit, so I was able to yield only to the Holy Spirit. He was working in our hearts mightily in a wonderful way. You talk about a new-found joy and a new life, we really had it there. So, I would go to the prayer place at home or even down in the woods. We lived on 78 acres of land. I'd have as many as three different places around over the farm where I had little altars and where I'd go to pray. No one told me to do that. I had no one to go along with me, but the Lord was just real. The hope of His coming was much alive.

The very first thing that happened after being saved is I began to sing when I went to prayer. I don't know how it happened, so it had to be real. I'd never go to prayer without taking my guitar along. Most of the time I began waiting before the Lord by singing such songs as this:

> There's a song in my heart
> Says Jesus save me;

> My all I'm giving;
> For Him I'm living;
> Anywhere Jesus leads me I'll be willing
> To tell the story of His great love.

Another little chorus we'd found that I would begin to sing to the Lord as well as to pray was this:

> I am determined to hold out to the end;
> Jesus is with me, on Him I can depend;
> I know I have salvation, I feel it in my
> soul;
> I am determined to hold out to the end.

The Holy Spirit just began to bring little songs to me. I would sing alone there with the little guitar. So prayer and praise is certainly not a new step in the Christian life. We're grateful for services where we go and find people who are singing and worshipping and praising the Lord. Then, later a message is preached. Listen, Friends, truly that is wonderful. If there is any way to improve upon our worship, it's to learn to get alone with the Lord and begin to worship him with no hindrances or distractions. There is nothing more wonderful than that.

A couple who truly falls in love, if their love is what it should be and the purpose of their togetherness is for the right reason, then it's not long until they just want to be alone and talk about their plans for a future life together. You may have to turn back a few pages to find such things existing, but it was there. That was the way we came to know the Lord. You didn't have to be in church to find the blessing. You didn't have to be among friends to find the blessing. All you had to do was go before the Lord with a hungry heart and with a thirsty soul.

You know, if you were to go to a well to get a drink of water, you wouldn't have to have company there to drink the water and enjoy it. And *somehow if the Lord gets on the inside of our heart, it doesn't take a crowd to bless you.* It doesn't take a crowd to bring commitment and joy to you. What God has brought over to our heart in The Secret Place is to come before Him with prayer, with praising and singing unto the Lord.

"Rejoice in the Lord always..." Did you notice the word *always*? Have you ever rejoiced and tears were flowing down your cheeks? That's odd, isn't it? But it can happen. You will be surprised the tears that can flow because of such joy that's filling your soul.

Has a friend ever blessed you and you actually felt their care and their concern for you? Their gift to you was from such a heart of love that you had to cry instead of rejoice. Well, that's the way the blessings of the Lord come at times... rejoicing with tears. "Rejoice in the Lord alway: and again I say, Rejoice. Let your moderation be known unto all men. The Lord is at hand" (Philippians 4:4-5).

I say here that one revelation that swept through my heart in The Secret Place was that, "the coming of the Lord is at hand." Honestly, I can hardly believe that years have gone by and the Lord has not come. Really, after I first found the Lord and He moved in my heart at home in the prayer time, if they had come and told me it would be ten years before the Lord would come, I would have just known they all were false prophets. I would have known they were unbelievers. So you can tell, because of my feelings back then, that I must have found something to still have that strong confidence today that truly He's coming again.

That confidence was built by getting in The Secret Place before the Lord and laying His Word down before me. I was getting so much understanding of His Word, developing patience and long-suffering. I know that His delay doesn't mean that God isn't true. James tells us, "Be patient therefore, brethren, unto the coming of the Lord. Behold, the husbandman waiteth for the precious fruit of the earth, and hath long patience for it, until he receive the early and latter rain. Be ye also patient; stablish your hearts: for the coming of the Lord draweth nigh" (James 5:7-8).

By staying in touch with the Lord in prayer, I'm not

stumbling in the least over why the years have gone by, and the Lord still hasn't come. If I had the time, I could give many reasons why there is still a longing, a strong confidence that the coming of the Lord is at hand. I believe the reason is because staying in the presence of the Lord and the revelation of truth today is just as real as it was years ago.

How true the saying is where Jesus said, "Verily, verily, I say unto you, Moses gave you not that bread from heaven; but My Father giveth you the true bread from heaven. For the bread of God is He which cometh down from heaven, and giveth life unto the world. I am the bread of life. Your fathers did eat manna in the wilderness, and are dead. This is the bread which cometh down from heaven, that a man may eat thereof, and not die" (John 6:32-33,48-50).

I find that if I stay in His presence, the Word of the Lord is just as powerful now even if years have gone by. You learn after all which way to turn. Paul says, "If in this life only we have hope in Christ, we are of all men most miserable. But now is Christ risen from the dead, and become the firstfruits of them that slept" (1 Corinthians 15:19-20).

He is coming again. He wants to find us watching, waiting, even longing, for His coming. He wants to do things in our heart and in the hearts of others. The time will come He will return. "Henceforth there is laid up for me a crown of righteousness, which the Lord, the righteous judge, shall give me at that day: and not to me only, but unto all them also that love His appearing" (2 Timothy 4:8).

Then, Philippians 4:6-7 says, "Be careful for nothing; but in every thing by prayer and supplication with thanksgiving let your requests be made known unto God. And the peace of God, which passeth all understanding, shall keep your hearts and minds through Christ Jesus." What a statement to read, but what a revelation to receive of this wonderful truth because no one wants to be ugly in their life. "Let the peace of God passeth all understanding, shall keep your hearts and minds through Christ Jesus." More and more I can see the importance of staying before the Lord and allowing God to remove things that hinder me from receiving.

The more of Christ that comes into our hearts, the more opportunity and the greater is the blessing. To maintain it is almost unbelievable. The enemy wants to make you think you're going to lose it. It's important to be cautious enough to embrace what God has done for you in The Secret Place yesterday so you will be faithful to be there today and keep seeking His face.

Honestly, I could actually pretty well hold a revival and talk nothing about praising and singing while I prayed. I did notice a unique move of the Lord. I studied it, but the satisfaction I was getting in the move that was being made satisfied that it was the Lord. The time did come when there were little seasons that I would pick up my guitar and go to prayer and seek His face and, for minutes and sometimes for an hour, not play or sing. I just began to pray and meditate in the Word where normally at first I started with singing and praising. I think the Lord was trying to teach me just to let Him lead me and guide me less I take it and go one direction all the time.

I have seen it happen in recent years and months when it seemed it would be a good time to change to another song, they would sing or stay with the same song. Then, they would change to another. So really, I would say this, the whole thing is good, and what makes it better is to be led of the Spirit as you pray and as you praise.

It hasn't been too long ago when we typed and copied on our copy machine a little booklet we called, "Put Your Prayer And Your Praise In A Song" or "Put Your Prayer In A Song." I began to sing little choruses. One of them was:

> I want to *be* what You want me to be;
> I want to *say* what You want me to say;
> I want to *do* what You want me to do;
> Help me Lord, help me, Lord, I pray.

The Lord spoke to me and said, "Now that's the greatest prayer you've ever prayed." I put it on a tape immediately, so I could remember the melody of it.

I noticed the arrangement of that little song was first "I Want To *Be.*" You know, so many times we try to do things we can't do because we're not being something. The Lord made me see that we are first *to be.* Before we *can say* things right, we have *to be* right. Before we *can do* things right, we have *to be* right. So, the Lord said that's the greatest prayer. You've got *to be* first before you *can do* and before you *can say.* In other words to be what He wants you to be is to be born again, to be filled with the Spirit, to be led by the Spirit. Then, we can begin to learn to say and to do what He wants us to do. That was easy to understand.

Jesus, when He was in the cradle and Herod was seeking to destroy Him, couldn't get out of the cradle, but the Lord told Joseph to take Him and Mary, His mother, and flee into Egypt. So then actually growing is expected, and God has the patience to teach us. The prayer began to come I noticed there, and that's why I called it "Let Your Prayer And Praise Be In A Song." I noticed that every one of the twelve little choruses the Lord gave me was a sincere prayer...but I was singing them. That was so real.

So our thoughts from The Secret Place began to grow and become more real. I saw then that the Lord had helped us to be in harmony with His way of worship, and we had hardly realized it. The only thing I knew was that there was something good about it because we were so blessed. So we need to practice today to give thanks in everything. Jesus prayed, "Father, I thank Thee that Thou hast heard Me. And I knew that Thou hearest Me always: but because of the people which stand by I said it, that they may believe that Thou hast sent Me" (John 11:41-42).

So, God has a way of doing things. There's no better way to find that way and to be able to operate and be motivated and led in the way God wants us than just staying in His presence in The Secret Place. *How beautiful to have Prayer And Praise In A Song, and it will go places with us. God bless you!*

– 12 –

THE CORNER POST

I think it's important that we understand all of God's Word, but He does put some emphasis and cautions upon certain phrases of scripture. These scriptures are important to the Christian's journey and faith. The emphasis today is "The Corner Post."

Being a farm boy, I did a lot of fence building. I learned by walking along beside my dad why some posts were different than others and why some posts had greater responsibility and were even more important than others. A lot of our posts in the fence are called line posts. And all they are to do is just to hold up the wire. They don't have any other pressures on them but to hold up the wire. But the corner posts are larger and, as my father would say, they are posts that are put there that will last a long time. Where the little line post can be small and can be easily replaced, these corner posts are special.

That's what we have seen in the Scripture in God's ways of doing things. He put great emphasis upon putting things in our lives that we won't forget. Some things we need to remember because it's so easy to forget some important things. But the Lord is purposing and aims to put some things in our life that we won't easily forget.

He tells Moses to bring the children of Israel to the foot of Mount Horeb. He said He wanted to speak to them there in a way that they would fear Him. "Specially the day that thou stoodest before the Lord thy God in Horeb, when the Lord said unto me, Gather Me the people together, and I will make them hear My words, that they may learn to fear Me all the days that they shall live upon the earth, and that they may teach their children" (Deuteronomy 4:10).

Think of how important this message is. To actually have God do something for us so that we will get hold of the life and of the move of God that will direct us all the days of our life. That's why we have spoken much on the importance of the fear of God. That's a subject that very few people look into. The first thing they think is that God wants them to get rid of the fear. He doesn't want them to be afraid.

But there's a vast difference in what God says about fearing Him and fearing man and the things that are coming upon the earth. He says we are to fear Him. "And I say unto you My friends, Be not afraid of them that kill the body, and after that have no more that they can do. But I will forewarn you whom ye shall fear: Fear him, which after he hath killed hath power to cast into hell; yea, I say unto you, Fear him" (Luke 12:4-5).

So the purpose of this chapter today in *Stones From The Secret Place* is to find out the importance of God doing something in our lives that will work for us all the days of our life so we can't forget. Most people do remember some things that happened years ago, but some things that happened yesterday they forget.

In fact, my little wife said a few times about how it shocked her to think how easily I could forget some things that happened yesterday and talk about something that happened years ago. But there are things that impress us more than other things and get hold of us differently than other things. That's why God said, "I want to do something for Israel. I want to bring them to a service. I want to bring them into a place where I can talk to them. And I'm going to talk to them in a way that they will fear Me all the days of their lives."

Deuteronomy 4 presents to us the beautiful picture, the important picture of having corner posts put into our life. And this corner post then was a visitation of God that they were to remember. So whenever He appeared to them as they were standing at the foot of the mountain, He caused the Heavens to turn dark and there was a great cloud and thick darkness upon it. "And the Lord spake unto you out of the midst of the fire: ye heard the voice of the words, but saw no similitude; only ye heard a voice." You know Israel was bad to make images of other men and other creatures, but the Lord didn't show

Himself openly like that. They just heard a voice.

So He goes on with His visitation. "And He declared unto you His covenant, which He commanded you to perform, even ten commandments; and He wrote them upon two tables of stone" (Deuteronomy 4:4-13). But whenever He spoke there, the people were so much afraid that they cried out to Moses and said, "Moses don't let God speak to us. You speak to us."

I read on in the scripture where they did not choose the fear of God. Then I recognized to get the fear of the Lord, we have to choose it or it makes no difference what the Lord does if fear of God doesn't take hold. We have to choose it. And the Word says they didn't choose the fear of God. They'd rather have Moses. "For that they hated knowledge, and did not choose the fear of the Lord: They would none of my counsel: they despised all my reproof" (Proverbs 1:29-30).

You might be surprised to find out what you can feel in the ministry of God's Word, especially when you begin to talk about God's judgment or things that displease God, how quickly you lose an ear today. I really do believe if we read the Scripture, there is already enough there to teach us that the greatest thing that could happen to a person is for them to say, "Lord, give me the fear of God in my life." The fear of God will move you whether you understand why you are moving. You hear things. You see things. You feel things. The fear of God will work for you, and you can understand why later. "The fear of the Lord is a fountain of life, to depart from the snares of death" (Proverbs 14:27).

So, in a message we called that a "Corner Post." The Lord has done things, and He still wants to do things in your life that you just can't forget. Can you think of it now?

Have you received a visitation of the Lord that means so much to you that you just can't forget? Really, we have. I've seen the time, my friends, that I'd forget God's blessings in some ways, but there are some things that He has spoken and I just cannot forget. We call that a "Corner Post."

Now then, He blesses us daily and we daily forget a lot of things He does. "Blessed be the Lord, Who daily loadeth us with benefits, even the God of our salvation" (Psalm 68:19).

But He says, "I want to bless them. I want to speak to them in a way they will fear Me, not just for a day, tomorrow, or when they are just in trouble, but they will fear Me all the days of their life." God wants us to have it. Let's you and me choose it and ask God to do something in our life so we will learn to fear Him all the days of our life.

Really, I think that's one reason the Lord actually sends terrible judgment, and even in the house of God, why He sends real judgment a lot of times. In fact, He said judgment begins at the house of God. "For the time is come that judgment must begin at the house of God: and if it first begin at us, what shall the end be of them that obey not the gospel of God?" (1 Peter 4:17).

A lot of people have a testimony that would help others to learn to fear God. If they would tell them how God spoke and warned them not to do certain things but they went ahead and did it, how they suffered because they ignored the warnings of God. The Lord wanted to speak in such a way that they wouldn't have to just be told over and over and over again not to do certain things. The fear of God itself would actually be a fountain of life to depart from the snares of death. "Whoso despiseth the Word shall be destroyed: but he that feareth the commandment shall be rewarded. The law of the wise is a fountain of life, to depart from the snares of death" (Proverbs 13:13-14).

We've talked so much about the Corner Post to the extent that we made a small pamphlet and named different things that happened in our lives that we cannot forget. I actually remember talking back to an elderly man after I was saved. I was working on the job with this man. As an elderly man, he was really hard to work with. I understood later that he had the name of just being hard to please. My joy really was to please the man that I worked for. Just being saved and filled with the Spirit, I aimed with all my heart to keep that relationship with the Lord. But, this man was so hard to please on the job. He would get after me for many different little things that I wasn't really guilty of.

This is a very simple illustration, but it got a truth over

to me anyway. We were up on the barn nailing shingles, and we were putting them on straight. I had a brother-in-law who was a road commissioner. It was his barn. He came by and got up on the barn and just started nailing the shingles on. He caused bad curves in the shingles between the three of us. The elderly man looked and said to me, "Don't do that. Look how crooked it is." He began to quarrel about it when really it wasn't me. That made me feel bad. I wanted to tell him, "It's not me," but I wanted to keep peace. He ought to be able to see it himself.

I won't go into full details, but finally, it got really rough. I was hoping the day would end soon and I would to be able to leave the job before I lost my cool, as some would say. Then I would feel bad when I knelt down to pray and seek the Lord, so I tried to hold on and say nothing. Sure enough we started to quit, but he looked at his watch and said, "We got about an hour before quitting time. We're going to work around on the front of the house and put up a form for a concrete walk." Oh, I dreaded it because it seemed like he was so hard to work with and found fault in everything we did and didn't mind expressing it. Then I prayed, "Lord, help me keep right."

So, I got some little stobs ready to stob down the form for a cement slab and he began to gripe about the way I was aiming those little stobs that were to hold the form together for the cement to be poured. Finally, it seemed like it was just more than I could bear, so I said to him, "I wish that I could please you." And I said it in a wrong tone of voice...I felt bad about it. He looked up at me as he was on his knees driving the stobs down in the ground and said, "I'll knock you in the head with this hammer."

Well, I was just young enough, you might say, just in the stage that I didn't like that at all. Anyway, I calmly said, "You'll not be Mr. Willis either when you do." And when I did, I knew that I had answered him wrong, for this man had stood out on the street several times while I was out there singing and witnessing for the Lord. And the thought came to me: the next time he sees me on the street he'll remember me talking back to him. I went around the side of the house crying and my sister asked me what was wrong. I told her and she said, "No one gets along with him. Don't worry about it."

Nevertheless, what could I do about it? But, when I knelt down in prayer the next morning, the Lord spoke to me and said, "I want you to go to that man and ask his forgiveness." Well, I'll tell you, really, I knew enough about that man that he could care less about my apology, and what would he say? But the Lord just seemed to put it upon my heart. And I said, "Lord, if you'll let me see him whenever I get to town, why I'll sure ask him to forgive me."

The very next morning I went to town and he was one of the first people I saw...in that little country town where they tie off their teams in the back alley and stand around and talk to one another. He was back there talking to somebody and I thought to myself, "Well, I'll wait until he quits talking and ask him to forgive me later." But the Lord must have known that was the best time and something just seemed to almost get a hold of my collar and pull me over there. So I said, "Listen, Mr. Willis, I'm trying to live a Christian life and I'm sorry that I talked back to you yesterday evening." He said to me, "Well, you had no business doing it." And I said, "I know it and I want you to forgive me for it." And he just turned away and walked over and started talking to the man again. But did I feel better? Yes, I felt better.

I've used these experiences as guidelines as time has gone by. The more room we make for the Lord, the more He puts in our heart, the same feelings that He has towards others. So, don't fall out with one another. Find a place in the Lord that we can share with others the Christ-likeness that we want the Lord to share towards us. Give it a try...*it's worth it.*

– 13 –

IF I DON'T DO IT WITH LOVE, IT PROFITETH ME NOTHING

I know of nothing that is made plainer in Scripture than the responsibility we have in our labor and work for God to love. In fact, all of the things that Jesus had to accomplish and do for us started and stemmed with love. In spite of our condition the Bible reveals that, "God so loved the world that He gave His only begotten Son that whosoever believeth in Him would not perish but have everlasting life" (John 3:16).

We know and are instructed in the Word that Jesus loves the ungodly. "For when we were yet without strength, in due time Christ died for the ungodly. For scarcely for a righteous man will one die: yet peradventure for a good man some would even dare to die. But God commendeth His love toward us, in that, while we were yet sinners, Christ died for us" (Romans 5:6-8).

The Scripture speaks of loving your enemies. We've set our focus towards pressing to the mark of being more like Jesus. "Ye have heard that it hath been said, Thou shalt love thy neighbour, and hate thine enemy. But I say unto you, Love your enemies, bless them that curse you, do good to them that hate you, and pray for them which despitefully use you, and persecute you; That ye may be the children of your Father which is in heaven: for He maketh His sun to rise on the evil and on the good, and sendeth rain on the just and on the unjust" (Matthew 5:43-45).

The Stone from The Secret Place at this time is…"If I Don't Do It With Love, It Profiteth Me Nothing." An experience and a visitation of the Lord had come to me and I realized this truth, but I must have needed it again or the Holy Spirit wouldn't have said it over again. I didn't hear it in a camp-meeting. I didn't hear it from the neighbor. I heard it from the Lord.

My dear wife and I had moved to Cameron, Texas, to be in full-time ministry and work with the young people and help the pastor there.

We were unloading our furniture, and before we got it fully unloaded and in place, the pastor came up to the apartment and said, "Brother Murdock, I have an elderly lady who is unable to go to church. Would you and your wife take your instruments and go sing for this lady? She would enjoy it so much." We had an accordion and a guitar.

Now I'm a young person who has just come from a job working at a dairy, and this was certainly a new field to give myself totally to... full time in the ministry. But, I was glad to, and felt God had certainly opened this door for us to fulfill His will for our lives.

I picked up my guitar and walked across the big, long porch there at the apartments. I got into the Sunday school bus the pastor had come in and wanted us to see. I didn't speak out loud, but I thought to myself very clearly, "Well, this is your job now. To pick up the guitar and go sing to the elderly and those who desire to have a song or a prayer." Immediately the Spirit of the Lord said, "Yes, but if you do this without love, it will not profit you anything." Now, I'll tell you, it's one thing for your friend to tell you that. It's another thing for you to be aware that the Holy Spirit and the Word of God is relating that to you.

I wasn't out there to just labor in vain. I didn't want to just beat the air. "I therefore so run, not as uncertainly; so fight I, not as one that beateth the air:" (1 Corinthians 9:26). If I had to have love for it to count, you know that's exactly what I certainly began to do. As the song says...

> Fill my way every day with love.
> And let me walk with that heavenly dove;
> Let me go all the while,
> With a song and a smile,
> Fill my way every day with love.

Now that's easy to say, but we have found for sure that it takes a relationship with God to do things in love. "But woe unto you, Pharisees! for ye tithe mint and rue and all manner of herbs, and pass over judgment and the love of God: these ought ye to have done, and not to leave the other undone" (Luke 11:42). There's one thing that the Lord cautioned the disciples about. He said to them, "Beware of the leaven of the Pharisees and of the Sadducees" (Matthew 16:6).

They thought Jesus had found fault with them because they had forgotten to bring bread along with them. He had already performed a miracle with the loaves and fishes, so that was not a problem on Jesus' mind. He had something else in mind. But they thought, "Oh, we may have to feed the multitude again, and didn't bring any bread." But the Lord made it clear. "Then understood they how that He bade them not beware of the leaven of bread, but of the doctrine of the Pharisees and of the Sadducees" (Matthew 16:12).

In other words, don't just say you love somebody, say, "Lord, fill my heart with love. Don't let me be a hypocrite. Don't let me act as if I love somebody when I don't." That may not seem like much to some of us, but listen, Friends, it means a whole lot the *way* you do it. It's going to count if you do it in love.

You and I would feel mighty bad if we tried to send a counterfeit dollar across the counter to pay for our gas or groceries. Wouldn't you feel terrible to think, "Oh, if he looks real close, he'll find that money isn't real...it's counterfeit?" But, think of actually working for God and not having the real love of God. "He that loveth not knoweth not God; for God is love. In this was manifested the love of God toward us, because that God sent His only begotten Son into the world, that we might live through Him. Herein is love, not that we loved God, but that He loved us, and sent His Son to be the propitiation for our sins. Beloved, if God so loved us, we ought also to love one another. No man hath seen God at any time. If we love one another, God dwelleth in us, and His love is perfected in us" (1 John 4:8-12).

We're not saying this to put anyone down. We're saying

this to caution and help us to find out how not to labor in vain. We must ask God to give us a love that will cause our ministry to profit. "And hope maketh not ashamed; because the love of God is shed abroad in our hearts by the Holy Ghost which is given unto us" (Romans 5:5). That doesn't mean that everyone will be glad to see us, but know this, God will see what kind of spirit or attitude we have. Let's labor hard to do it.

You'll find 1 Corinthians 13 speaks of this love. "Though I speak with the tongues of men and of angels, and have not charity, I am become as sounding brass, or a tinkling cymbal" (1 Corinthians 13:1). What is He saying? He is saying that you can speak with tongues of men, and you can speak with tongues of angels and still not have charity. You can say one thing and be something else. That's why the Lord wants to touch the heart for He says, "Out of the abundance of the heart the mouth speaketh" (Matthew 12:34). If it's not real, it'll prove it's not in a very short while.

Friends, we must urge and encourage ourselves to stay before the Lord until the Holy Spirit can work in our lives and shed abroad His love in our hearts. "And hope maketh not ashamed; because the love of God is shed abroad in our hearts by the Holy Ghost which is given unto us" (Romans 5:5). Oh, there's been times I've wondered after I ministered if I had the proper love. It doesn't hurt to wonder. It doesn't hurt to examine yourself. It doesn't hurt to be more sure of yourself. My friends, grow in the love of God.

The Word says, "Though I have the gift of prophecy, and understand all mysteries, and all knowledge; and though I have all faith, so that I could remove mountains, and have not charity, I am nothing" (1 Corinthians 13:2). Did you ever see how far we are off without charity? Oh, nothing is plainer than the word brings out there concerning the love of God. And say, it is not your love. It's His love, and we get that when we seek His face. As the old song says...

Fill my way every day with love.

And how important it is.

Then he goes on to says, "And though I bestow all my goods to feed the poor, and though I give my body to be burned, and have not charity, it profiteth me nothing" (1 Corinthians 13:3). Isn't that strange that we can actually see the possibilities of giving our body to be burned for a cause, and it profits us nothing? We may be forced, my friends, to give ourselves to things that we have no desire for, but we can seek the Lord and He will strengthen us. Whatever comes our way, He will help us to do it with the right spirit and with the right attitude.

We see that a lot of real operations and services can be rendered that do not have charity. I don't know about you, but I want to work for God and I want it to count when I do. And the only way it's going to count is that I do it in the love of God.

And then the Bible gives a description of love. "Charity suffereth long, and is kind; charity envieth not; charity vaunteth not itself, is not puffed up, Doth not behave itself unseemly, seeketh not her own, is not easily provoked, thinketh no evil; Rejoiceth not in iniquity, but rejoiceth in the truth; Beareth all things, believeth all things, hopeth all things, endureth all things. Charity never faileth: but whether there be prophecies, they shall fail; whether there be tongues, they shall cease; whether there be knowledge, it shall vanish away. For we know in part, and we prophesy in part. But when that which is perfect is come, then that which is in part shall be done away. And now abideth faith, hope, charity, these three; but the greatest of these is charity" (1 Corinthians. 13:4-10,13).

So don't labor in vain. Be sure to labor with love. The love that comes only from a relationship with the Lord. "And we have known and believed the love that God hath to us. God is love; and he that dwelleth in love dwelleth in God, and God in him. Herein is our love made perfect, that we may have boldness in the day of judgment: because as he is, so are we in this world. There is no fear in love; but perfect love casteth out fear: because fear hath torment. He that feareth is not made perfect in love" (1 John 4:16-18).

If I don't do it with love, it profiteth me nothing.

You've Got To
Be Right First...
Before You Can
Do Right...
Before You Can
Say Right.

-J. E. Murdock

–14 –

OUT OF SODOM, YET LOOKING BACK

We went on in the preaching of the gospel, and the television age came. I tried to be broadminded enough to take in things that would be helpful, but I've always seen the necessity of shunning the very appearances of evil…to be careful. I've said this a lot of times. I don't even back my car out of the garage without being careful and watching, much less when I get on the highway. So I will say it gently, but I want to say it in the fear of God. I wish that our generation could get hold of it before it's too late.

We chose the Scriptures concerning Samson. He was a man with strength, a man who was not afraid of the enemy, a man who was not afraid to go against the Philistines. God was with him. The anointing was with him…the presence of God was with him. "And the woman bare a son, and called his name Samson: and the child grew, and the Lord blessed him. And the Spirit of the Lord began to move him at times…" (Judges 13:24-25).

Samson saw a woman of the Philistines and he told his mother and father he wanted to marry her. "And he came up, and told his father and his mother, and said, I have seen a woman in Timnath of the daughters of the Philistines: now therefore get her for me to wife. And he went down, and talked with the woman; and she pleased Samson well. And after a time he returned to take her" (Judges 14:2,7). In the first place he should not have been over there. He was there because of a wrong influence. He might not have said that when he first went, but he went again and talked to her.

She actually began to be used to allure Samson. "And it came to pass on the seventh day, that they said unto Samson's wife, Entice thy husband, that he may declare unto us the riddle, lest we burn thee and thy father's house with fire: have ye called us to take that we have? is it not so? And Samson's wife wept before him, and said, Thou dost but hate me, and lovest me not: thou hast put forth a riddle unto the children of my people, and hast not told it me. And he said unto her, Behold, I have not told it my father nor my mother, and shall I tell it thee? And she wept before him the seven days, while their feast lasted: and it came to pass on the seventh day, that he told her, because she lay sore upon him: and she told the riddle to the children of her people" (Judges 14:15-17).

Later, he saw another Philistine woman and loved her. Her name was Delilah. He went over to her place again and again. And, although he didn't realize it, he had begun to miss God's will for his life. "And it came to pass afterward, that he loved a woman in the valley of Sorek, whose name was Delilah. And the lords of the Philistines came up unto her, and said unto her, Entice him, and see wherein his great strength lieth, and by what means we may prevail against him, that we may bind him to afflict him: and we will give thee every one of us eleven hundred pieces of silver" (Judges 16:4-5).

So, she began to brag on him and question about his strength. She would, we might say, just pet him. This would have been a good time for God to have helped raise a standard in Samson. He didn't tell her at first. "And Delilah said to Samson, Tell me, I pray thee, wherein thy great strength lieth, and wherewith thou mightest be bound to afflict thee. And she said unto him, How canst thou say, I love thee, when thine heart is not with me? thou hast mocked me these three times, and hast not told me wherein thy great strength lieth" (Judges 16:6,15).

She kept on and finally he told her. "Really, this long hair of mine speaks of a dedication that my parents made to God for me. And the Lord has honored the dedication and His presence is with me. If you cut that hair off, then I will be like anybody else. And it came to pass, when she pressed him daily with her words, and urged him, so that his soul was vexed unto death; That he told her all his heart, and said unto her,

There hath not come a rasor upon mine head; for I have been a Nazarite unto God from my mother's womb: if I be shaven, then my strength will go from me, and I shall become weak, and be like any other man" (Judges 16:16-17).

He didn't plan on her cutting his hair off, but she finally got him to lay down in her lap enough that he finally told her. Even at that, when he lay down, she had called for the Philistines to come three times before and Samson would arise and overcome the Philistines. Actually, sometimes victories can mean a deception to us. Many people think if God is with me at all, He's with me all the way. But listen, He was not with Samson all the way. He was dealing with Samson. He was patient with Samson.

But finally, Delilah prepares to give him a haircut. "And when Delilah saw that he had told her all his heart, she sent and called for the lords of the Philistines, saying, Come up this once, for he hath shewed me all his heart. Then the lords of the Philistines came up unto her, and brought money in their hand" (Judges 16:18).

That's when we made a little track, "Watch Those Scissors, Samson." I put it this way. "Samson, I know you are strong, but watch those scissors." And he laid his head down in her lap, and went to sleep. "And she made him sleep upon her knees; and she called for a man, and she caused him to shave off the seven locks of his head; and she began to afflict him, and his strength went from him" (Judges 16:19).

He woke up to find that the Philistines had been called in again upon him. Delilah says, "Arise Samson. The Philistines be upon thee." And he arose. He didn't know what had happened. The Word said he shook himself and went out as before to go against the Philistines not knowing that the presence of God had departed from him. And when he reached for the Philistines they reached for him. They caught Samson, the strong man who had won many victories, and punched out his eyes and made sport out of him. "And he awoke out of his sleep, and said, I will go out as at other times before, and shake myself. And he wist not that the Lord was departed from him. But the Philistines took him, and put out his eyes, and brought him down to Gaza, and bound him with fetters of brass; and he did grind in the prison house" (Judges 16:20-21).

I'll tell you what. I didn't altogether condemn Samson. I felt really touched about him, but before I was overcome with too much pity, the Lord let me see something. Samson didn't get this haircut while the Holy Spirit was off somewhere visiting. The Holy Spirit talked to him before it ever happened. He just drifted to a point that he wasn't hearing the Holy Spirit. And it wasn't long until, through the pride and flattery that Delilah was giving, he was overcome. He fell for it. I was very touched about what I saw in the Scripture. I saw the importance of obeying God at this point...that is to shun the very appearances of evil.

Then when the television age came in, I never will forget thinking back to whenever the radio came in. There was one preacher that I wanted to hear. His program was on every morning at 7:15 out of Beaumont, Texas. I knew that there were things on the radio that would not be very good, that would not edify us in the Lord. So, after I brought the radio to my house, I decided to take it back because it might not be very long until a member of the family would be ready to turn on any kind of program. In the fear of the Lord, to protect my own relationship with the Lord, I took it back.

A time came later, when I sought the Lord, I really felt like the Lord had given me strength to overcome wrong listening. So, I got me a radio. It wasn't all that easy to shut out wrong programs, but I knew it was important. Some way it became an easy matter for me to just hear the preaching of the Word or the news that was worth listening to and shut it off. I really never felt the wrong things that came over the radio affected me.

But, here comes *the television.*

I saw it as a *dangerous* weapon, as well as a weapon that could provide good.

I saw it as one of the most dangerous inventions that could ever come to the world. I didn't have to look at all the things that are shown. More and more, the Lord helped me. I never did say I wouldn't have a television. I didn't have to say that.

I put it this way to try to comfort those who maybe have two or three, I said, "Well after all, you can go into the room and close the door and still miss Heaven. So, it's not altogether just the radio or the television, but we must learn to shun the very appearances of evil."

Then the phrase came to me like this. If it can happen in the garden of Eden that there was one tree in the midst of all of the others that if you eat of it, you will die, that was going to take some real watchfulness. Go ahead and eat of the trees that are good, but remember, don't eat of this one or you will die.

I feel like this. God does things His own way, and that's the only way to go. But, He puts things before us sometime just to try us and to prove us that tells us which way to go and what to do. That is to shun the appearance of evil. So, I said down deep in my heart, "I must not take one of those in because Samson didn't intend to get his hair cut. He didn't intend to get his eyes punched out. He didn't intend for his enemies to begin to laugh at him. He certainly didn't intend to wake up and find God had departed. But, that's exactly what happened." And that's why we used the statement, "Watch those scissors though you are strong."

I've never told people not to have a television. We'll leave it up to the individual. But, by the help of the Lord, we're seeking hard to be ready when Jesus comes.

Then, the Lord impressed me to write the little track, "Flee for the Life of Jesus for Herod Seeks to Destroy Him." That's when He was a babe in the house near the manger place where the wise men came to worship the Lord. They were to go back another way, and then they were to flee into the land of Egypt and escape Herod. That's why we called King to the TV...King TV...because he is after to destroy. It's a testing moment. It's a testing time. The Word speaks of it this way. That people have sinned by these inventions. There are a lot of inventions that have been displeasing to the Lord. It is good, at least, that the gospel can be preached. I wish the gospel was preached every moment of the day. In fact, we were encouraged many years ago that the religious world should buy a station of their own where the gospel alone could be published. We saw in the future that it would be hard to find space where the gospel could be preached because of the many wrong advertisements and entertainments that go through. They are here, and they are doing their work. My heart really goes out for what has already happened.

I believe the Lord impressed me concerning a lukewarm church like you read about in the book of Revelation. The Lord said to them, "Listen you have left your first love." One of the churches was lukewarm. "I know thy works, that thou art neither cold nor hot: I would thou wert cold or hot. So then because thou art lukewarm, and neither cold nor hot, I will spue thee out of My mouth" (Revelation 3:15-16).

I felt impressed and concerned about this lukewarm church of today although I don't fuss about it like I did in my younger days. The Lord spoke a Scripture to my heart, "Their ways will correct them." They don't listen to God's word or shun the appearance of evil. They'll understand one day what has happened. I just trust it won't be too late. Anyway, to shun the very appearances of evil is what it's all about. "Thine own wickedness shall correct thee, and thy backslidings shall reprove thee: know therefore and see that it is an evil thing and bitter, that thou hast forsaken the Lord thy God, and that My fear is not in thee, saith the Lord God of hosts" (Jeremiah 2:19).

Then, the Lord impressed me to write the little tract, "Fleeing for the Life of Jesus for Herod, or King TV, Seeks to Destroy Him." I really felt that the Lord whispered in the Spirit to my heart that the TV is like an incubator, and the lukewarm church will be born sitting around at the feet of King TV. They won't know just when it happened, but the first thing you know something gets into them and they are lukewarm. They are neither cold or hot. They may be talking about God, but their heart is not with God. You cannot serve two masters.

Then, we noticed this, and I used the little track that we called "The Last Look at Sodom." The Word says He revealed to Abraham that He was about to destroy Sodom and

Gomorrah. "And the Lord said, Shall I hide from Abraham that thing which I do; Seeing that Abraham shall surely become a great and mighty nation, and all the nations of the earth shall be blessed in him? For I know him, that he will command his children and his household after him, and they shall keep the way of the Lord, to do justice and judgment; that the Lord may bring upon Abraham that which He hath spoken of him" (Genesis 18:17-19).

Abraham interceded for the righteous. He said, "Wilt Thou also destroy the righteous with the wicked? That be far from Thee to do after this manner, to slay the righteous with the wicked: and that the righteous should be as the wicked, that be far from Thee: Shall not the Judge of all the earth do right?" (Genesis 18:24-25). Finally he said, "Oh let not the Lord be angry, and I will speak yet but this once: Peradventure ten shall be found there. And He said, I will not destroy it for ten's sake" (Genesis 18:32).

But, there were not enough righteous for God to spare the city, not enough right going on, so the angels told Lot and his family to leave the city for the Lord is going to destroy it. "And there came two angels to Sodom at even; and Lot sat in the gate of Sodom: and Lot seeing them rose up to meet them; and he bowed himself with his face toward the ground; And when the morning arose, then the angels hastened Lot, saying, Arise, take thy wife, and thy two daughters, which are here; lest thou be consumed in the iniquity of the city" (Genesis 19:1,15).

The angel said one little phrase there that means a lot, "Look not behind thee" (Genesis 19:17). And the Word says they left Sodom but Lot's wife turned and looked back. And when she did, she turned to a pillar of salt. "But his wife looked back from behind him, and she became a pillar of salt" (Genesis 19:26).

Now we love to hear of the deliverance of Lot, but we are told to remember Lot's wife. "But the same day that Lot went out of Sodom it rained fire and brimstone from heaven, and destroyed them all. Even thus shall it be in the day when the Son of man is revealed. In that day, he which shall be upon the housetop, and his stuff in the house, let him not come down to take it away: and he that is in the field, let him likewise not return back. Remember Lot's wife" (Luke 17:29-32).

She just looked back. This thought came to me about looking back, and I don't think it should be ignored. I think there's good in it. Just don't look back. She's out of Sodom, but she's looking back. In my mind and spirit I could remember testimonies of believers who had truly turned to the Lord and told how God had removed wrong things from them. But, now they are looking back. I've known some who have stopped going to the little theater across town because the programs didn't seem to be in harmony with their relationship with the Lord. They stopped going, but now they are looking back at even worse things on the TV across the living room. I'm not accusing. I'm just saying this. "Save yourselves from this untoward generation" (Acts 2:40). Don't look back. Remember, and watch those scissors! What happens happens quickly, and it's too late to do anything about it sometimes.

Friends, the test is on. We've made this statement not to be unkind, but to warn you from the depths of our heart to be careful and shun the very appearance of evil. You won't know when the enemy has bitten you until it's too late. "Abstain from all appearance of evil" (1 Thessalonians 5:22). How are we going to overcome the very appearance of evil? We can overcome by staying in The Secret Place with the Lord until the truth has taken hold of our lives and set us free from the desire of the things that our flesh lusts after. We cannot serve two masters.

The stronger statement is..."Be not deceived: evil communications corrupt good manners" (1 Corinthians 15:33). Be careful, Friends, judgment is on it's way.

Let's flee for the life of Jesus.

Protect your relationship by getting in The Secret Place.

Keep it by abiding in The Secret Place.

In crisis times of Jesus' life, He went into the garden of prayer. He had prayed all night when He was ministering to the public. This time before Calvary He went to pray, and He took His disciples with Him. "And He cometh unto the disciples, and findeth them asleep, and saith unto Peter, What, could ye not watch with me one hour? Watch and pray, that ye enter not into temptation: the spirit indeed is willing, but the flesh is weak" (Matthew 26:40-41).

Friends, have a relationship with the Lord that you can know the difference between right and wrong. Have a relationship with the Lord that enables you to not only depart from evil, but to shun the very appearance of evil. You can save yourself from this untoward generation.

Remember, it came to Lot's wife when she just looked back. Disobedience began when Eve was attracted to look at the tree that once registered in her heart and in her mind, "Oh, I cannot touch that tree. I cannot eat of that tree, or I will die." God told Adam, her husband. "And the Lord God commanded the man, saying, Of every tree of the garden thou mayest freely eat: But of the tree of the knowledge of good and evil, thou shalt not eat of it: for in the day that thou eatest thereof thou shalt surely die" (Genesis 2:16-17).

But then, she listened to a voice that said, "Yea, hath God said, Ye shall not eat of every tree of the garden? And the woman said unto the serpent, We may eat of the fruit of the trees of the garden: But of the fruit of the tree which is in the midst of the garden, God hath said, Ye shall not eat of it, neither shall ye touch it, lest ye die" (Genesis 3:1-3).

She told the serpent, "Yes. God did say not to eat of it or we would surely die." So the message wasn't forgotten. It was just about to be shown that it was ineffective in the life of Eve for the serpent said, "You really won't die." Can you see the picture? He called the Lord a liar. He said, "Ye shall not surely die For God doth know that in the day ye eat thereof, then your eyes shall be opened, and ye shall be as gods, knowing good and evil" (Genesis 3:4-5). So, now a different picture comes before Eve. She saw one God which said will actually destroy you, and now, she sees the same picture as one to make her wise.

I've had people say, "Brother Murdock, you need a TV." Well I never have said I wouldn't get one. I don't intend to, but I don't have to make statements like that. I just thought to myself, "Listen, the TV is there, and the first thing you know it will be offering something of which God says to shun the very appearance. The Word also, "But put ye on the Lord Jesus Christ, and make not provision for the flesh," (Romans 13:14).

I told those who said, "Brother Murdock, you need to know what's going on through the TV"..."Listen, I know more about it than you do." That might sound a little foolish. It might not sound just right. But, that's the reason I don't have one. And they would laugh a little bit about that. Then I said, "Listen, there's a lot of good. There needs to be more good on it because there's so much bad when we to try to save those who are trying to stay on both sides of the fence and let God get hold of them where they'll be able to turn the dial."

I made a little track, and on it, I said, "It's Time to Reset the Dial." There was a picture of a TV and the hand was up. Then over inside this little track, there was a picture of a young man sitting at a table with a lamp reading God's Word. I called it, "It's Time to Reset the Dial." Then I quoted that scripture, "Blessed is the man that walketh not in the counsel of the ungodly, nor standeth in the way of sinners, nor sitteth in the seat of the scornful. But his delight is in the law of the Lord; and in His law doth he meditate day and night. And he shall be like a tree planted by the rivers of water, that bringeth forth his fruit in his season; his leaf also shall not wither; and whatsoever he doeth shall prosper" (Psalm 1:1-3).

Think of it. *Turn off your television with programs that do not edify and spend a few minutes in The Secret Place.* Your Secret Place and mine must get strong enough to keep our lives from being exposed to wrong things. So you won't be..."Out Of Sodom, Looking Back." The Bible says to shun the appearance of evil. Don't even look that direction. And go on with God. "Prove all things; hold fast that which is good. Abstain from all appearance of evil" (1 Thessalonians 5:21-23).

God doesn't expect this out of you and I if we don't build a relationship with Him. You can't do this in yourself, but save yourself by getting into The Secret Place. "And the very God of peace sanctify you wholly; and I pray God your whole spirit and soul and body be preserved blameless unto the coming of our Lord Jesus Christ. Faithful is He that calleth you, Who also will do it" (1 Thessalonians 5:23-24).

Reevaluate the importance of praying through and touching God and getting strength to walk in the way that's pleasing. *You'll be glad!*

Enter The Calm... It Was Made For Thee.

-*J. E. Murdock*

WORDS FROM THE HEART

A COLLECTION OF POETRY

DR. J. E. MURDOCK

The Power Of A Day

How powerful is the day?
Well, really it's all we have in hand.
What? How can this thing be, we would question.
So much to be done...and do it in a day?

Yes, the Master would say,
"My child, all that I ask you to do, or be today,
Can be done *in a day.*
Believe Me My child, yesterday is a today gone.
Tomorrow that you hear about, has never come."

Makes sense, doesn't it My child?
So why not put all in today,
And discover it to be the day—
That the Lord has made—you'll be glad.

Yesterday.
Are you troubled about yesterdays?
Many are.
This need not be...remember, your today is Lord over all.

May not sound true, but it is...
You can handle today...your yesterdays.
All that you are is what you are today.
Believe me, make it a good day.
And make it...today.

Tomorrow.
What about tomorrow, many are saying.
The very thought of it...
Hearts are failing.

Powerful, isn't it?
Who can deny it?
But really, it is true?
Tomorrow? No not really,
If we faint...it will be today.

You can win...
Do it.
And do it—
Today.

HEAVEN ON EARTH

Heaven on earth, just listen to me.
Yes, a bit of Heaven for you and me.
So lift thine eyes, look and see;
A lot of Heaven on earth is meant to be.

Heaven on earth, did I hear Him say?
Yes, Heaven on earth has been heralded today.
To gladden your heart, didn't you hear Him say?
I bring peace and good will, in earth today.

Heaven on earth, amid storm and rain;
May seem hard to see, in the hour of restrain.
Let us look up and we'll see, and hear it so.
A bit of Heaven will come, in our world below.

Heaven and earth, that we so long for;
Is not out of reach, for those who seek.
So, let us pray and believe, His will be done;
That we can know, Heaven on earth has begun.

February 8, 1989

"...on earth peace, good will toward men."
Luke 2:14

Promotion Day

Promotion day with Jesus,
What a promise to you and me.
As we travel this road with Jesus,
Promotion day, is sure to be.

Promotion day with Jesus,
Is a natural cry you see.
For in God's plan for you and me,
Promotion day is *meant to be.*

Promotion day with Jesus,
The cry will surely be.
For in this world of sorrow,
Promotion day, we *long for thee.*

Promotion day with Jesus,
What a Heavenly bliss to see.
To a world of joy, peace and love;
Promotion day, we welcome thee!

February 12, 1989

*"For promotion cometh neither from the east, nor from the
west, nor from the south. But God is the judge: He putteth
down one, and setteth up another.
...the righteous shall be exalted."*
Psalm 75:6,7,10

Rumbling In The Land

There is a rumbling in our land today.
A rumbling of *voices,* that seem to say;
There is unrest, in our world you see;
Such rumbling, such rumbling,
Has come, to you and me.

There is a rumbling of *feet,* in our land today.
There is unrest, unrest; what does it say?
Such rumbling, great rumbling, we hear it so;
There is more about this rumbling,
That we should know.

There is a rumbling too, in our *hearts* you know.
Such rumbling here, and where're we go.
Makes one to think, what's happening here?
This rumbling, rumbling, makes one to hear.

The rumbling you hear, will rumble on you see;
Till a Voice comes through, to you and me.
We must step in line, if we're to see;
There is freedom from the rumbling,
That has gripped you and me.

February 23,1989

"...in this we groan..."
2 Corinthians 5:2

"...the whole creation groaneth..."
Romans 8:22

The Rumbling

There is a rumbling in our heart today;
Such rumbling, rumbling, in this house of clay.
A rumbling so; should we hear it say?
There is rest, for your rumbling soul today.

There is a rumbling in our heart today;
For God Who knows, we're not here to stay.
A rumbling cry, that seems hard to know,
Just what to do, in our world of woe.

A rumbling came to a man one day;
Who en route was found on Damascus way.
A rumbling so, some thought it had thundered;
Not so with Saul, who on this road had plundered.

A rumbling, rumbling, now loud and clear;
Saul, Saul, why do you wander here?
Brought blindness to eyes, who thought could see.
Rumbling, such rumbling, makes way to be.

A rumbling cry, from the man called Saul;
Who are Thou? Must be Lord of all.
Sought the man who to the ground did fall.
The rumbling cry, now made plain;
Come with Me. There's much to gain.

February 23, 1989

"...be not silent to me: Lest,
if Thou be silent to me, I become like them
that go down into the pit."
Psalm 28:1

GOD'S MIRROR

God gave Jesus, as a mirror to thee;
Revealing Himself to you and me.
A mighty God of power you see;
All came shining through, God's mirror to thee.

God gave Jesus, a mirror to be;
A reflector of His love, for the world to see.
Through the mirror God has chosen for thee;
Should leave no doubt, that He loves you and me.

God gave Jesus, a mirror to show;
Of His grace, He longs for us to know.
A grace so strong came shining through;
All this was given for me and you.

God gave Jesus, a mirror to say;
Come unto Me ye that are weary today.
I'll give you rest from your heavy load;
His care for you, this mirror doth show.

April 1, 1989

I'VE CHOSEN YOU

I make of you, a mirror to show,
Of My saving power that others may know.
There is forgiveness of sin and a cleansing within;
And you, a mirror, can make to know.

You, a mirror, Jesus said would be;
For I go to the Father, and you will see,
Through the Comforter that He will send to thee;
You, are a mirror to be.

You, a mirror, that others may see;
A love that I gave at Calvary's tree.
The change that's been wrought in you and me;
This mirror should make it plain to see.

You, a mirror, chosen of God to be;
A light on a hill for others to see.
There is grace for all who are willing to be,
A mirror to God, Who has chosen you and me.

TELL US PLAINLY

Tell us plainly, if Thou be the Christ;
These words came to Jesus, not once, but twice.
Tell us plainly, if this be so;
There are many others, too, who want to know.

Tell us plainly, was a sincere cry,
From many that day who walked by His side.
Tell us plainly, so we will know;
And may we tell others, who are wondering so.

Tell us plainly, if Thou be the Christ;
This question was answered, not once, but twice.
Tell us plainly, I heard you say;
Now, come with Me, I am the Way.

Tell us plainly, was His purpose here;
To many that day, this was made clear.
So plainly it came, left no doubt or fear,
This is truly the Christ, Who has come to us here.

What More?

What more could I have done?
Was the question asked.
As to his vineyard he had come to last.
What more? What more? Again he cried;
In a fruitful hill, did my vineyard lie.
And I fenced it in, there to abide.
What more? What more? Could I have done?

What more? What more? What more He thought;
I've gathered out stones,
And planted the choicest of vines. What more?
I've built a tower in the midst thereof.
I've made a winepress therein.
What more? What more? Could I have done?

What more? What more?
Was the question to thee;
What more could I have done to my vineyard to be?
A vineyard of good grapes I did not see;
But lo, wild grapes hang here and there,
This should not be.
That's why my question comes once again to thee;
What more? What more? Could I have done?

January 14, 1988

THE RING YOU WORE

The ring you wore, that I gave to you;
Just seemed to touch you, through and through.
You may never know what that means to me;
When with pride you would speak,
Of the ring I gave, you see.

The ring you wore, that I gave to you;
Seemed small in my sight, for such a one as you.
Yet, a little ring, helped me to show;
A little bit of the much I wanted you to know.

The ring you wore, that I gave to you;
Has not failed to touch me, as well as you.
For not one time, have you made me think,
That the ring I gave was not distinct.

The ring you wore, that I gave to you;
Speaks more and more as days we go through.
I can hardly believe you could say so much to me;
Through just a little ring, that I gave to you,
from me.

May 10, 1989

"I rejoice with you, the wife of my youth."
Proverbs 5:18

Glimmering Hope

Glimmering hope, *I felt your presence today;*
As I awoke this morning, while in bed I lay.
Glimmering hope, I heard you say,
I'll shine again, as bright as day;
For in God's promise, I'm built to stay.

Glimmering hope, *though dim you seem to be;*
Still gives light in our world, for us to see.
Glimmering hope, I'll ever reach for thee;
For only in God's promise, you're found to be.

Glimmering hope, *though you come and go;*
I'll cleave to you for His blessings to know.
Glimmering hope, I'm amazed to see,
What reading His Word does, to you as well as me.

Glimmering hope, *I'll build with you;*
Brighter hope will come shining through.
Glimmering hope, is a token you see,
While looking through a glass darkly,
we're found to be.
Glimmering hope, will then fade away;
As face to face, we have come to now stay.

July 14, 1989

Walking With God

Our walk with God is *a walk to be;*
If we His will, do plan to see.
Our walk with God, if not begun,
Should start today, that His will be done.

Our walk with God *holds much in store;*
For all who will this walk implore.
Our walk with God is a walk to see,
A burden lifted from you will be.

Our walk with God *can surely be;*
For know it well, it's His plan for thee.
Your walk with God will prove to be,
A joy, a peace, as you walk with me.

This walk with God is *a walk for thee;*
If you hope to know of the life to be.
This walk with God *has much to give,*
To all who will this walk to live.

July 9, 1989

If We Walk With God

If we walk with God, we must need to see;
We must be agreed, for this walk to be.
If we walk with God, we will come to see,
There's commitment to make if this walk is to be.

If we walk with God, no darkness will be;
For all is light, in Him, we will see.
If we walk with God, a fellowship will come;
Fulfilling His will, when this walk has begun.

If we walk with God, a newness of life will be;
For in pride it's said, you can't walk with me.
If we walk with God, His Glory to see;
We need know it well, how this walk must be.

If we walk with God, every learning will be;
That a walk in the flesh, is a no-no' you'll see.
If we walk with God, we soon come to know,
That serving two masters, can never be so.

July 9, 1989

SPRING UP O WELL

Spring up O well, the cry was made;
A thirsty soul, for water to be.
Spring up O well, I long for thee;
A thirst so strong has come to me.

Spring up O well, I long for thee;
A fainting heart so longs to see.
Spring up O well, Oh let it be;
A refreshing to all, who drink of thee.

Spring up O well, many look to thee;
To give water, to bless a fainting world you see.
So dry and thirsty, many do call,
Spring up O well, lest this comes to all.

Spring up O well, we depend on thee;
To give living water, my soul to see.
Spring up O well, we believe in thee;
There's hope, there's joy and victory.

July 9, 1989

To My Children

To you, my children, I write this day.
In the presence of Him, Who showed me the way.
Of the One Who saved me, Who filled me;
And called me and put me in the right way.
This all took place before your day...
My children, I write.

To you, my children, I write today.
To share with you some things that have
come my way.
When lonely—and as some would say—blue.
It seems so good to know just what to do.
This remember—I write to you.

To you, my children, I write today.
Of a joy and peace...though mixed with tears,
Has led me down a path that leads to a hill.
There strength did come to steady my feet,
Mid storm and rain and utter defeat,
He did not fail me.
Children...to you I write.

To You My Children

To you, my children, I write today.
I'm thinking of the pleasure you brought,
When you came our way.
A pleasure others cannot bring, you see.
I want so much for you to know,
That is why to you I write today.

To you, my children, I write today.
Your coming to us was not a surprise,
We desired you to be by our side.
So God loved it so to be;
As children are His heritage you see.
This my children...I write to thee.

To you, my children, I write today.
Though not possible at this time
to call each by name.
But know this well, you are loved the same.
When I talk to God and call your name,
Then I know well you are the same.
This, I write to you.

To Know Him

To know Him, a cry is made, *to know Him;*
A deep cry, a loud cry, yes, even a desperate
cry is made,
To know Him.
The whole creation crieth, *to know Him.*
Hear the cry that is made, made in each of us;
To know Him.

To know Him, a cry too often misunderstood,
And even more often unheeded.
Yes, the cry *to know Him.*
To know Him, though misunderstood;
comes again the cry...
To know Him.
Though often unheeded yet comes again the cry...
To know Him.

To know Him?
Yes, it's God's plan that we know Him;
The loneliness of your heart seeks *to know Him.*
Your hope for tomorrow is *to know Him,*
So stop, look, and listen; if you do, you'll find
your Heart is crying out,
To know Him.

*"As the hart panteth after the water brooks, so
panteth my soul after Thee, O God."*
Psalm 42:1

*"In the last day, that great day of the feast, Jesus stood and
cried, saying, If any man thirst, let him come unto Me, and
drink. He that believeth on Me, as the scripture hath said,
out of his belly shall flow rivers of living water."*
John 7:37-38

*"Blessed are they which do hunger and thirst after
righteousness: for they shall be filled."*
Matthew 5:6

ENTER THE CALM

"Enter The Calm," a small Voice said to me one day.
As I was searching in all directions
for such a place to be.
When again, the Voice so vivid came:
"Enter The Calm My child.
It was made for thee."

"Enter The Calm," a third time it came,
With great feeling it brought into my spirit to be
a light so clear gave witness to me,
Left no doubt in my mind,
Truly this was made for me.

"Enter The Calm," more plain than ever it seems.
Bringing desire into my heart,
For such a place to be.
When already I had noticed a foretaste to see,
That the calm I needed *was really made for me.*

"Enter The Calm *without struggle,"* He said to me.
I could hardly believe such achievement could be.
When so much time and struggle had been made
by me,
Yet little by little, I began to see,
The Calm I needed, He had made for me.

"Be still, and know that I am God:"
Psalm 46:10

"...in quietness and in confidence shall be
your strength:..."
Isaiah 30:15

"But they that wait upon the LORD shall renew
their strength;"
Isaiah 40:31

Enter The Calm
Afterthought

To Enter The Calm this too must be,
If we plan to labor to the end you see.
Amid frustrations, we are found to be,
That's why The Calm was made for you and me.

To The Calm, He called His disciples to be,
From a long day of toil among multitudes you see.
A rest from your labors, He knew should be.
That's why He prepared The Calm for thee.

He's Coming Again

This same Jesus, the angel said...is coming again.
A timely message it was
To hearts of men bewildered that day.
He's coming again!

He's coming again, He coming again,
A message with power how it fell that day.
On hearts so sad and filled with dismay.
Yet powerful it came...this Word,
He's coming again!

He's coming again—was what they said,
Repeated the men as toward Jerusalem they turned.
From fear to faith, to the Upper Room they came,
What hope, what peace, what joy within,
Since the good news...*He's coming again!*

TOGETHER

Together, you and I had after eleven months of
courtship days.
Together, we chose a life with each other.
Together, we walked a long sandy road.
Yes, just for the reason to be,
Together.

Together, you and I have traveled a path not so
plain at first it seemed...
Together, a joy, a tear, a prayer, a song,
All this seemed had to be.
Together, a good word to use that describes
why we still go through,
Together.

Together, it was meant by our Lord above,
To comfort, to help, and truly to love.
Together, it's great, that's plain to see,
Though trials do come to you and me.
Together, how bliss can it be since fifty-four
years have passed,
Together.

Written to one so dear to me (my sweet wife)
May we have a Happy Anniversary
Love you, Daddy (Your Honey)
54th Anniversary...May 26, 1988
Daddy's Poem to Mother 3:30 A.M. 1934-1988

The Will Of God

The will of God, what could it be?
A will to break, to make, to mold, a one like me.
A will to change, to talk, a walk,
An ear to hear, the eye to see.
How bliss can it be...*His will for me?*

The will of God, what could it be?
A will so strong, to love you and me,
A will to give His life for thee,
A will to save a wretch like me.

The will of God, what could it be?
A will to lead a one like me,
A will for me to win the fight,
A will to know the way that's right.

THE PART I DIDN'T KNOW

The part I didn't know,
I faced more often
than one would think.
Almost each passing day it comes—
the part I didn't know.
Be not dismayed with this My child.
There's much good to be found...yes, found!
In the part you didn't know.

The part I didn't know,
Which is much I now see,
Seems to have a special way in it's approach to me.
Yes, *the part I didn't know* seems to say,
And says it gently,
You have need of Me you see,
I'm the part you didn't know.

The part I didn't know,
It's easy now to see.
There's much, much reason that I should follow after Thee.
Though it seems I face it daily...*the part I didn't know,*
Yet I hear the Master say, "Follow on, My child,
I have much for thee,
Yes, and in *the part you didn't know.*"

COMMITMENT

Be not afraid of Commitment,
It's a powerful *instrument* in your hand.
Commitment, yes, it is a *Key* all your own.
Commitment is a *Gift* to thee; use it today.

Commitment!
Many are not afraid of Commitment.
Why should you be?
They set their sail at any cost,
To reach for that which in the end is lost.
They toil for a life of riches and fame,
Commitment they make...but make it in vain.

Commitment for thee, it need not be,
Toward things so void as to satisfy thee.
Commitment I say is a gift to thee,
Make it today,...and *make it to Me.*

Does It Pay?

Does it pay?
Is the question often asked.
Asked more often than we think, Does it pay?"
Does it pay to think as I think?
To say what I say?
To do what I do?
Does it pay?

Does it pay that I should ask the question,
Does it pay?
A good question, My child, ask it again and again...
Yes, again and again,
Does it pay?

Does it pay? That's the question at hand—
Does it pay?
A good question indeed, Does it pay?
Think right, talk right, do right—IT PAYS.
Yes, in the end, *it really pays.*

*"Then shall ye return, and discern between the
righteous and the wicked, between him that serveth
God and him that serveth him not."
Malachi 3:18*

*"...we count them happy which endure..."
James 5:11*

Thoughts

We may not speak them where others may hear,
We may not write them, that others can read,
Thoughts, yes, thoughts.
They will be
The first to affect us.
For good or for evil.
Thoughts, yes, *Thoughts!*

Choose today
What your thoughts will be.
Choose
What God has chosen for thee.
Which is; the "What-so-ever-formula."

"Whatsoever things are true, whatsoever things are honest, whatsoever things are just, whatsoever things are pure, whatsoever things are lovely, whatsoever things are of good report; if there be any virtue, and if there be any praise, think on these things."
Philippians 4:8

"As he thinketh in his heart, so is he:"
Proverbs 23:7

SHOCKED

I'm really shocked to see how far from right
I've gone;
How hard it is to admit I'm wrong.
Yet, have no peace to call my own.
To find myself in such a state—
I'm really shocked.

Are you shocked to learn that God loves you?
To learn that His hand reaches out to thee—
In a world that's lost you see?
Are you shocked at this, my friend—
That He cares?

Shocked? Well, you need not be.
After all, God is love you see.
Yes, God reaches for you and me.
In Him you'll find forgiveness—
Of sin and peace within.
At this my child, you will have reason—
To be shocked.

*"Behold, what manner of love the Father hath bestowed upon
us, that we should be called the sons of God:"*
1 John 3:1

The Order

The Order I give is The Order to *Be*.
Fulfilling My will, this you need to see.
The order I give will bring order to thee.
Fulfilling My joy, My peace within thee.

The Order I give is The Order to Be,
If real life and real joy you hope to see.
The Order I give will bring harmony, too.
Such happiness you'll know what this Order will do.

The Order I give is an Order you'll *know,*
If you'll believe in Me, My Order to see.
The Order I've promised will come to you,
Though it may appear not to be true.

The Order I give is The Order to *Be*.
If any expect a life of victory.
The Order I give will bring order in thee,
great hope, great faith, and love will be.

August 24, 1989, 3:20 A.M.

I Found You For Real

When I think of you, I can hardly say,
Of the much that fills my mind,
And just seems to stay,
Now, if I can explain, I surely will try,
To share things that's down inside.

Along the way I've been busy, yes,
But time enough to know you were there,
Of course, this brought a pleasure to me,
But I didn't take time to really see.

Time moves on for you and me,
This I'm sure gives reason for what we now see.
Looking now beyond the outer walls where real
beauty is found,
E're we both would fall.

As coming to see beyond these outward walls,
To discover the One we fell for after all,
A heart who said it in the face of all,
I love you dear, with this we still stand tall,
Believe me, YOU ARE FOR REAL.

The Seasons (No. 1)

The Season of Spring, comes to one and all.
Yet, there are those who walk on the summer,
the Season is called,
It's here, many blessings come through;
It's there a Voice will say, "Go ahead."

The Season of Autumn many will find,
That spring and summer are left behind.
No, not a time to despair, it's *meant here to be.*
But, a step closer to Him, Who planted the
Season to be.

The Season of Winter does come around.
And many behind walls in this Season are found.
Yet, His grace in this Season doth truly abound,
Through faith in all, Who in this Season are found.

All Seasons have come and gone, may we see.
Now a bliss eternity awaits you and me.
The Bridegroom will call, "Come away My love,
the winter is past."
The flowers bloom again—not for a Season
but for eternity.

THE SEASONS (NO. 2)

The Seasons that I write about today,
Cover a span of life, that comes our way.
The Seasons are planned by the One Who knows,
To give to each who travel this road.

The Seasons that come are in His plan,
Makes it even more important that we understand.
Each Season that comes has purpose to be,
Fulfilling His will, this we need see.

The Seasons do come, as we plainly can see.
And a reason for each are meant to be.
A real blessing to all,
What'er the Season may be.

The Season that comes your way or mine,
Are never to dim your vision, no not for a time.
But brighter and brighter the day should shine,
As Seasons roll, by His great wisdom to find.

May 2, 1989

Your Talk

Your talk is your walk, my child,
no matter what you say.
Your talk will be your walk each day along the way.
May you watch your talk, which is your walk,
That others may see you clear.

If you plan your walk, you must plan your talk;
For the walk you walk, will be the talk you talk
no matter what you say.
You must remember, your destiny depends not only
in the talk you talk, but in the walk you walk.

Jesus Talk

Jesus said it well, day after day,
Yet many did wonder along the way.
Questions arose as they heard Him say:
If thou wouldest know who I am today,
Follow on.

As Jesus' talk began to walk,
Leaving tracks along the way;
As lame did walk and the dumb did talk,
What revelation did come each passing day;
And on and on as His talk did walk,
Many believe in the talk He talked
by the walk He walked.

CONCERN

Since Concern has come my way,
I'm really not the same I'd say.
Concern, has got my attention too,
I feel He's talking to me tis true.
A bit hard to see why Concern thinks so
much of me.

Since Concern has made Himself known to me,
It seems I can't get Him off my mind, you see.
I guess that's why I'm writing to thee.
Concern has left His mark on me.

Since Concern knocked on my door one day.
I saw immediately He had something to say.
So I stopped for a moment to see,
And shocked I was of what Concern said to me.

Since Concern got my attention as I'm sure by
now you can see.
It's because of what Concern did for me
that has opened my heart to say,
I'm concerned about thee.

April 13, 1989

CROWN HER QUEEN

She was thirteen years of age when I met her.
My thoughts about her, "She is beautiful."
"I want to sit beside her," and I did.
Something inside me said, "I want to marry her,"
and I did.
She is a perfect wife. She loves me. She proves it
in every way.
She answered the call of God to the ministry
with me.
She was ready to sing with me, anytime, anywhere.
She can sing.
She went to prayer meeting and church with me.
She sacrificed all to work with me in the ministry.
She is the mother of my children.
She made a home for me.
She prays with us. She talks to us. She works for us.
She gets up early and sits up late to keep harmony
in the family.
She loves and wants to be loved.
She, at age fourteen, walked eight miles from her
house to mine to marry me.
Needless to enumerate all the rugged places, she
has gone through to stay with me.
Yet, after thirty-six years she shows me that she
still loves me. You understand now, why I suggest
that she be Queen.
Be it known to all. She, who was Miss Willie
Dunnam became my wife, Mrs. J.E. Murdock, the
mother of my children.
She is Queen of this home.

May 26, 1970

FOLLOW ON

They follow the Lamb wheresoever He goeth.
They hear His voice like no other to be.

They sit at His feet to hear His words clear.
So they can walk this road, without fear.

They follow the Lamb, that peace they may know.
They find it for real as onward they go.

They come soon to green pastures, so rich and free.
Yes, and beside still waters, you can plainly see.

Yes, they followed the Lamb, and so can we,
Just hear that Voice, that is calling for thee.

His call will come clear,
You need not fear.

Just seek with faith His joy to find,
You too can know of His peace sublime.
Follow On.

"...These are they which follow the Lamb
whithersoever He goeth...And in their mouth was
found no guile: for they are without fault before
the throne of God."
Revelation 14:4-5

Growing And Going

Growing and going, just listen to me.
I would like to tell you what this rhyme can be.
Growing and going was meant for thee.
Growing and going will lead to victory.

Growing and going what a shout 'twill be,
As you see that growing and going was in His
plan for thee,
So let growing and going do it's work in thee,
You'll be surprised what growing and going will be
doing for thee.

Growing and going, what a joy to me,
Since growing and going are becoming
a part of me.
Yes, growing and going, I say welcome to thee,
What a blessed hope you're giving to me.

Growing and going, go hand in hand.
Let growing and going take a more permanent stand.
You see, growing and going are in great demand,
Oh, that we may see that growing and going was in
His plan.

Christ In You

Christ in you, did I hear Him say?
What a challenge could it be.
To a one as me, all that I am, I give to thee,
So think it not strange that I say to thee,
Come follow Me and you will see.

Christ in me did I hear Him say?
For every need that has come my way,
To a lonely heart, you will hear Him say,
Come unto Me, I'll be your friend today.

Christ in me, I've heard Him say,
For hope, for joy, and love within.
For peace, not fear, but rest you see,
This life we seek comes only from Thee.

Christ in me, the hope of Glory, 'tis written.
Christ in you, the hope of Glory is found.
Christ in us, the whole world round.
Christ in all, may His grace be found.

September 18, 1989, 3:00 A.M.

"...Christ in you, the hope of glory:"
Colossians 1:27

CHANGES

So many changes now appear,
Along the highway that once was so clear.
Makes it hard to travel with ease you see,
As so many changes seem now to be.

The changes that now appear,
Are not really meant to confuse us while here.
For really the road is the same, may we see.
For He Who changeth not, leadeth not.

A disciple one day, saw plainly the way.
Across troubled waters, a plain path now lay.
And a Voice he heard clearly say unto him,
Be not afraid, it is I.

A plain path now lay, before the disciple you see,
But this do remember, keep your eyes on Me.
For changes will appear, but not from Me.
Remember, I am the same, this you need see.

May 13, 1989, 1:00 P.M.

THE WILDERNESS

The Wilderness My child, was one chosen by Me,
Leading toward a land flowing with milk and honey,
you see.
The Wilderness My child, I deemed the best way to go,
To this land I had promised a long time ago.

The Wilderness My child, was one chosen you see,
A one that I knew to be fitting for thee.
To prove thyself to Me you see,
Then on into the land from The Wilderness to be.

The Wilderness My child, a testing place you see,
To teach you to trust and to lean on Me.
I gave you water in abundance of supply,
Yes, in The Wilderness My child My wonders to thee.

The Wilderness that I chose for thee,
Was a place to prove your love for Me.
So dwelling in you and you in Me,
We then leave The Wilderness forever to be,
In the city He has prepared for you and me.
A City Built By God.

March 22, 1989 3:30 A.M.

His Plan

The Father's plan of which I speak,
Is a plan so powerful and unique.
His plan like no other was drawn to save,
To heal all His own,
What a plan! *His plan.*

His plan so strong was built by love,
Came forth to us, through His Son above.
And on to a cross where for my sins He died,
That I could forever in Him abide.
What a plan! *His plan.*

His plan unveiled one day for all.
A plan though may seem hard now to see,
There's a Father Who loves you and me,
But for real it is as some looked to see.
What a plan! *His plan.*

The Father's plan of which we speak,
Has proven true to those who seek.
A plan that will save through His Son you'll see,
What a plan! *His plan.*

April 8, 1989 1:00 A.M.

ALL THAT I HAVE IS THINE

To an angry son the father said one day,
Why do you stand off and act that way?
This should not be in a time of rejoicing as you now see.
So stand up my son and come with me.
Remember all that I have is thine you see.

To the angry son, the father went on to say,
Don't feel that way but look and see today.
A one who was dead and is alive again,
So come to the house and rejoice with me.
For all that I have is thine you see.

The angry son still could not see.
Why such dancing over a one so wicked as a
brother could be.
A fatted calf—you gave none to me.
Though all my time I've spent with thee.
But oh my son lift your head and see,
All are thine, can't ye now see?

The angry son must understand,
There's a loving Father still in great demand.
To all who may have wondered from the fold need see,
There's much in His house for such a one as he.
For all who serve Me I say to thee.
All Mine are thine, can ye now see?

September 18, 1989 2:30 A.M.

*"And he said unto him, Son, thou art ever with me, and
all that I have is thine."*
Luke 15:31

I Am Grateful

To You, dear Lord, I am grateful today,
Since after so long I've heard You gently say.
Come away from behind your walls, My love.
Winter is over now, for this I am thankful.

To You, dear Lord, I am grateful today,
As I think of the favors You have shone,
Such as: Calling to me while in sin I did lie,
To let me know that it was for me that You truly died.
For the Lord, I am grateful.

To You, dear Lord, I am grateful today,
As gain, I think of the forgiveness You gave,
To my heart that cried, have mercy Lord I pray.
Yes, when I think of this, Lord I am grateful.

To You, dear Lord, I am grateful today,
As numerous blessings now come my way,
Blessings such as the abiding Comforter,
the Holy Spirit to stay.
To lead, to guide me through the day,
To make your Voice clear and known to me,
For this Lord, I am grateful.

A Wilderness

There is a wilderness that turns out to be,
One that was chosen by you, not me.
This wilderness we did not see,
Eyes being blinded by the deceiver,
the serpent you see.

There is a wilderness in parts of the land.
But not one so dry as the one that now stand.
In the heart more and more you can see,
There is a wilderness that grips the heart of
you and me.

There is a wilderness it is plain to see.
A one much bigger than either you or me.
A one we did not plan to be.
Just received by the serpent who seemed wiser
than we.

There is a wilderness we speak of that's plain to see.
Can be changed by Jesus of Calvary's tree.
Just ask of Him and a cleansing will come.
Now a change in your wilderness has truly begun.

There is a wilderness you'll see will blossom again,
Roses will bud and the flowers will bloom again.
Yes, winter will have passed,
And all because Jesus has come,
To your wilderness at last.

March 22, 1989 5:00 A.M.

Weep Not For Me

Weep not for Me, is what Jesus said,
As He walked the path Calvary led.
A path so strange that He walked that day,
Where many were crying along the way.

Weep not for Me, how strange can it be?
From lips of One that's so bound you see,
Chained by soldiers, so cruel to be,
Yet such words were said, and said unto me.
Weep Not.

Weep not for Me, how can this be?
From a one whose feet walks this road, you see.
A road so rugged as no other could be.
Yet stranger still, it was walked for me.

Weep not for Me once again I say,
From the Master's lips how they fell that day.
It's the Father's will that I've come this way.
Fulfilling His plan, It must be today.

June 23, 1988 3:00 A.M.

WEEP FOR YOURSELF

Weep for yourself, seems stranger still,
From Him Who walked up Calvary's hill.
Yes strange it seemed, to hear Him say,
Weep not for Me but for yourself today.
When really it was for me, He was Calvary led.

Weep for yourself, these words clear as could be.
Yet onward He climbed Golgotha's hill to see,
A Son so pure and holy as He,
Yet it was there I was told He was offered for me.

Weep for yourself, on this more light came unto me,
Letting me know that in darkness I did lie.
With a knowledge of this He had bled and died,
Gave clear reason that I should do as He said,
Weep not for Me, but for yourself instead.

THE SERVANT

Jesus, the Servant who else could it be?
A One Who served so willingly as He,
Jesus, the Servant said to you and me.
I come to serve this you need see.

Jesus, the Servant to all this you need know,
'Tis My Father's will Who has planned it so.
Jesus, the Servant our example you see,
To all who may choose a servant to be.

Jesus, the Servant was missed one day,
By Joseph and Mary who journeyed their way.
Jesus, the Servant they turned to seek,
Among kinfolk they did not find,
Jesus, the Servant Who had stayed behind.

Jesus, the Servant where could He be?
Searched Joseph and Mary so desperately.
Turned back to Jerusalem and there to find,
Jesus, the Servant about His Father's business.
A good place for you and me a servant to be.

May 17, 1989 10:00 P.M.

A NEW CREATURE

A new creature we are told must be,
If from the natural life we are to flee.
A new creature we are told must be,
If in the new world we hope to see.

A new creature what a change will surely be,
Old things passed away and new life now to be.
A new creature we are told would be,
New life makes way in you and me.

A new creature what a difference now to see,
As new desires arise, almost hard to believe.
A new creature though we are told must be,
If new hope, new joy and peace we would see.

A new creature now working with the power and might,
Moving the old nature by day and by night,
A new creature what a battle will rage,
Since new life must reign on page after page.
No more I, but Christ.

September 5, 1990 4:00 A.M.

Do It God's Way

Do it God's way, how unique it will be,
For there's no other like Him you'll see.
A peace will come in all that He's planned.
But do it God's way is His command.

Do it God's way, Jesus our example to be,
Though pressure did come against Him you see.
Yet never once did He waver from the plan to be,
But in every way, He did it God's way you see.

Do it God's way, we are told,
Though storms may come and winds may blow,
But in all will be well and you will know.
While others will see the great reason why,
You did it God's way.

Do it God's way, and assurance will be.
Your strength renewed and you will mount up with
wings as the eagle you see.
Run and not be weary, walk and not faint,
All because you did it God's way.

November 6, 1990 3:00 A.M.

Stay With God

Stay with God no matter the cost.
No valley too deep, no mountain too high,
He'll lead you to a place of rest.
You may never know until you follow on.
Stay with God.

Stay with God *till all is well.*
A peace He'll give that you can tell.
As He works in us from sun to sun,
You'll be glad for what He's done.
Stay with God.

Stay with God and *all will be well.*
He'll make you know, He'll make you tell,
Of a joy you'll feel, of a love to tell,
He knows the way.
Stay with God.

Stay with God *from day to day,*
He has much to do and much to say.
A care for you and a life to give,
In the eternal home for all who will,
Stay with God.

November 6, 1990 2:10 A.M.

BE FOR REAL

Be for real we are told you know,
For this is right you know, you know.
Be for real by day and by night,
Let no hypocrisy be found in sight.

Be real, be real, be real we are told,
Many about us are wanting to know.
Be real, be real, be real, make it so.
A make believe can never make to be.

Be real, be heard, in our world that's disturbed.
A cry for truth no hypocrisy to be found.
Be real, be heard the whole world around,
Is fainting, is fainting for someone that's sound.

Be for real, is the battle cry,
From all that are about us e're they sigh.
Be real not a cloud without rain,
Not a cistern without water.
Be real.

September 14, 1990 4:30 A.M.

ABOUT THE AUTHOR

Dr. J. E. Murdock is the president and founder of Highway and Hedge Ministry, an organization devoted to building churches. Pursuing this God-given vision, Dr. Murdock has pioneered and birthed eight different churches in Texas and Louisiana.

In more than 63 years of pastoring and preaching the Gospel, Dr. Murdock has discovered the profound impact of prayer upon the Christian life. "Prayer must move more than mountains, part more than seas, and bring down more than manna," explains Dr. Murdock. "It must bring Christ, Who is your hope, to your inner man." Dr. Murdock has dedicated his life to helping believers to discover the power of prayer.

He has been called by many "The Man of Prayer."

In 1986, Dr. Murdock began writing poetry, a new expression of his love for God and all of His creation. His words have inspired many to a deeper walk with their Creator.

Dr. Murdock was granted an honorary doctorate at the age of 80 years old. Dr. Murdock resides in Denton, Texas. He has 7 children 17 grandchildren and 24 great grandchildren. He is 87 years old and still preaching the gospel.

A Vision, A Tent, And A Gleaning

By Nola Mae McFillen

While driving through the outskirts of town one hot, sultry July day I noticed a large van parked on a lot, just off the highway. On the side of the van was written "Nation Wide Hi-Way and Hedge Evangelism." Beside it was a neat looking tent, complete with chairs, platform, pulpit and loud speaker system.

"That must be an old fashioned tent revival," I thought. My curiosity was aroused, but not enough to stop. After all, I was a member of a large denominational church and worshipped in a modern, expensive structure with beautiful stained glass windows and all the trimmings, so why should I be concerned with people who still bothered to hold a tent revival?

But for some strange reason this scene stuck in my mind. Two years later I could still have written a good description of it, even though I'd given it just one passing glance.

A short time after I'd seen this Hi-Way and Hedge van, I began to feel a great dissatisfaction in my own religious life. My church seemingly had everything to offer, yet somehow I couldn't find the heart of Christ in it! I couldn't find the reality of a closeness to God. Religion had become nothing more than a ritual to me; it had lost it's savour and it's spirit. Going to church had become a duty instead of a joy.

In my heart and soul, a great yearning was building up, a yearning to walk and to talk with God, and to hear from Him just like Paul and Isaiah and Jeremiah had. But most of all I wanted to see Jesus' miracles re-enacted again in this modern day!

I began to search through all the prestige avenues of my handsome, formal church, for the reality I was seeking, but I came up with exactly nothing. Then my search began to lead me through such unusual and unexplainable pathways that I know God had to be directing me.

Finally, one day, I found myself in the office of a Minister, whom I'd never seen before, and who pastored a church that I'd never bothered to understand or know anything about. While sitting across the desk from this pastor, telling him of my quest, I happened to glance out the window, and there on the vacant lot behind this study was a large van with the words, "NATION WIDE HI-WAY AND HEDGE EVANGELISM" written on it! Immediately my mind flew back to the time when I'd casually driven by this very same van in the outskirts of town.

"What a coincidence!" I thought. But as I started asking questions about it and as this minister – Reverend J. E. Murdock – began to unfold the vision God had given him for the Hi-Way and Hedge Evangelism, I suddenly realized that my being in this particular pastor's office was no coincident – it was God! Of all the places in our city I could have gone for information, unexplainably, I had come to just the right place, and I know it was right because as Brother Murdock told me about the vision that God gave him for Hi-Way and Hedge Ministry, it did more to satisfy my quest for reality, than any amount of "scripture-quoting" could have done!

For you see, I learned that day that God does still speak to man, just like He did to Moses; and that He does still give man visions, like He did Ezekiel, making him willing to give up family, home, prestige, a good pastorate – everything – to step out on nothing but pure faith in God!

The story I heard that day, of the Hi-Way and Hedge Evangelism, is a real story of faith and love of God! It's not a story of man's achievements but rather a story of God's achievements through man; a story of God's ability to make a man step out on the water just like Peter did with nothing to hold him up but the Master's promises.

As this quiet spoken, humble minister – J.E. Murdock – unfolded his vision before me, my own veil of formality and disbelief was pushed aside. "Through the years God has spoken to me many times and revealed many things," he explained. "He has given me visions, and blessings, and burdens, but never like He did that day in 1954 when He first spoke to me about the Hi-Way and Hedge Evangelism! That time God didn't leave any room in my mind for doubt, or in my heart for unbelief!"

"You see, He didn't just come to me and say, Go do this. Instead, He actually kept me under such a pressure and so burdened with troublesome visions for two whole weeks, that I felt like I would never get through this puzzling maze! For fourteen long days, whenever I'd quit praying or waiting on the Lord, a great faintness would sweep over my soul! I would be greatly depressed! It seemed like I couldn't exist unless I stayed in communion with God! I tried to throw off this feeling and go about my every day work, but I couldn't get the load off my shoulders. Like Job, I couldn't understand why God was leading me through such a puzzling place. I completely lost interest in natural things – because the visions and truths He was pouring over me while I was praying, were so real and so impressive that I couldn't get them out of my mind!

"God gave me such a clear picture of world conditions that I was fascinated, but also greatly troubled. An artist couldn't have painted the picture He showed me, or a writer couldn't have found words to describe the scenes He flashed in front of my eyes. And as He showed me world conditions He said, 'Man has turned to his own way of battling and struggling! He no longer relies on me to show him the way, like Joshua did. All this is vanity for man's glory. And it cannot survive unless there is a real return to Christianity in world affairs!'

"And then God flashed a picture of Spiritual conditions in front of my eyes that was plumb frightening! He showed that the Christian world has been polluted with man's theories rather than God's and that there had been a great falling away from His Word. Because the church world today works for denominations, it's lost it's true vision and is trying to use the Lord instead of letting Him use us. This has brought about great confusion and doubt and fear among Christians.

"As He was telling me the problems of the Christian world he brought the scripture to my mind that Paul wrote to the Galatians after they had drifted away from God... 'How turn ye again to the weak and beggarly elements?... Where is the blessedness ye spake of? ... if it had been possible ye would have plucked out your own eyes, and have given them to me... (but now)...I stand in doubt of you.'

"Then in a flash God painted a picture of the modern church world which had been founded on a firm rock, now drifting away and building modern temples on man's cardboard theories! And when the first strong 'trial' wind comes along, they waver and topple! He pointed out that, whereas at one time Christians were willing to die for their heritage, now they've drifted back to man's beggarly elements, and are in bondage to fear, and to nervousness, and to doubts! There is much faintness of heart in our modern church world because we've forgotten the blessedness of the Gospel!"

As Brother Murdock told his story with such complete simplicity there was a note of urgency in his voice – not an agitated hurry, but a sense of dedicated urgency! As he talked about his vision this minister seemed to fade into the background and it was no longer man's story that I was hearing but rather Christ speaking through man.

"Next God said to me, 'If you don't pray, you'll faint. You are just as obligated to be an intercessor as Jesus was!' Then He flashed before me a picture of Daniel praying, and weeping, and confessing his sins in order to save the children of Israel! And He showed me a picture of Job and his friends talking but not getting anywhere until Job began to pray and his captivity rolled away.

"After showing me these pictures God said, 'I want you to call the church world to prayer – not just rejoicing in prayer, but to intercessory prayer! The church world is obligated to intercessory prayer just like Esther was.' And quickly He flashed through my mind a vision of Esther and her uncle Mordecai, who sat before the King's gate mourning while Esther was inside with favor from the king. She could have had anything she wanted from the king. But she wanted to stop her uncle's mourning so she sent him new garments. When he refused them and warned her, 'Think not with thyself that thou shalt escape in the king's house, more than all the Jews... thou thy father's house shall be destroyed,'... Esther agreed to fast and to go unto the king, even if she perished. And when she took her share of intercessory prayer, her people were saved!

"After showing me this scene God brought the scripture to me, 'For truth is fallen in the street... and there was no intercessor'... And He said, 'In spite of all the wickedness and confusion that exists today, no one is weeping. Everyone is frustrated, but no one weeps!' And as He said that I had a clear picture of Jesus weeping over Jerusalem.

"As God brought each of these pictures through my mind and continued speaking to me, I felt that I could no longer go about my natural, normal life. I felt I couldn't rest or go to sleep! These visions were rolling over my soul in such a fascinating way that I could never forget them! Whenever I'd stop praying I'd have much the same feeling as you might have if your child was in another room crying and suffering. You just couldn't walk off and leave him. I kept hearing the words, 'The whole world groaneth for the manifestations of His power, yet do not know how to give themselves to intercessory prayer for it.'

"But I knew if the world could see what God was showing me there would be crying on the jobs, around the kitchen sink, and in the schools. The Lord kept saying to me, 'If you don't pray, you'll faint!' There was no doubt that He was trying to impress me with the importance of a prayer ministry –

especially intercessory prayer – and He was doing it in such a manner that no matter what trials I met, I'd stick to prayer for the answer!

"Then Christ warned me, 'You'll meet great indifference in this ministry – not just out and out opposition – but deadly indifference and unconcern. Remember how I spoke to My disciples and showed them many things, and did many miracles among them and they worshipped Me and knew I was the Son of God. Yet they forgot I was to come back to them! They didn't even know Me! I had to re-commission them and send them forth again with power.' And then He added, 'But don't strive with indifference. Just pray, and present My Word.

"As if to illustrate this, a woman came into the prayer room shortly after God had spoken this and knelt down across the room from me. And in a moment the Lord spoke to me and said, 'Go pray for that woman.' I walked over to pray for her and as I did I was almost overcome with the feeling that this person had suddenly become completely lifeless! She seemed to have turned to wood! I prayed for her and suddenly all her unconcern and lifelessness and indifference seemed to melt! She seemed to come back to life! She began crying and weeping and praising the Lord! This incident brought God's point home to me about unconcern and indifference in such a way that I'll never forget it!

"But as the Lord poured all these visions and revelations over my heart, during this two week period, I couldn't seem to get a release. I only felt more and more burdened! The things He was showing me were not comfortable. They were quite distressing. And it seemed that He would not let me rest. But finally He said to me, 'Remember Ezekiel in the valley of dry bones?' And He brought to my mind this scripture telling how He'd taken Ezekiel into the valley of dry bones and caused him to view them and then asked, 'Son of man, can these bones live?' Ezekiel answered, 'O Lord God, thou knowest.' Then God showed Ezekiel so many other scenes in the lives of the children of Israel that he was convinced the dead hope in Israel could be revived. God could have just told Ezekiel all that, but instead He actually took him out and showed him.

"And as I thought of Ezekiel, I suddenly realized that the Lord was dealing with me in the same way! Instead of just telling me, He actually drug me through a valley of dry bones, too! For fourteen days He presented such visions to me that I was thoroughly convinced that if we did not return to a prayer ministry, we'd completely lose God! He left me no room to ignore what He was showing me!

"Finally God spoke to me again and said, 'The Lord of the Harvest is calling you to a last day ministry, based on prayer and intercessory. I want you to go out into the hi-ways and hedges, and compel them to come in that My house may be filled. This is a last day ministry – a gleaning of the fringe areas and it will have to be an unselfish ministry, for they cannot recompense thee. And to carry out this last day ministry you'll have to have vision, or you'll perish! And if you don't pray, you'll faint!'

"And as He spoke the words, 'If you don't pray, you'll faint,' one more time, my heart and soul and mind were released as if God had suddenly flooded me with a great light, and a feeling of peace. I realized the reason for all the visions He'd been showing me. I knew He was giving me my commission to go and preach the gospel in the hi-way and hedges, and to do it with much prayer and supplication for God's people.

"But after that came the hard part!" J.E. Murdock added with a grin. "The magnitude of the task He'd put before me suddenly hit me full force! It dawned on me that in order to do this work I'd have to give up the security of 15 years in the ministry and of a good pastorate, and step out on nothing but God's command, spoken to me in a vision! There was absolutely no sign of financial backing and no guarantee of supplies – God hadn't mentioned that! After 15 years in the ministry, my family

– which included five children – had finally gotten established! We had a good pastorate and a home, and now suddenly God was telling us to leave all that! This was a hard place to go through!

"My wife and I talked the situation over and it suddenly became impressed on us that we'd spent much time teaching our children that the Lord would take care of them. And my sermons usually proclaimed that the Lord would sustain us and meet our needs. Yet when faced with the prospect of taking care of a family on nothing but God's promises, even I hesitated! Finally we agreed that either we did believe in God's Word that "He" takes care of us, or we didn't believe it! If we did, then when He said He'd take care of us it was just the same as a guaranteed income!

"Now, I'd learned through the years that obedience is the one great requirement of faith, so we made the decision to go! I resigned my pastorate and prepared to leave. The Lord took over from that moment on! He made a way, and provided for us in this ministry, at every turn of the road!

"It was truly amazing, during the next few years, how gifts would come in, often from unexpected sources as if to prove that only the Lord could have sent it. It really seemed that God used the Hi-way and Hedge Ministry as an example to show what great things can come from just relying on Him for everything. Each time a seemingly impossible mountain arose in front of us the Lord would always overcome!

"Many times we received money in the mail from people we didn't even know! One person who lived over 200 miles from us sent a regular monthly check. Another couple, who we'd known years before, suddenly took it upon themselves to send us money regularly. In one town where we held a revival, the people decided to build a church. When they went to purchase the lot they were faced with the question of money. So one dear old saint – in her eighties – said, 'I'll pay the down payment on the lot.' Of course when others saw her gift, they, too, gave, and established a church.

"My wife and children really felt the impact of God's hand continually supplying our every need," Brother Murdock continued. "In times when the going was rough, someone would bring us groceries or provisions. Because these gifts always seemed to come from unexpected sources, we knew the Lord had put us on these people's hearts. And we rejoiced with each miracle God worked for us."

"The Lord has really been with us in this ministry. As I went about forming Prayer Bands, the people already seemed to have had their hearts opened to us. It was as if the Lord had gone before! I could not possibly have made myself do the things I had to do if God had not been leading me every step of the way. This is strictly a faith ministry!

"And just before I left my pastorate, the Lord showed me the way to acquire a van and tent for this evangelism. As I parked in front of a grocery store one day, a large refrigerated ice cream truck stopped near me.

"What a wonderful thing it would be if we could get a van like that, for Hi-way and Hedge, I thought. Then the Lord seemed to say to me, 'How did that ice cream company get the money to buy their truck?' I know the answer – from the nickels and pennies of the people – the change that would ordinarily be wasted. Then the Lord said, 'You can build Hi-way and Hedge Evangelism from the crumbs off the people's tables. Remember how I sent Elijah to the poor widow, who had only enough meal and oil to make a small cake for her son and herself. Elijah was not embarrassed to ask for food because I told him to. And the widow and her son never hungered again.'

"After that revelation I no longer dreaded asking smaller churches and poorer people for their nickels and pennies – their crumbs. And that is where most of Hi-way and Hedge support has come from down through the years. Within a very short time I found a truck and van, complete with tent and equipment. I made arrangements to buy it – through faith – and soon was able to begin revivals in it.

"From then on Hi-way and Hedge Ministry was taken to the southern parts of Texas and Louisiana, which was a ripe and virgin territory for this gospel. Along with an evangelistic ministry, Hi-way and Hedge also provided tent and equipment for other ministers who were working in the fringe areas. It has helped bring the Gospel to the isolated bayou areas along the Gulf Coast of South Louisiana, as well as to help establish several churches in this area. It has truly been a ministry of gleaning, but a ministry that needs to be done and is often neglected. Even though small it has brought wonderful results."

As J.E. Murdock completed his story I felt as though I'd really been let in on one of God's greatest miracles – the miracle that can occur in human hearts when God gives them a vision! The complete results of the Hi-way and Hedge Ministry only God knows. I have asked others and have heard many thrilling testimonies from people who were saved under this evangelism – some of whom have gone on to serve the Master by bringing the Gospel to others.

But very little has been told about the Hi-way and Hedge work except to those directly involved. There is no room in Rev. J.E. Murdock's prayer-filled heart for concern about fame, or prestige, or organizations, or publicity! These things he has left to others. God is his record! But his has been a ministry that God put on his heart strongly, and no matter what happens, as long as he continues to walk in God's will, he will be able to do the job the way the Lord wants him to. His personal plans and concerns have long ago been pushed aside to make way for God's plans.

Recently I attended a revival meeting held in a Hi-way and Hedge tent and on this particular night, in an atmosphere of quietness and reverence and oneness with God, that can only be felt in the openness of a tent under a beautiful starlit sky, a man stood and gave a glowing testimony of how God had saved him from alcoholism! Tears came to my eyes as he told his story. He'd been saved as a result of an earlier Hi-way and Hedge missionary work. I couldn't help but think as I listened to him, that even if no more than just this one soul had come as a result of this Evangelism, it would have been worth it all!

But of course there have been many, many, such dramatic results – results that all my questioning could never uncover. The complete tabulation of this ministry will only be written in God's book and I cannot tell you of it. But one thing I can tell you, and that is of the marvelous change that has been wrought in my own heart and life because of the discovery that God is still present to give visions to man like He did in this ministry.

Just to discover that there are individuals like J.E. Murdock, who are willing to do God's work no matter how much sacrifice it requires; and who go quietly about their work with no fanfare, or loud trumpets, accomplishing the impossible in their humble ways – gently moving mountains – has brought me to the greatest realization of my life – the realization that God is just as real today to talk to me – and to you – and to give us visions and prophecies, as He was when Jeremiah and Noah walked the earth! And this realization has truly brought me to that closer walk with God that I had been searching for!

Memories From The Murdock's Photo Album

Me, Mother, Mike, David, Flo, Kaydonna and Deborah

Me, Mother, Barbara Ann, John, Jr. and Flo

Herman Stone called to be a missionary to India under my ministry

My "Willie." I married her when she was 14 years old

Howard Holton - one of my dearest minister friends

My son, Mike, with Sunday School members

One of My First -
Cameron Church

My "Tent" Meetings at Cameron, Louisiana

My Church Pastorate
of 10 years
Calcasieu Tabernacle
Lake Charles,
Louisiana

Me and my wife, Willie

*The Big Lake,
Louisiana Pastorate*

*"Our Water Fountain" in
Big Lake, Louisiana*

*Some of my men from Big Lake
church...I am kneelng...looking
a bit younger than my 87 years
old today!*

In my younger days!

Our Sweetlake Church

*Some of our
Sweetlake Members*

*Our Sweetlake
Musicians -
My wife, Willie,
on the accordion*

Our "Satellite" Church - Southside Tabernacle in Lake Charles, Louisiana

The church I pioneered Franklin Gospel Tabernacle Franklin, Louisiana

I started Prayer Bands in all the churches I pioneered - Waco, Texas Highway & Hedge Ministry

My childhood home in Grapeland, Texas

Me with my wife, Willie

Me with my 3 sons, John, Mike and David

My longtime pastor friend, Burl Stephens, who wrote poems and songs for country singer, George Jones

God impressed me to go to small towns to birth churches where the Holy Spirit had never been emphasized...

Me with my oldest daughter, Barbara Ann

Me with my brother and sisters

My son, David with his wife, Sondra, and their children David, Evan and Erin

Me and Willie with our oldest son, John, Jr. and my twin sister, Flo

My daughter, Flo, and her husband, Lee

My daughter, Deborah, and her children, John, Sissy and Misty

The Ark...my special place of prayer in DeRidder, Louisiana. God stirred me to become the intercessor for my family as Noah, who had built the Ark for the preservation of his family and the coming judgments of God.

Me, Willie, and our son, Mike

Me with my grandson, Charles

Me and my son, Mike, out on the family pond

*John, me, Barbara Ann,
Mike and Willie*

*My daughter,
Flo*

*Here fishing on my pond in
DeRidder, Louisiana*

Me and my "catfish"

*My brother, Earl, me
and my sister, Flo*

I have always loved gardening!

Kneeling here at the gravesite of my precious wife of 63 years. I married her at 14 years old.

Me with my great-grand-children, Jared and Brittany

My grandson and his wife, Todd and Pam

My great-grandson, Ryan

My granddaughter, Sissy, and her son, Isaac

My great-grand-son Tristan

My great-grandchildren L'il John and Regan

My grandchildren, Damon and Daryn

*My granddaughter,
Pam*

*Me with my grandchildren,
Dusti and Damon*

*My grandson,
Jason*

Great-grandson Ryan with me

*Me with my son,
David, 2 of my
daughters, Kay and
Deborah and her
son, John*

Me with my grandson, John III, and his wife, Sherry

My son, David

Me with 2 of my sons, John, Jr. and Mike

My daughter, Deborah and her husband, Robert

My daughter, Barbara, with 2 of her daughters, Cindy and Cheré

My grandchildren, Charles, Cindy, Cheré and Cylyce

My granddaughter, Pam, and her husband, David, with children Casey, Katy and Geoffrey

DECISION

Will You Accept Jesus As Your Personal Savior Today?

The Bible says, "That if thou shalt confess with thy mouth the Lord Jesus, and shalt believe in thine heart that God hath raised Him from the dead, thou shalt be saved" (Romans 10:9).

Pray this prayer from your heart today!

"Dear Jesus, I believe that You died for me and rose again on the third day. I confess I am a sinner...I need Your love and forgiveness...Come into my heart. Forgive my sins. I receive Your eternal life. Confirm Your love by giving me peace, joy and supernatural love for others. Amen."

☐ Yes, Rev. Murdock, I have received Jesus as my Savior through reading your book. Please keep me on your daily Prayer List.

NAME _____ BIRTHDAY _____

ADDRESS _____

CITY _____ STATE _____ ZIP _____

PHONE _____ E-MAIL _____

Mail form to:
c/o The Wisdom Center · *P. O. Box 99* · *Denton, TX 76202*
Phone: 1-888-WISDOM-1 (1-888-947-3661)
*Website: **thewisdomcenter.tv***

488